Revolutionary Classics

State Capitalism in Russia

Tony Cliff

With a new introduction by the author

BOOKMARKS

London, Chicago, Sydney

State Capitalism in Russia – Cliff
This edition published July 1996
First published in duplicated form in June 1948
Bookmarks, 265 Seven Sisters Road, London N4 2DE, England
Bookmarks, PO Box 16085, Chicago Il. 60616, USA
Bookmarks, PO Box A338, Sydney South Australia
Copyright c Bookmarks Publications Ltd

ISBN 090622446

Printed by Cox and Wyman

The Socialist Workers Party is one of an international grouping of socialist organisations:

- **Australia:** International Socialists, PO Box A338 Sydney South
- **Belgium:** Socialisme International, Rue Lovinfosse 60, 4030 Grivengée, Belgium
- **Britain:** Socialist Workers Party, PO Box 82, London E3
- **Canada:** International Socialists, PO Box 339, Station E, Toronto, Ontario M6H 4E3
- **Cyprus:** Ergatiki Demokratia, PO Box 7280, Nicosia
- **Denmark:** Internationale Socialister, Postboks 642, 2200 København N, Denmark
- **France:** Socialisme International, BP 189, 75926 Paris Cedex 19
- **Greece:** Organosi Sosialisliki Epanastasi, c/o Workers Solidarity, PO Box 8161, Athens 100 10, Greece
- **Holland:** International Socialists, PO Box 9720, 3506 GR Utrecht
- **Ireland:** Socialist Workers Party, PO Box 1648, Dublin 8
- **New Zealand:** International Socialist Organization, PO Box 6157, Dunedin, New Zealand
- **Norway:** Internasjonale Socialisterr, Postboks 5370, Majorstua, 0304 Oslo 3
- **Poland:** Solidarność Socjalistyczna, PO Box 12, 01-900 Warszawa 118
- **South Africa:** Socialist Workers Organisation, PO Box 18530, Hillbrow 2038, Johannesberg
- **United States:** International Socialist Organisation, PO Box 16085, Chicago, Illinois 60616
- **Zimbabwe:** International Socialists, PO Box 6758, Harare

Contents

<u>Also in the Revolutionary Classics Series from Bookmarks</u>

Labour in Irish History
James Connolly
'Left Wing' Communism: An infantile disorder
Vladimir Lenin
Lessons of October
Leon Trotsky
The Mass Strike
Rosa Luxemburg
Reform or Revolution
Rosa Luxemburg
Socialism, Scientific and Utopian
Frederick Engels
Wage Labour and Capital plus Wages, Price and Profit
Karl Marx

Introduction

At the graveside of the Stalinist regime

The first edition of *State Capitalism in Russia* was written in 1947 and appeared in duplicated form. It was a time when Stalinism was at its peak: after Russia's victory over Nazi Germany, after the Russian occupation of Eastern Europe and before the split between Tito and Stalin. Mao's army was spreading quickly over China and was on the verge of total victory.

Forty two years later, in 1989, the Stalinist regimes collapsed in Eastern Europe and then in Russia. The death of the Stalinist economic, social and political order made it possible to test conclusively the validity of the 1947 theoretical analysis of this book. A post mortem reveals the sickness that affected a person when he was alive. The moment of death of a social order can also be its moment of truth.

The perception of the Stalinist regime as a socialist state, or even a degenerated workers' state—a transitional stage between capitalism and socialism—assumed that it was more progressive than capitalism. For a Marxist this had to mean fundamentally that Stalinism was able to develop the productive forces more efficiently than capitalism. However, the deepening crisis in Eastern Europe and USSR cannot be explained except by reference to the slowing down of economic growth in the late 1970s and early 1980s. This lead to stagnation and a growing gap between these countries and the advanced West.

In the USSR the annual rate of growth of gross national product was as follows; The first five year plan—19.2 percent (probably an exaggerated figure); 1950-59—5.8 percent; 1970-78—3.7 percent. In 1980-82 it was down to 1.5 percent and over the last ten years there has been a negative rate of growth. Clearly then the productive forces were not developing efficiently.

If the productivity of labour had been more dynamic in Eastern Europe and USSR than in the West, there would be no reason for the rulers of these countries to turn to the market mechanisms of the West. If Eastern European economies were superior than the reunification of Germany, for example, should have seen the flourishing of East German industry in comparison with that of West Germany. In fact the economy of East Germany collapsed after unification. The number of workers employed in East Germany in 1989 was 10 million while today it has fallen to 6 million. Productivity of labour is only 29 percent of the Western level[1]. Thus the East German productivity level, though the highest in Eastern Europe, was still low compared with West Germany and the other advanced economies that it found itself openly competing with after 1989.

If the USSR was a workers' state, however degenerated, then when capitalism assaulted it workers would have come to the defence of their state. Even Trotsky, the sharpest critic of Stalinism, always considered it axiomatic that if capitalism attacked the state the workers of the Soviet Union would come to its aid, however corrupt and depraved the bureaucracy dominating it.

But when it came to the crunch in 1989, the workers in Eastern Europe did not defend 'their' state. If the Stalinist

---

1. *Financial Times* 12 May 1992

state had been a workers state one cannot explain why its only defenders were the secret police forces of the *Securitate* in Rumanian and the *Stasi* in East Germany, nor why the Soviet working class supported Boris Yeltsin, the outspoken representative of the market.

If the regimes in Eastern Europe and USSR were post capitalist and in 1989 there was a restoration of capitalism, how was the restoration achieved with such astonishing ease?

The 1989 revolutions in Eastern Europe were remarkable for the absence of large scale social conflict and violence. Except for Rumania there was no armed conflict. In fact there were fewer violent clashes in East Germany, Czechoslovakia and Hungary during the fall of these regimes than there were between the police and striking miners in Thatcher's Britain of the mid 1980s.

The transition from one social order to another is necessarily accompanied by the replacing of one state apparatus by another. The state machine was hardly touched anywhere in 1989. The Soviet army, the KGB and the state bureaucracy are still in place in Russia, as are many of their equivalents elsewhere. In Poland the military helped to promote the change from Polish state capitalism to a market based economy. General Jaruzelski, the architect of the 1981 coup and the Interior Minister and chief administrator of martial law General Kiszcak, played crucial roles in negotiating the round table agreement with *Solidarity* and the formation of Mazowiecki's coalition government. If a counter revolution had taken place, if a restoration of capitalism had taken place, there should have been a wholesale replacement of one ruling class with another. Instead we witnessed the continuity of the same personnel at the top of society. The members of the *nomenklatura* who ran the economy, society and state under 'socialism' now do the same under the 'market'.

The collapse of the Stalinist regimes in Russia and Eastern Europe created havoc in the world communist movement and amongst those on the left not armed with a state capitalist understanding. Millions of members and supporters of the communist movement across the world accepted the claim that the Stalinist regime embodied socialism. Millions who belong not to the communist movement but to the socialist movement, also accepted it. This did not only apply to those on the left of the movement. The right wing Fabians, Sidney and Beatrice Webb produced a book entitled *Soviet Communism; a New Civilisation* (1936) which was a massive panegyric to the Stalinist regime. For the majority of those who had identified Stalinism with socialism the collapse of the these regimes led to a shattering ideological and moral crisis.

For example, in February 1990 Eric Hobsbawm, the guru of the British Communist Party, was asked; 'In the Soviet Union, it looks as though the workers are overthrowing the workers' state'. Hobsbawm replied, 'it obviously wasn't a workers' state, nobody in the Soviet Union ever believed it was a workers' state, and the workers knew it wasn't a workers' state'.[2] Why hadn't Hobsbawm told us this 50 years ago, or even 20 years ago?

The extreme ideological disorientation of the British Communist Party is clearly demonstrated by the minutes of their Executive Committee meetings in the wake of the collapse. Nina Temple, General Secretary of the Party said; 'I think the SWP was right, the Trotskyists were right that it was not socialism in Eastern Europe. And I think we should have said so long ago.'

Chris Myant, International Secretary of the CPGB, went further. He said that the October Revolution was 'a mistake of historic proportions... Its consequences have been severe.' He went on to blame Lenin and the Bolsheviks for the Second World War, the Holocaust, the Gulag, the show trials, third world fascist dictatorships and the arms race, famine in Ethiopia, world poverty and the Vietnam war!

The ideological collapse of the British Communist Party in

---

2. *Independent on Sunday*, 4 February, 1990.

effect has led to its total disintegration. From some 60,000 in 1945, with very broad influence in the working class, it dwindled to tiny group of a couple of hundred, old and passive. Similar stories could be told about Communist Parties world wide.

The ideological crisis also very much affected the British Labour left. While in 1981 Tony Benn received some 3.2 million votes in the deputy leadership campaign for the Labour Party and probably had a couple of hundred thousand active supporters, in April 1995 the total number of individual members of the Labour Party who voted for the retention of Clause 4 was only 8,500. Of course, the bankruptcy of Stalinism was only one factor, although a significant one, in the decline of the Labour left.

Socialism is the child of the self activity of the revolutionary emancipation of the working class. Stalinism has been a constant drain on that self activity and the gravedigger of the revolution. The idea that Stalinism was socialism has now ended in calamity for those taken in by it.

I am convinced that the analysis of Stalinist Russia as state capitalist, as elaborated some 48 years ago, has proved its value and is a necessary rebuttal of Stalinism and the reaction to its decay.

Tony Cliff

July 1996

From the 1988 Introduction

This book was first distributed in duplicated from in June 1948, under the title *The Nature of Stalinist Russia*. An amended version was published in 1955 as *Stalinist Russia: A Marxist Analysis*. In 1964, it appeared as the first part of a larger work, *Russia: A Marxist Analysis*. The book was first published with the title *State Capitalism in Russia* by Pluto Press in 1974.

The main text of this edition is based on that of 1955 which differed in a number of ways from the original duplicated version (mainly in terms of chapter order, but also by the addition of material referring to the split between Yugoslavia and Russia in 1948, and amendments to the section dealing with crisis in state capitalism).

What is published here as the first appendix, on Trotsky's view of Russia, was an integral part of the original text. It remains a devastating reply to those influenced by Ernst Mandel or Isaac Deutcher, who claimed to hold to Trotsky's analysis throughout the post war period.

The second appendix was written as a separate essay in 1948, just after the completion of the original text, and deals with the view that Russia is a new sort of class society, quite distinct from both socialism and capitalism. At that time the view was mainly associated with the American ex Trotskyist Max Shachtman; it has been revived in recent years by various writers such as Rudolf Bahro, Antonio Carlo, Hillel Ticktin, and George Bence and Janos Kis (writing jointly under the pseudonym Rakovski). It showed signs of being the 'common sense' of a whole section of the non Stalinist intellectual left. Cliff's critique destroys both the old and the newer versions of the argument.

One final point. As the 1964 edition of Cliff's classic work warned: 'The reader unused to the conceptual scheme of Marxist theory may experience some difficulty in reading the following pages from cover to cover. Chapters V, VI and especially VII are liable to present some difficulty and should be left till the end.' It only needs to be added that these are nonetheless important chapters where Cliff grapples with the key issues facing those who want to fit Russia into Marx's account of the dynamics of capitalism.

Chris Harman
March 1988

Chapter 1: Socio-economic relations in Stalinist Russia

The control of production · The workers are not
allowed to organise in defence of their interests · The
atomisation of the working class · The denial of any
legal freedom to the worker · Female labour · Forced
labour · The subordination of consumption to
accumulation – the subordination of the workers
to the means of production · The accumulation of
capital on the one hand and of poverty on the other ·
The subordination of industry to war · The
productivity of labour and the workers · The
expropriation of the peasantry · The turnover tax ·
The subordination of man to property · Changes in
the relations of distribution · Bureaucratic
mismanagement · Russia, an industrial giant

Let us begin the study of the nature of the Stalinist regime
by describing some of the salient features of the economic
and social relations prevailing in Russia. A factual survey will
serve as a basis for later analysis and generalisation.

The Control of production[1]

Immediately after the revolution, it was decided that the
management of every plant would be in the hands of the
trade unions. Thus the programme of the Communist Party
of Russia, adopted at the Eighth Party Congress (18–23
March 1919), declared:

> The organised apparatus of social production must primarily
> depend upon the trade unions . . . They must be transformed into

huge productive units, enrolling the majority of the workers, and in due time all the workers, in the respective branches of production.

Inasmuch as the trade unions are already (as specified in the laws of the Soviet Republic and as realized in practice) participants in all the local and central organs administering industry, they must proceed to the practical concentration in their own hands of the work of administration in the whole economic life of the country, making this their unified economic aim. By thus protecting the indissoluble union between the central State authority, the national economy, and the broad masses of the workers, the trade unions must in the fullest possible measure induce the workers to participate directly in the work of economic administration. The participation of the trade unons in the conduct of economic life, and the involvement by them of the broad masses of the people in this work, would appear at the same time to be our chief aid in the campaign against the bureaucratisation of the economic apparatus of the Soviet Power. This will facilitate the establishment of an effective popular control over the results of production.

The Party cells participated in the running of industry together with the workers' plant committees. Together with these, and under their control, worked the technical manager: the combination of these three formed the Troika.

With the strengthening of the bureaucracy in the party and the trade unions, the Troika became more and more a mere label, it progressively rose above the mass of workers. Nevertheless, it remained amenable to workers' pressure and retained some element of workers' control until the advent of the Five-Year Plan. A.Baykov, who is no supporter of workers' control, but praises Stalin's activities, says:

> De facto, during that period [before the Five-Year Plan] the director was largely dependent on the works' trade union organ, the 'Zavkom' (the factory trade union committee) and on the party cell, the organ of the Communist Party at the enterprise. Representatives of these organisations considered it their duty to supervise the director's activities and usually interfered with his decisions.[1]

With the big drive towards industrialisation, the Troika could no longer be tolerated, because its very existence would have prevented the complete subordination of the workers to the needs of capital accumulation. Hence, in February 1928, the Supreme Economic Council issued a document entitled *Fundamental Regulations Regarding the Rights and Duties of the Administrative, Technical and Maintenance Staffs of Industrial Enterprises*, which aimed at putting an end to the Troika and at establishing complete and unfettered control by the manager.[3] In September 1929, the Party Central Committee resolved that the workers' committees 'may not intervene directly in the running of the plant or endeavour in any way to replace plant administration; they shall by all means help to secure one-man management, increase production, plant development, and, thereby, improvement of the material conditions of the working class.'[4] The manager was placed in full and sole charge of the plant. All his economic orders were now to be 'unconditionally binding on his subordinate administrative staff and on all workers.'[5] L.M. Kaganovich, the well-known trouble-shooter in the economic field, stated: 'The foreman is the authoritative leader of the shop, the factory director is the authoritative leader of the factory, and each has all the rights, duties, and responsibilities that accompany these positions.'[6] His brother, M.M.Kaganovich, a senior official of the Commissariat of Heavy Industry, stated: 'It is necessary above everything to strengthen one-man management. It is necessary to proceed from the basic assumption that the director is the supreme chief in the factory. All the employees in the factory must be completely subordinated to him.'[7]

One textbook on Soviet economic law, published in 1935, even went as far as to state: 'One-man management [is] the most important principle of the organisation of socialist economy.'[8]

The Troika was officially buried in 1937 when, at a Plenum of the Central Committee, Zhdanov, then Stalin's second-in-command, said: 'the Troika is something quite impermissible . . . The Troika is a sort of administrative board, but our economic administration is constructed along totally different lines.'[9]

The new system of management was very clearly defined in an official manual: 'Each plant has a leader – the plant manager – endowed with the full power of decision, hence fully responsible for everything.'[10] Further, 'one-man control implies strict demarcation between the administration on the one hand and Party and trade-union organisations on the other. This strict demarcation must be applied on all levels of industrial management. Current operations in fulfilment of the Plan are the task of the administration. The chief of a workshop, the manager of the plant, the head of the Glavk, a board of industry or branch of industry, has full powers, each within his field, and the Party and trade-union organisations may not interfere with their orders.'[11]

In the light of these quotations, how preposterous are the words of the Dean of Canterbury: 'The democracy of the workshop is the bulwark of Soviet liberty.'[12]

During the first few years after the revolution, both in law and in fact, only the trade unions were entitled to fix wage rates. During the NEP period they were fixed by negotiation between the unions and the management. Now, with the introduction of the Five-Year Plan, they were determined more and more by the economic administrative organs, such as the Commissariats and the Glavki, and the individual factory manager. This subject is dealt with in detail in a later section of this chapter, but a few typical quotations are given here in order to illustrate the views of the Soviet leaders on the right of the manager to fix wages. In June 1933, Weinberg, one of the principal trade union leaders, declared:

'The proper determination of wages and the regulation of labour demand that the industrial heads and the technical directors be charged with immediate responsibility in this matter. This is also dictated by the necessity of establishing a single authority and ensuring economy in the management of enterprises ... They [the workers] must not defend themselves against their government. That is absolutely wrong. That is supplanting the administrative organs. That is Left opportunistic perversion, the annihilation of individual authority and interference in the administrative departments. It is imperative that it be abolished.'[18]

The following year, Ordzhonikidze, then Commissar of Heavy Industry, speaking at a conference of managers of heavy industry, said:

as directors, administrative heads and foremen, you must personally occupy yourselves with wages in all their concrete detail and not leave to anyone this most important matter. *Wages are the most powerful weapon in your hands.*[14]

Some time later, Andreev, a member of the Political Bureau, declared:

The wage scale must be left entirely in the hands of the heads of industry. They must establish the norm.[15]

And the anomalous situation was created that the 'Piece Rates and Conflicts Commission', while retaining its name was specifically excluded from intervening in the establishment of wage-rates and work-norm![16]

The workers are not allowed to organise in defence of their interests

Under Lenin and Trotsky the workers had the right to defend themselves even from their own state. Thus, for instance, Lenin said: 'Our present state is a workers' state with bureaucratic deformation ... Our state is such that the completely organised proletariat must protect itself against it and we must utilise these workers' organisations for protecting the workers from their own state, in order that the workers may protect our state . . .'[17]

It was taken for granted that strikes were not to be suppressed by the state. At the Eleventh Party Congress only one party leader, V.P.Miliutin, proposed 'not to permit strikes in state enterprises.'[18] All the others stated that it was the duty of party members to participate in them even if they did not agree with the majority who were in favour of striking. And indeed the first few years following the revolution witnessed a large number of strikes. Thus in 1922, 192,000 workers went on strike in state-owned enterprises; in 1923 the number was 165,000; in 1924, 43,000; in 1925, 34,000; in 1926; 32,900; in 1927, 20,100; in the first half of 1928, 8,900. In 1922 the number of workers involved in labour conflicts was three and a half million, and in 1923, 1,592,800.[19]

Today the trade unions, if they can be called trade unions, do nothing in defence of the workers' interests. Their disregard is clearly illustrated in the fact that seventeen years elapsed (1932–49) between the Ninth and Tenth Congresses of the Trade Union Congress, years which witnessed far-reaching changes in workers' conditions – such as the abolition of the seven-hour day, the introduction of Stakhanovism and of many draconic laws. When the Congress finally did meet, it did not represent the workers at all, as its social composition shows: 41.5 per cent of the delegates were full-time trade union officials, 9.4 per cent were technicians, and only 23.5 per cent were workers.[20] (At the previous Congress, in 1932, 84.9 per cent of the delegates were workers.)

In addition, the 'unions' have no say at all in the determination of wages. In 1934, collective agreements ceased to be drawn up.[21] In 1940, Shvernik, chairman of the Central

Council of Trade Unions, gave the following explanation for the abrogation of collective agreements:

> When the Plan becomes the decisive element of economic development, questions of wages cannot be decided independently of it. Thus the collective agreement as a form of regulating wages has outlived its usefulness. *[22]

In February 1947, so-called collective agreements were again drawn up, but the Stalinist leaders made it quite clear that these new agreements had no relation whatever to what is accepted elsewhere as collective agreements, as wages were not covered by them. As Shvernik wrote in the trade union monthly: 'Any change in wages ... may be brought about only by government decision.'[23] And an official commentator on the labour law wrote accordingly: 'It is taken for granted that present-day collective agreements must have a different content to those agreements which were made when wage rates and some other labour conditions were not established by government decree.'[24]

Textbooks on labour law published between 1938 and 1944 do not even mention the subject. However, in a textbook published somewhat later (in 1946) it is stated that:

> Life itself has shown that the restoration of the practice of collective bargaining is not expedient. *The collective agreement as a particular form of legal regulation of labour relations of wage-workers and salaried employees has outlived itself.* Detailed regulations of all aspects of these relations by normative acts of the state do not leave a place for any contractual agreement concerning this or that labour condition.[25]

Thus a text-book on labour legislation, published in 1947, reproduced the Labour Code without including Article 58,

---

* It is interesting to note that books published for foreign consumption, such as Lozovsky's *Handbook on the Soviet Trade Unions*, Moscow, 1937, pp 56–57 continue to describe collective agreements as if they still existed.

which reads: 'The amount of an employee's payment for his work shall be determined by collective agreements and individual employment contracts.'[26] Instead we are told: 'The amount of wages and salaries is at present fixed by the decisions of the government (or on the basis of its directives) ... In the determination of the amount of wages and salaries the agreement of the parties plays a subordinate role. It should not be contrary to law, and is allowed only within limits strictly provided for by law, for example, where the precise amount is fixed in instances in which the approved list of wages defines the rates as "from" – "to"; or fixing the payment for part-time employment of a person having another job, and the like.'[27]

Likewise, A.Stepanov, Director of the Wages Division in the Central Council of Trade Unions, wrote: 'Wage tables and wages are fixed by the government.'[28]

It is obvious that collective agreements which exclude any bargaining on wages – and that, after all, must necessarily be the workers' main interest in any such agreement – and that are arrived at by means of a procedure that allows the government the decisive voice as regards all its main points, are nothing but a bureaucratic formality and a sham.

The atomisation of the working class

Although the vast industrial plants of modern capitalism undoubtedly act as a powerful objective factor in the integration of the workers as a class, the employers have at their disposal a number of effective methods of disrupting this unity. One of the most important of these is the fostering of competition between workers by means of piece-work systems. The same threat of hunger which can impel workers to unite against their employers, may also be made to lead to a fight for survival between one worker and another.

For instance, piece-work systems were used on a large scale in Nazi Germany for the same purpose. Franz Neumann wrote:

> The class wage of the Socialist trade unions has been replaced by the 'performance wage' (*Liestungslohn*) defined in Section 29 of the [Nazi] Charter of Labour. 'It has been the iron principle of the National Socialist leadership,' said Hitler at the Party Congress of Honour, 'not to permit any rise in the hourly wage rates but to raise income solely by an increase in performance.' The rule of the wage policy is a marked preference for piece work and bonuses, even for juvenile workers. Such a policy is completely demoralising, for it appeals to the most egotistic instincts and sharply increases industrial accidents.[29]

Neumann goes on to explain why the Nazis went to such lengths in applying the piece-work system:

> The preponderance of the performance wage brings the problem of wage differentials into the forefront of social policy. It is essential that this problem be understood not as an economic question but as the *crucial political problem of mass control* ... Wage differentiation is the very essence of National Socialist wage policy ... the wage policy is consciously aimed at mass manipulation.[30]

The Stalinists use piece-work methods for the same purpose. After the introduction of the Five-Year Plans, the proportion of industrial workers paid on piece-rates rose very steeply: by 1930 it stood at 29 per cent of the total number of workers; by 1931 it had risen to 65 per cent of the total; by 1932 to 68 per cent.[31] By 1934 nearly three-quarters of all industrial workers were taking part in so-called 'socialist competition'.[32]

In 1944 the following percentages of workers and employees in various industries participated; petroleum industry, 82 per cent; aviation, 81 per cent; armaments, 85 per cent; machine-tool construction, 81 per cent; munitions, 81 per cent; automobile industry, 86 per cent; electrical-machine building, 83 per cent; rubber, 83 per cent; cotton industry, 91 per cent;

the shoe industry, 87 per cent.[33] In 1949 more than 90 per cent of the workers participated in 'socialist competition'.[34]

To make the competition even sharper, instead of simple piece-work in which payment is in direct proportion to output, as is the practice in other countries, progressive piece-work has been introduced in Russia. A couple of examples will illustrate how this operates.

A manual on the oil industry cites the following scale of payment:[35]

Percentage of overfulfilment of norm	Percentage of increment over basic piece rate
1-10	5
11-20	10
21-30	20
31-50	40
51-70	70
71 and above	100

Thus a worker producing 50 per cent above the norm is paid 110 per cent above the norm; if his output was 70 per cent above the norm, his payment is 189 per cent above the norm; if it was 100 per cent above the norm his payment is 300 per cent above the norm, and so on.

The rise is even steeper in some other industries. Thus, for instance, in the plants of the Ministry of Machine-Tool Construction, the following progressive piece rates exist:[36]

Percentage of overfulfilment of norm	Percentage of increment over basic piece rate
1-10	30
10-25	50
25-40	75
40 and over	100

Thus a worker producing 50 per cent above the norm is paid 200 per cent above the norm!

The progressive piece-rate system is doubly reactionary under Russian conditions. Since the amount of consumers' goods available is predetermined by the Plan, and since workers who surpass the norm are able to buy a much larger share than is warranted by their output, it follows that workers who do not achieve the norm get even less than the share their output really warrants.

The progressive piece-rate system enables the state to depress the workers' standard of living by continually raising the basic production norms. In fact, the launching of the Stakhanovite campaign at the end of 1935 was followed by changes in the norms of output in every industry. The new norms were not determined by the output of the average worker, but by 'averaging the production of Stakhanovites with the average of other workers.'[37]

At the beginning of 1936 the norms of work in most major industries were raised as follows: coal by 22–27.5 per cent, iron and steel by 13–20 per cent, machine-building by 30–40 per cent, non-ferrous metallurgy by 30–35 per cent, oil industry by 27–29 per cent, chemicals by 34 per cent,[38] textiles by 35–50 per cent and building by 54–80 per cent.[39]

There were further considerable rises during 1937 and 1938. As a result of these rises 60 per cent of the workers in the metal industry were unable to achieve the norm.[40] Later, on 16 April 1941, Shvernik stated that 22–32 per cent of the workers in all industries did not fulfil the norms.[41]

One preposterous result of the drive for the atomisation of the working class, and at the same time an inevitable effect of bureaucratic mismanagement, is the huge number of norms established. Thus, for instance, in 1939 the Commissariat of General Machine and Vehicle Construction alone had 2,026,000 work norms![42]

Originally there was an institute responsible for checking these norms so as to ensure that they were compatible with maintaining workers' health at a reasonable standard. Its abolition in 1936[43] was a clear indication of the government's determination to impose the full rigours of 'free' competition between workers. And, of course, the Stakhanovites were a powerful instrument in the process. 'The British worker, from his own peculiar point of view, as one who seeks to checkmate efforts to hasten the pace, would probably call them [the Stakhanovites] blacklegs,'[44] wrote Maynard. That the Russian workers are of the same opinion is shown by the numerous cases of 'sabotage' or even murder of Stakhanovites by workers.[45]

Sometimes Stalinist writers are careless enough to draw a parallel between Stakhanovism and the most refined method of capitalist exploitation – Taylorism. Thus, for instance, in a manual approved by the Ministry for Higher Education, designed for higher educational institutions of the petroleum industry, this remark is made: 'The views and methods of Taylor in the field of increased utilisation of implements of labour are unconditionally progressive.'[46] (One should compare this with Lenin's characterisation of Taylorism as 'the enslavement of man by the machine.'[47])

The denial of any legal freedom to the worker

Until the First Five-Year Plan, workers were free to change their places of work at their own discretion. Their right to work where they pleased was, in fact, guaranteed by the Labour Code of 1922: 'The transfer of a hired person from one enterprise to another or his shipment from one locality to another, even when the enterprise or institution moves, can take place only with the consent of the worker or employee concerned.'[48] Workers could also migrate, unhindered, from one part of the country to another. Even as late as 1930, it was stated in the *Small Soviet Encyclopaedia* that, 'the custom of internal passports, instituted by the autocracy as an instrument of police oppression of the toiling masses, was suppressed by the October Revolution.'[49]

Nevertheless, by 1931 no worker was allowed to leave Leningrad without special permission. From 27 December 1932, this system was applied to all parts of Russia, and an internal passport system, much more oppressive than the Tsar's, was introduced to prevent anyone changing his place of residence without permission.[50]

As early as 15 December 1930, all industrial enterprises were forbidden to employ people who had left their former place of work without permission,[51] and Article 37 of the 1922 Labour Code, to which reference is made above, was abolished on 1 July 1932.[52]

Labour Books were introduced for industrial and transport workers on 11 February 1931, and on 20 December 1938, for all other workers.[53] These books must be shown to the director of the enterprise when a job is first taken on. Directors are instructed to specify in the book the reasons for dismissing the worker. No worker can obtain a new job unless he shows his Labour Book. The vicious way in which this works in practice was clearly illustrated by Victor Serge, when he wrote that: 'The passport is visaed at the place of work. With each change of employ, the reason for the change is entered into the passport. I have known of workers discharged for not having come on the day of rest to contribute a "voluntary" (and, naturally, gratuitous) day of work, in whose passports is written: "Discharged for sabotage of the production plan".'[54]

Under a law of 15 November 1932, any worker who is absent from work for one day without good reason is liable to be dismissed, and, much more serious under Russian conditions, is liable to be evicted from his home, if it is tied to his place of employment,[55] which is usually the case for industrial workers, miners, and so on.

On 4 December 1932, the Council of People's Commissars and the Central Committee of the Party issued another decree aimed at absenteeism. This time, food supplies and other necessities were put under the control of the factory directors.[56]

A decree of 28 December 1938,[57] was aimed against those either arriving late at work, leaving before the scheduled time, unduly prolonging the lunch period or idling while at work. Offenders were liable to be transferred to work of a lower grade, and, if they committed three offences during one month or four in two months, to be dismissed. The official interpretation of the decree was that penalties milder than dismissal should be imposed only when the worker was less than twenty minutes late, or was idling for less than twenty minutes. If he were later than this on any one occasion, then he should be immediately dismissed. Besides losing his living accommodation, if attached to his place of employment, a dismissed worker suffers in other ways. For instance, not only pensions for disability, old-age and dependents, but also rates of sickness benefit depend upon the length of employment at one enterprise. To ensure the fulfilment of this new decree, it was stipulated that directors of enterprises and factory shops who did not impose these penalties would be liable to dismissal and penal prosecution. Nevertheless, after less than two years, it became obvious that, because of the shortage of labour, the threat of dismissal was not bringing about the desired results, and the punishments were revised.[58] As from 26 June 1940, instead of dismissal, any worker absent even for a single day without a reason satisfactory to the authorities was now liable to compulsory labour without confinement for up to six months at his usual place of work and to a reduction in wages of up to 25 per cent. Under this revised law, no worker may leave his job unless he is either physically unfit to work, or is accepted into an educational institution or is given special permission by a higher authority.

After the issue of this decree, unjustified attempts on the part of workers to get doctors' certificates excusing them from work were punished very severely. Thus, for instance, *Izvestia* of 27 August 1940, reported: 'The case of T.V. Timonin, born in 1915. On 23 August [the defendant] appeared at a clinic where he demanded that he be issued a doctor's certificate excusing him from work. Becoming chagrined because the thermometer indicated only normal temperature, he indulged in debauchery and used unprintable language. He was sentenced on 23 August to three years in gaol and was not permitted to live in nine specified cities of the Soviet Union after the completion of the sentence.'

A few months after the promulgation of this law, some women wrote to the press suggesting that domestic servants should be made subject to this law.[59] It is an amazing commentary on the developments within the USSR that, although disagreeing with the suggestion, *Izvestia*, the newspaper concerned, showed no astonishment that it should be made in a period of alleged 'transition from socialism to communism'!

From the law against labour truancy it is merely a step to such a declaration as was made in the journal of the Department of Propaganda and Agitation of the Moscow Party Committee: 'No-one who does not use all 480 minutes for productive work is observing labour discipline.'[60] One may be sure that outside Russia not one worker in the world observes this necessary 'socialist' standard!

On 19 October 1940 a decree was issued which allowed the administration of industry to carry out the 'compulsory transfer of plant engineers, technicians, foremen, employees and skilled workers from one enterprise or institute to another.'[61]

A further savage curtailment of working class freedom was introduced by a decree of 26 December 1941. This decree imposed penalties ranging from five to eight years in prison for workers who left military industries without permission (the offenders to be tried by military tribunal).[62] Yet another, issued on 15 April 1943, placed railway workers under complete military discipline. They could be kept under arrest quite legally by order of their superiors for up to twenty days without trial and without an opportunity of appeal to the courts.[63] Similar regulations were applied to maritime and inland waterways workers,[64] post, telegraph and radio employees, electric power employees and others. Offences such as leaving a job without permission were henceforth punished very harshly.[65] It is clear that these war regulations have continued in force after the war.

Very soon after the triumph of the Stalinist bureaucracy, in the late twenties, strikes were prohibited and strikers rendered liable to the death sentence. Since the abolition of capital punishment, the penalty has been twenty years' penal servitude. It is true, of course, that strikes were not referred to by name, so that the following Article, decreed on 6 June 1927, is the only item in the *Collection of Laws* which could be interpreted by the courts as dealing with strikes: 'Counter-revolutionary sabotage, i.e., knowingly *omitting to discharge a given duty*, or discharging it with deliberate carelessness, with the specific object of weakening the authority of the government or the government machine, entails deprivation of liberty for a period of not less than one year and confiscation of property in whole or in part, provided that where there are aggravating circumstances of a particularly serious nature, the penalty shall be increased to the supreme measure of social defence – death by shooting, with confiscation of property.[66]

The significance of Stalinist labour legislation has been well summed up in these words: 'in comparison with the legislation of the New Economic Policy period, when private enterprise was tolerated, the legal status of labour has changed for the worse. All the channels through which labour can plead its case in the capitalist world – legislation, courts, administrative agencies and trade unions – are in the Soviet Union the agency of the principal employer of industrial labour – the government. Another feature of the present Soviet labour law is the numerous penal provisions. The labour law is to a large extent criminal law.'[67]

Female labour

The conditions of the workers as a whole are certainly grim; those of women workers are simply appalling.

The Labour Code of 1922 prohibited the employment of women (and young persons) 'in particularly heavy and un-healthy production, and in work underground.'[68] An order issued by the Commissariat of Labour and the Supreme Economic Council on 14 November 1923, prohibited the employment of women for work consisting *entirely* of carry-ing or moving loads exceeding 10 Russian pounds (4.1 kilo-grams). The carrying of loads up to 40 pounds (16.4 kilo-grams) was allowed only if it was directly connected with the woman's normal work, and if it did not occupy more than one-third of her working day.[69] Today not one of these safeguards remains. For instance, women work in mines, often on the heaviest work in the pit, and the Soviet author-ities describe this as a great achievement. The same applies to the carrying of heavy loads in the building industry, work as stevedores, railroad builders, and so on.

In 1932, the Scientific Council of the Commissariat of Labour asked four institutes charged with research into occupational disease in various coal-mining districts to in-vestigate the effects of underground employment on women. The institute in the Caucasus coal district carried out a clinical investigation of 592 female coal workers, of whom 148 were employed in surface work and 444 underground, and arrived at the conclusion that underground work is no more harmful to expectant mothers than is surface work. Furthermore, 'it was the unanimous consent of all institutes charged with this research that a considerable increase in female employment in coal mining, including various operations underground, is possible without any harm to the female body.'[70] Women in mines are doing all types of jobs, including loading and hewing, as is testified by the Russian press. One organ wrote: 'For the first time in the Donetz Basin, a team of women loaders has been organised. Now 10 women of the Babicheva's Brigade daily load fourteen to fifteen tons of coal each. This team has already its own hewing machine operator, Paulina Tantsyura.'[71]

Another official writer had this to say in 1937: 'The most interesting point is that Soviet women have gained and continue to gain in those branches of industry which are closed to women in capitalist society, and which in capitalist countries are regarded as a man's job from which women are "by nature" excluded. Women thus play a very negligible role in capitalist mining industry. The proportion of women to the total numbers employed in the mining industries is, for France (1931), 2.7 per cent; for Italy (1931), 1.8 per cent; for Germany (1932), 1.0 per cent; USA (1930), 0.6 per cent; and in Great Britain, 0.6 per cent. In the USSR women represent 27.9 per cent of the total number of people working in the mining industry. The building trade offers a similar picture. In the countries mentioned above, the percentages for this trade range from 0.5 per cent (Italy) to 2.9 per cent (Germany). In the USSR women constitute 19.7 per cent. In the metal industries the percentages range from 3.0 per cent (USA) to 5.4 per cent (Great Britain). In the metal industries of the USSR, 24.6 per cent of all workers are women.'[72] The Stalinist author omitted to mention that there *are* two other countries besides the USSR where many women are employed in the mines – India and Japan,[73] both notorious for the terrible conditions of the workers.

The following eye-witness account of the harsh conditions under which female labour is employed in building railways was given by Charlotte Haldane, who at the time was very well disposed to Stalin's regime:

> In Archangel it was necessary to lay down a light railway track for about five miles along the docks . . . I watched this being done, entirely by women. The track, complete with points, was laid in forty-eight hours. They went at it day and night, by daylight and electric light. It was snowing and freezing nearly all the time, but this made no difference to their labours. All the cargo checkers were women too. They worked in shifts, twenty-four hours on, twenty-four hours off. During their working period they had occasional brief rests of an hour or two, when they retired to a wooden hut on the quay, ate their cabbage soup and black bread, drank their imitation tea, had an uneasy doze in their clothes, and returned to work.[74]

Hindus, another of Stalin's well-wishers, wrote:

> One of the remarkable aspects of Russian life is the presence of women as day labourers. They work with pick and shovel, they carry heavy loads of lumber, they cart wheelbarrows. At the time that Moscow was building the subways women worked underground side by side with men. A common sight in any city is that of women laying bricks, putting in rafters, performing the other heavy tasks in construction. On night shifts they are as conspicuous on such jobs as on day shifts.[75]

Side by side with reports like these, how ironical sounds Stakhanov's statement: 'For the Soviet people work has become a pleasure.'[76]

Forced labour

In Russia forced labour exists in a number of forms and in varying degrees. For instance, contracts are made between kolkhoz chairmen and industrial plants, mines or transport undertakings, by which the kolkhoz undertakes to supply a certain number of workers. Such types of forced labour will, however, not be dealt with in this section. We shall deal only with forced labour in its extreme form, in the slave camps where labour power is not bought and sold as a commodity, because the labourer himself has no legal freedom.

Until the First Five-Year Plan, prison labour was on far too small a scale to have any real significance in the Russian economy. In 1928 there were only 30,000 prisoners in camps, and the authorities were opposed to compelling them to work. In 1927, the official in charge of prison administration wrote that: 'The exploitation of prison labour, the system of squeezing "golden sweat" from them, the organisation of production in places of confinement, which while profitable from a commercial point of view is fundamentally lacking in corrective significance – these are entirely inadmissible in Soviet places of confinement.'[77] At that time the value of the total production of all prisoners equalled only a small percentage of the cost of their upkeep.

With the inauguration of the Five-Year Plan, however, the situation changed radically. 'Kiseliov-Gromov, himself a former GPU official in the northern labour camps, states that in 1928 only 30,000 men were detained in the camps ... The total number of prisoners in the entire network of camps in 1930 he gives as 662,257.'[78] On the evidence available, Dallin concludes that by 1931 there were nearly two million people in labour camps, by 1933–35 about five million, and by 1942, from eight to fifteen million.[79] The one-time leader of the Yugoslav Communist Party, Anton Ciliga, who was held in Russian concentration camps for many years, estimates that the number of prisoners at the height of the purges of the thirties reached about ten million.[80]

The extent of slave labour in USSR may be gauged not only from the reports published in the Russian press of heavy punishments for the most elementary crimes, such as theft of bread,* but indirectly, from the statistics of voters. Everyone of eighteen years of age and over has the right to vote, except the inmates of forced labour camps. According to the census of 1939, 58.4 per cent of the population were aged eighteen and over at that time. By 1946, this percentage had almost certainly risen. For one thing, there was a smaller proportion of children in the new areas added to the USSR, such as Lithuania and Latvia, than in her 1939 territory, and, for another, the war not only caused a greater increase in the death rate of children than of adults, but also caused a sharp decline in the birth rate. But even assuming that the proportion of people aged eighteen and over was nearly the same in 1946 as in 1939, out of a population of 193 million there must still have been 112.7 million people in that age group. Yet only 101.7 million had the right to vote in the elections. According to this method of calculation, at least eleven million must have been in slave labour camps.

There are other pointers to the mass character of the forced labour camps. For instance, during the second world war the German Volga Republic was dissolved for alleged lack of loyalty to the regime, and its population was banished, in all probability to labour camps. In the areas of the USSR formerly occupied by the Germans a number of republics were dissolved. These dissolutions were not even mentioned in the press. And it was only when *Pravda*, on 17 October 1945, gave a list of the constituencies for the coming general

---

*See below, pages 71-74

elections that it was discovered that a number of republics had disappeared, since when one cannot know. They were the autonomous Crimean Tartar Republic, the Kalmuk Republic, and the Checheno-Ingush Republic, as well as the autonomous Karachev region.[81] The Kabardinian-Balkar autonomous Republic became the Kabardinian Republic after the expulsion of the Balkars.[82] The population of these regions was more than two million. No official information is available as to their whereabouts. Again, in all probability, they have been sent to labour camps.

But the clearest indication of the extent of slave labour in Russia from a Soviet official source is to be found in *State Plan of the Development of the National Economy of USSR for 1941*.[83] According to this source the value of the gross output of all enterprises managed by the NKVD was planned to be, in 1941, 1,969 million roubles at 1926/27 prices.[84] What an advance since 1925, when the total output of all convict labour was 3.8 million roubles[85] – an increase of more than 500 times! If the output per prison worker was the same in 1941 as in 1925, there would have been as many as fifteen million slave labourers. Probably the productivity of labour in the camps was considerably higher in 1941 than in 1925, and probably the estimate of the output of NKVD enterprises in 'fixed 1926/27 prices' was somewhat inflated. But even after making the necessary corrections, it is clear that slave camps hold *millions* of people.

The impossibility of computing exactly how many slaves there are in the camps is due to the complete absence of official statistics. Until the beginning of the thirties a considerable bulk of statistics was published relative to trials, prisons and prisoners, but since then, publication of such figures has ceased entirely. It is symptomatic, that a book called *Court Statistics*, by A.A.Gertsenzon (Moscow 1948), gives actual figures for the United States, Britain, Germany,

Canada, India, Belgium, Denmark, Finland, Italy, Greece, Holland, Austria, Sweden, Switzerland, and Norway, but for the USSR gives only years I, II, etc. – without mentioning which they are – and about regions I, II, etc. – without mentioning where they are. It merely notes that in these regions there is a population of 4.7 million. Since that figure is a very small percentage of the total population of the USSR, neither absolute figures nor even general trends can be adduced therefrom.

It is highly significant that the published results of the 1939 census do not include the distribution of population according to districts. This information, which normal census tables always include, would have made it possible to estimate the number of people in slave camps with considerable accuracy, because there are certain districts that are definitely known to have almost no free population.

A clear proof of the presence of children, mothers, pregnant women, old men and women, in Russia's labour camps was given by the amnesty decree of 27 March 1953. This released from prison and labour camps 'women with children under ten years of age, men over 55 and women over 50, and also convicted persons suffering from grave, incurable illness.'[86]

Slave labour is generally very unproductive. The Russian government resorts to it on such an enormous scale simply because it is relatively so very much poorer in capital than in man-power compared with the advanced countries of Western Europe and the United States. At the same time, paradoxically, it serves to overcome bottlenecks caused by labour scarcity in certain regions and industries. At all periods of history, when labour has been scarce, the state has imposed legal restrictions on the freedom of the workers, as in Western Europe in the fourteenth and early fifteenth centuries, and again in the seventeenth century. The slaves in Stalin's camps are a crude version of the 'army of unemployed' of traditional capitalism, that is, they serve to keep the rest of the workers 'in their places'. In addition to this, it must be remembered that in the USSR there are many highly distasteful tasks to be accomplished (in the far north, for instance), which free or even semi-free workers could be induced to undertake only by the offer of very powerful incentives. In spite of its extremely low productivity, slave labour is, in such cases, the cheapest, if not the only, possible method. This is exemplified by the following extract from *Izvestia*. Describing operations on a new railway line built in Siberia by forced labour, it points out that: 'Up to the present it was thought that the building season does not go beyond a hundred days in a year. The winter is very cold, 50° below zero. But the builders have proved, that even under such conditions, it is possible to work the whole year through without interruption.'[87]

One could not end the present section better than by quoting Vyshinsky's words: 'Work enthusiasm, socialist consciousness and the lofty feeling of duty towards the state, the fatherland and the Soviet people, decide questions of work discipline among us – not penalties or threats of criminal punishment as in capitalist countries.'[88]

The subordination of consumption to accumulation - the subordination of the workers to the means of production

Under capitalism the consumption of the masses is subordinated to accumulation. Sometimes consumption increases at the same time as accumulation, at other times it decreases while accumulation rises; but always, in every situation, the basic relationship remains.

If we follow the history of Russia from October, we find that until the advent of the Five-Year Plan this subordination did not exist, but from then on expressed itself in unprecedented brutality. This will become clear from the following table: [89]

Division of gross output of industry into means of production and means of consumption (in percentages)

	1913	1927-8	1932	1937	1940	1942 (planned)
Means of production	44.3	32.8	53.3	57.8	61.0	62.2
Means of consumption	55.7	67.2	46.7	42.2	39.0	37.8

Even if these figures do not tell the whole story, for it is almost certain that this official calculation has not given due weight to the facts that the turnover taxes are imposed mainly on means of consumption and that the subsidies are devoted almost exclusively to means of production (see below) with consequent distortion of the price system.

The figures available concerning the actual change in the volume of output of consumer goods are very meagre and in their interpretation we meet great difficulties indeed.

It is inadvisable to include products, like bread, whose rise in output is not the reflection of a total increase in production, but simply of a shift from home-processing, not covered by statistics, to industry, which *is* covered. [90]

	1913	1928/9	1932	1937	1945	1949	1950
Cotton goods (thousand million metres)	2.9	2.74	2.7	3.4	1.7	3.7	3.8
Woollen goods (million metres)	95.0	96.6	91.3	108.3	56.9	153.9	167.0
Leather shoes (pairs)		23.2	82.0	164.2	60.0	156.0	205.0
Raw sugar (thousand tons)	1,290.0	1,340.0	828.0	2421.0			2,522.0
Paper (thousand tons)	197.0	316.0	478.5	831.5			
Hosiery (million pairs)			154.0	401.0	83.0	340.3	
Linen (million metres)		162.0	130.0	278.0			
Soap (thousand tons)			357.2	495.0			866.0

This table shows only a very modest increase in the output of consumer goods – except for the case of leather shoes, paper and sugar.

Regarding the interpretation of these figures, it must be pointed out that while the figures for 1913 are adjusted to the reduced territory of USSR after the Revolution, the figures for 1945 and 1949 are not adjusted to the greatly enlarged post-war territory. (Russian annexations from 1939 onwards, included it will be recalled, Lithuania, Latvia, Esthonia, the Eastern part of Poland, etc.) Furthermore, until 1928 at least, very small factories made an important contribution to the production of means of consumption. In 1929, large-scale industrial plants – defined as employing more than thirty people, or having a motive power keeping more than fifteen people occupied – employed 3.2 million persons, while small-scale industry employed 4.5 million persons.

However, goods produced in this way during the Plan era were excluded from the Stalinist statistics. This, perhaps, explains the tremendous increase (on paper) in leather shoe production, an increase that cannot be squared with what is known about available supplies of leather. The number of animals slaughtered annually after the big collectivisation drive could never have reached the number slaughtered previously, as it was not until 1938 that the total number of livestock again approached the 1929 level. (In 1929 cattle numbered 68.1 million, in 1938, 63.2; sheep and goats numbered 147.2 and 102.1 respectively).[91] Furthermore, the surplus of imported hides, skins, and leather over those exported was 45.3 thousand tons in 1927–28, as against only 15.6 thousand tons in 1939.[92] Obviously only a miracle could increase leather shoe production simultaneously with a decreasing supply of leather. In the case of hosiery one overwhelmingly important fact is overlooked: the majority of hose used to be produced by artisans. As regards paper, output *has* undoubtedly increased enormously due to the propaganda needs of the government, the needs of administration and the cultural needs connected with industrialisation.

The subordination of consumption to accumulation is clear enough if we put side by side the series of targets of output of consumer goods in the different Five-Year Plans and those of production goods. It will be found that the Soviet government, while promising a rise in the production of means of consumption with every Five-Year Plan, fixes the actual target of the Plan at a volume of production which does not exceed the target of former Plans. This is shown clearly by the following table:[93]

Targets of production for the end of the Five-Year Plans

Some means of consumption	1st	2nd	3rd	4th	5th
Cotton goods (000m metres)	4.7	5.1	4.9	4.7	6.1
Woollen goods (million metres)	270.0	227.0	177.0	159.0	257.0
Linen (million metres)	500.0	600.0	385.0		
Socks (million pairs)		725.0		580.0	
Shoes (million pairs)	80.0	180.0	258.0	240.0	318.0
Soap (thousand tons)		1,000.0	925.0	870.0	
Sugar (million tons)	2.6	2.5	3.5	2.4	4.3
Paper (thousand tons)	900.0	1,000.0		1,340.0	1,740.0
Vegetable oil (thousand tons)	1,100.0	750.0	850.0	880.0	1,372.0
Some means of production					
Electric current (milliard kwh.)	22.0	33.0	75.0	82.0	162.5
Coal (million tons)	75.0	152.5	243.0	250.0	372.0
Pig iron (million tons)	10.0	17.4	22.0	19.5	34.1
Steel (million tons)	10.4	17.0	28.0	25.4	44.2
Oil (million tons)	21.7	46.8	54.0	35.4	69.9

However, when the Russian government boasts that 'in 1950 we will reach the level of 4.7 milliard metres of cotton goods', they are not embarrassed by having made the same promise twenty years ago, when the population of USSR was about fifty million less than now, as their police and propaganda combine to keep memories as short as goods.

To turn to actual production, we find that not only are

the *targets* for consumer goods much more modest than those for capital goods, but also (still according to official figures) the *rate* of realisation of these targets is much lower for the former than for the latter:

Percentage fulfilment of the planned increase in the First, Second & Fourth Five-Year Plans[94]

Means of production	1st	2nd	4th
Coal	72.3	71.5	112.9
Crude oil	107.1	33.6	154.5
Electricity	49.1	93.5	124.6
Pig Iron	43.3	83.8	97.8
Steel	24.4	106.4	126.8
Rolled steel	19.3	100.0	163.8
Cement	36.3	49.1	95.7

Means of consumption	1st	2nd	4th
Cotton goods	—3.0	31.0	—8.8
Woollen goods	—3.3	10.6	119.3
Shoes	26.1	83.3	0.0
Paper and cardboard	32.2	52.1	72.3
Matches	1.6	25.4	—
Soap	36.9	21.7	96.7

The accumulation of capital on the one hand and poverty on the other

Until 1928, notwithstanding the increasing bureaucratisation, the slow accumulation of wealth in the statified economy was not accompanied by a growth of poverty, as the following table shows:

Capital of large-scale industry

Year	Million roubles 1926/7 prices[95]	Index 1921 = 100	Year	Real wages[96]
1921	7,930	100	1913	100
1922	7,935	100.1	1922/3	47.3
1923	7,969	100.5	1923/4	69.1
1924	8,016	101.1	1924/5	85.1
1925	8,105	102.2	1925/6	96.7
1927	9,151	115.4	1926/7	108.4
1928	9,841	124.1	1927/8	111.1
			1928/9	115.6

Thus, even according to the calculations of Professor Prokopovicz, ex-Minister of the Kerensky government whom no-one would suspect of partiality towards the Bolsheviks, real wages of Russian workers in 1928–29 were 15.6 per cent higher than before the war. At the same time working hours were cut by 22.3 per cent. If we also took social services into account the rise in real wages would be even more pronounced. Another point that comes to light from this table is that in the last few years before the inauguration of the Five-Year Plan, as the bureaucracy strengthened itself, real wages almost ceased to rise, and the rate of the rise lagged a little behind the rate of accumulation.

The situation changed radically with the inauguration of the Plan. From then on accumulation leaped ahead tremendously, while the standard of living of the masses not only lagged far behind, but even declined absolutely compared with 1928. The following table gives an indication of the rate of accumulation:[97]

Investment of capital
(thousand million current roubles)

	Total	In industry
1923/4–1927/8	26.5	4.4
1928/9–1932	52.5	24.8
1933–1937	114.7	58.6
1938–1942 (Plan)	192.0	111.9
1946–1950 (Plan)	250.3	

Even making due mental allowance for the decline in the value of the rouble in these years, it is clear from a glance at this table that a tremendous accumulation of capital took place. In 1933 prices, the fixed capital of Russian industry was 10.3 milliard roubles in 1928 and rose to 22.6 milliard roubles in 1932 and to 59.9 milliard roubles in 1937.[98]

From 1928 the Russian authorities stopped publishing the index of real wages and of the cost of living and, from 1931, wholesale or retail prices. It is, therefore, very difficult to calculate changes in the level of real wages. All the available evidence shows, however, that, on the whole, the level has not risen since the introduction of the Plans. Thus, for instance, the purchasing power of average wages measured in food changed as follows:[99]

Year	'Food baskets' per monthly wage	
	Number	Index
1913	3.7	100
1928	5.6	151.4
1932	4.8	129.7
1935	1.9	51.4
1937	2.4	64.9
1940	2.0	54.1

This calculation of the changes in the purchasing power of wages expressed in food is confirmed by statistics of the actual consumption of some foodstuffs per head of the population.

Annual consumption of milk and meat per head of population (in kilograms)[100]

Year	Milk			Meat		
	Total	Rural	Urban	Total	Rural	Urban
1927-8	189	183	218	27.5	22.6	29.1
1932	105	111	85	13.5	10.3	21.8
1937	132	126	144	14.0	8.5	25.5

A comparison of the consumption of, say, meat, in the USSR in 1937 with that of Germany and France during the last decades of the nineteenth century shows how abysmally low the level of food consumption in the USSR has fallen. In 1898 meat consumption in Berlin fluctuated between 130 and 150 pounds (61 and 68 kilograms) per head, and in Breslau it averaged 86 pounds (39 kilograms) per head, in 1880–89. France showed the following position in 1852: in Paris consumption was 79.31 kilograms, in other towns 58.87 kilograms, in the villages 21.89 kilograms, France as a whole, 33.05 kilograms.[101]

As regards the consumption of some industrial consumer

goods, the following information has been culled from Soviet sources.

Basing his calculations on the official figures of the output of cotton goods and shoes, and on Voznessensky's statement of the portion taken by the army, occupational clothing, and so on,[102] Jasny comes to the following conclusion regarding the civilian consumption of these goods:

The quantity of cotton goods available for private consumption fell from 15.2 metres per capita in 1927–28, to less than 10 metres in 1940.'[103] Although the number of shoes available per person increased from 0.40 pairs in 1927–28, to 0.83 pairs in 1940; there was during the same period 'a great deterioration in the quality of shoes owing to the shortage of leather.'[104] The per capita consumption of woollen goods, excluding the portion taken by the army, occupational clothing, etc., was 0.66 metres in 1929, and 0.65 metres in 1937; of sugar (raw), 8.5 kilograms in 1929 and 14.7 kilograms in 1937.[105]

One can see how low these figures are by glancing at the figures of the output of consumers' goods in other countries: in Britain, in the same year, 1937, 60 square metres of cotton goods, 7.4 metres of woollen goods, and 2.2 pairs of leather shoes were produced, per capita. In the face of stubborn facts like these, one might assume that Kuibyshev, the late chairman of Gosplan, had a fine sense of humour when he declared to the Seventeenth Conference of the Party (January 1932):

We think it absolutely necessary to ensure, in the Second Five-Year Plan, such an expansion of the output of food and light industries and agriculture as will secure an increase in the level of consumption of not less than 2-3 times ... An approximate calculation of the consumption level in 1937 allows us to assert that in this year the Soviet Union will be, as regards the level of consumption, the most advanced country in the world.[106]

But the most extreme expression of the subordination of

workers' standards to the needs of capital accumulation is to be seen in the housing conditions of the Russian people.

The housing construction plans of the government and the co-operatives have never been realised since the Five-Year Plans were inaugurated, as the following table shows:[107]

Housing	Target	Fulfilment	% fulfilled
	(million sq. m.)		
First Five-Year Plan	53	22.6	42.6
Second Five-Year Plan	61.4	26.8	43.9

The Third Five-Year Plan was interrupted by the war, and so it is difficult to estimate the extent to which its housing target was realised.

At the same time the urban population grew very quickly. Unavoidably, therefore, this failure to achieve housing construction targets has meant that housing space per capita of the urban population declined even below the meagre standards of 1928:[108]

Year	Urban population millions	Living space in towns* Total mill. sq. m.	Per person sq. m.
1923	18.9	118.4	6.2
1927-8	26.3	160.2	6.1
1932	39.7	185.1	4.66
1937	50.2	211.9	4.5
1939	55.9	225.0	4.0

The living space available throughout the period covered by the table was far below the minimum sanitary norm, which according to a 1947 official statement, was 8.25 square metres.[109]

The housing area per person in 1949 in some other countries was: Denmark, 21 square metres; Ireland, 17; Sweden, 23; Belgium, 15; France, 23; Greece (estimated), 16; Italy 12.[110]

Some idea of what a living space of four square metres means may be gained by considering that in Britain the

---

* Kitchen, bathroom, hall, etc., space not included.

minimum allowed in new buildings is from 550 to 950 square feet per dwelling,[111] or about 51–88 square metres.

The decrease in the average floor space per person is more pronounced in Moscow and Leningrad and in the newly established industrial centres than elsewhere.

An article in *Soviet News* praising Soviet housing conditions, says of Moscow: 'An idea of the Soviet Union's progress in housing may be obtained from the example of Moscow, which is a model in modern town development for all other capitals of the world. Since the advent of Soviet power, 65 million square feet of housing have been built in Moscow, or half as much as was built in the city during its whole existence before the Revolution. Every year Moscow is building on an increasing scale.'[112] The fly in the ointment, one that the official handout delicately ignores, is that the *population* of Moscow has increased to an even greater extent than have the housing facilities. In 1912 there were 1,600,000 inhabitants, and 11,900,000 square metres of housing space, an average of 7.4 square metres per head; in 1939, 4,137,000 inhabitants and 17,400,000 square metres of housing space, an average of only 4.2 square metres per head; and by 1950 the number of inhabitants had risen to 5,100,000, and the housing space to only 18,600,000 square metres, an average of a mere 3.65 square metres per head.

Houses built under the plans were most primitive. For example, of all urban houses built in 1935, 32 per cent had no water supply, 38 per cent had no sewerage, 92.7 per cent had no gas supply, and 54.7 per cent had no central heating.[113] In 1939, in new houses controlled by town Soviets in the RSFSR (which included most of the best residential buildings), the percentage of housing space with the following amenities was: piped water supply, 60.5 per cent; sewerage, 43.7 per cent; central heating, 17.5 per cent; electric light 93.8 per cent; baths, 11.7 per cent.[114] Whole towns are entirely lacking in the most elementary communal amenities. It is rather shocking, for instance, to discover that the Fourth Five-Year Plan undertook to instal sewerage in thirteen cities, among them Archangelsk (with a population of 281,091 in 1939), Tomsk (with a population of 141,215 in the same year), Irkutsk (with 243,380), Kherson (with 97,186).[115] Out of 2,354 towns and workers' settlements only 460 had a piped water supply, 140 had sewerage, and 6 a gas supply.[116]

These are the facts on which the following official declaration is 'based'. 'The tempo and scale of housing construction in the USSR has no parallel anywhere in the world,' as is a similar one made some fifteen years earlier, that 'The housing conditions of the workers in the Soviet Union are incomparably better than in any capitalist state.'[117]

The claim in *Soviet News*, that house-building in Russia outstripped that of any other country, is quite ridiculous, as the following figures show. In the sixteen years between 1923 and 1939 there was an increase of only 106.6 million square metres in housing accommodation in Russian towns, whereas in England and Wales, in the four years 1925–1928 alone, a total floor space of not less than 70 million square metres was built.[118]

Is it necessary to give additional proof that the accumulation of wealth on the one hand means the accumulation of poverty on the other?

Industry subordinated to war

It is very difficult to get a clear picture of the extent of the war industries. The budget figures on defence mean very little as is shown in the following comparison of the amounts devoted to defence and 'social-cultural welfare' (education, health, physical training, pensions, etc.)[119]

	Defence	Social and cultural welfare
1935	8.2	13.1
1936	14.9	20.0
1937	17.5	25.7
1938	23.2	35.3
1939	39.2	37.4
1940	56.1	40.9
1946	73.6	80.0
1947	66.3	106.0
1948	66.3	105.6
1949	79.2	116.0
1950	82.9	116.9
1951	93.9	118.9

Note that in 1940, on the eve of the Nazi invasion, the defence budget was only very slightly more than that devoted to social and cultural welfare, and in 1949, when the 'cold war' was already raging fiercely, it was less. This is indeed strange.

Some factors contributing to this purely statistical phenomenon are: (1) Part of the expenditure of the Ministry of the Interior (NKVD or MVD) serve military purposes; (2) Expenditure on building munitions factories, military installations, barracks, etc., is included in the budget of ministries other than that of defence; (3) Expenditure on military schools is included in the budget of the Ministry of Education. But all these factors, and other similar ones, go only a short way towards explaining the small defence budget. The main explanation lies in the extreme cheapness – artificially induced – of armaments. As a result of heavy turnover taxes on means of consumption and huge subsidies to heavy industries, especially armaments, the price relationships between the products of heavy industry and those of the rest of the economy is drastically distorted. The coal and steel that go into the production of the machine tools which produce the armaments, the coal and steel that go into the direct production of armaments themselves, the transport of all these elements, etc., are heavily subsidised. Thus the prices of armaments are cumulatively reduced by the subsidy system. Insofar as turnover taxes made up about two-thirds of the prices of consumers' goods, and as subsidies, directly and indirectly, probably reduce the price of armaments to about one-third of the actual cost of their production, one should, to obtain a true picture, multiply their price by nine, and compare this figure with that of the total price of consumers' goods (including social and cultural services). Unless this is done, the picture remains quite out of touch with reality. For instance, the plan for 1941 stipulated that the total price of the products of all defence industries would be 40,300 million roubles, while that of the textile industry, at 46,000 million roubles, would be higher.[120]

Despite all these difficulties, however, we have, thanks to Professor M.Gardner Clark, of Cornell University, a reasonably accurate picture of the weight of armaments production in the Russian economy.

Relying solely on official sources he calculated the portion of all the iron and steel output of Russia which was used in the production of munitions, as well as the portion of all iron and steel utilised for the construction of munitions factories. The results of his research are summed up in the following table:[121]

Consumption of iron and steel by munitions industries in the USSR, 1932-1938 (in 1,000 metric tons and percentages)

Item	1932	1933	1934	1935	1936	1937	1938
1 Total tonnage consumed by munitions	1646.6	1378.1	2204.6	2667.9	2873.3	4019.1	4986.2
2 Munitions as % of machine building	40.4	32.6	38.2	38.0	35.4	47.1	57.5
3 Munitions as % of total USSR construction	21.8	17.5	17.5	19.3	17.4	23.2	29.2
4 Tonnage consumed by munitions for construction	252.3	135.6	164.4	290.8	745.5	793.0	880.1
5 Munitions as % of machine building construction	45.8	65.9	72.8	73.4	82.5	84.5	94.3
6 Munitions as % of total USSR construction	17.1	12.8	11.3	13.5	21.8	24.7	30.6

Thus, as early as 1932, munitions accounted for 21.8 per cent of all iron and steel – a very high percentage, as may be seen by comparison with the percentage of 29.2 for 1938, a year when war preparations were in full swing. Munitions plants accounted for nearly half of all iron and steel used in the construction of machine-building plants, and by 1938 nearly all other machinery plant construction had ceased, munitions construction accounting for 94.3 per cent of all iron and steel consumed in machine-building construction.

The armed forces also took a large part of the output of consumers' goods. Thus N.A.Voznessensky, writing as chairman of the Planning Commission (Gosplan), stated that in 1940 only 46 per cent of the cotton goods produced and 79 per cent of the shoes were sold 'on the broad market', the rest presumably going almost entirely to the army (except for a small portion given over to the production of working clothes for factories, transport, etc.)[122]

During the whole Plan era, the armament industry occupies a *decisive* place in Russia's economic system.

The productivity of labour and the worker

In a workers' state a rise in the productivity of labour is accompanied by an improvement in the conditions of the workers. As Trotsky said in 1928, real wages 'must become the main criterion for measuring the success of socialist evolution'. The 'criterion of socialist upswing is constant improvement of labour standards'. Let us see what the relation between the rise in the productivity of labour and the standard of living of the workers was in Russia. The following table gives an indication of this:

	Productivity of labour[132]	Number of 'food baskets' per average monthly wages[134]
Year	index	index
1913	100	100
1928	106.0	151.4
1936	331.9	64.9

Thus till 1928 not only were wages above pre-war, but they rose much more than the productivity of labour. Between 1928 and 1936, while the productivity of labour more than trebled, real wages were actually cut by more than 50 per cent.

The same conclusion can be reached in another way by comparing the level of productivity in Russia with that of other countries on the one hand, and the standard of living of the Russian workers with that of workers in other countries on the other.

In 1913 the average productivity of labour in Russian industry was about 25 per cent of that in the USA, 35 per cent of that in Germany, and 40 per cent of that in Britain. A committee of the Gosplan, appointed in 1937 to investigate the productivity of labour in Russian industry, found that it was 40.5 per cent of productivity in US industry, and 97 per cent of that in Germany.[125] There is ground for the assumption that this calculation is exaggerated, and that the productivity of labour in Russian industry in 1937 was about 30 per cent of that in the USA, 70 per cent of that in Germany, and about the same percentage of that in Britain. A detailed explanation of how we arrived at this conclusion would be too lengthy. But as the conclusions of the Gosplan committee do not invalidate our argument, and on the contrary only strengthen it, the exact figure is of minor importance. To resume, while the Russian worker produces about 70 per cent as much as a British worker, his standard of living is very much lower.

In the following table we assume that the Russian worker earns 500 roubles per month, which is the average wage of all state employees (the bureaucracy included), planned for the end of the Fourth Five-Year Plan in 1950. On the other hand, we have taken as the basis of the price calculation prices from Zone 1, where prices are lowest in Russia.[126] For Britain we have taken the *workers'* average weekly earnings of £5 3s. 6d.[127] The basis of the price calculation is the official figures published by the Board of Trade.

Number of units average weekly wages can buy

	Unit	Russia	Britain
Wheat bread (first grade)	lbs.	41.7	480.7
Wheat bread (second grade)	lbs.	63.3	—
Rye bread	lbs.	91.0	—
Beef	lbs.	9.0	79—127
Butter	lbs.	4.1	77.2
Milk	pints	57—81	247.2
Sugar	lbs.	18.5	412.0
Eggs	number	82—115	706.3
Tea	lbs.	1.6	36.4
Coffee	lbs.	3.4	41.2
Beer	pints	14.4	88.2
Cigarettes	number	464.0	618.0
Men's shoes	pairs	0.4	2—4.5
Women's shoes	pairs	0.4	1—4.0
Women's jackets, semi-wool	number	0.6	1.1—2.3
Stockings, women's cotton	pairs	16.2	25—27.0
Crêpe-de-chine	yards	1.4	23—25.0
Men's suits, single-breasted, semi-wool	number	0.3	0.6—1.5
Men's suits, wool	number	0.1	0.2—0.3
Rubber overshoes	pairs	2.6	9.5
Women's cotton dresses	number	0.2	3.5—6.0
Women's woollen dresses	number	0.6	0.8—2.1
Matches	boxes	577.0	824.0
Combs, women's toilet	number	28.8	103—154
Gramophones	number	0.12	0.6
Radio receiving sets (5 valve)	number	0.20	0.17
Wrist watches	number	0.12	0.3—0.5

If the productivity of labour of a worker in Russian industry is about four-fifths of that of a worker in Britain, while his standard of living is a quarter or a third of that of the British worker, can we conclude otherwise than that if the British worker is exploited, his Russian brother is much more so?*

The expropriation of the peasantry

The October Revolution expropriated the big landlords, the Church and the monarchy. The rural bourgeoisie – the kulaks – were not expropriated, and during the NEP period not only did the old kulaks thrive, but many new ones rose out of the middle peasantry. The kulaks, together with the private merchants, exploited the rural poor. Private capitalism continued to rule agriculture until 1928.

Collectivisation changed the situation fundamentally. We shall not discuss the effect of collectivisation on the class differentiation *among* the agriculturists, but shall deal with only the following question: How did collectivisation affect the *total* income received by the agricultural sector of the economy? The most important factor to deal with in answering this question is the influence collectivisation had on the state's cut out of agriculture, that is, its influence on obligatory deliveries: taxes, payment for work done by Machine Tractor Stations (MTS) and government flour mills. Obligatory deliveries are taxes in kind, in fact if not in name, for the prices paid to the kolkhoz are extremely low. In 1935, the price fixed for obligatory delivery of oats, which the government was re-selling retail for 55–100 kopeks per kilogram, was 4–6 kopeks per kilogram. The figures for rye were 60–100

---

* That the Russian worker today compared to the British worker today is worse off than the Russian worker under the Tsar compared with the British worker of that time is clear if we compare the above table with the following remark of M.Dobb: 'In Tsarist Russia . . . the average wage in mines and factories in 1913 is usually estimated to have been between 20 and 25 roubles per month, or the equivalent of between 40 shillings and 50 shillings in English money at its purchasing power at the time (i.e., about 10 to 13 shillings a week). This represents a figure rather less than a half the level in Britain at that date.' (M.Dobb, *Soviet Economic Development Since 1917*, London, 1948, p. 59).

kopeks and 4.6–6.9 kopeks respectively. The retail price of farina (of poor quality) was 60–70 times the price at which wheat was bought.[128] The price paid for other agricultural products was equally niggardly, and, since then, the differences have become greater. 'The government still pays producers about 10 kopeks per kilogram for delivered wheat, while – since the fall of 1946 – charging the consumer 13 roubles for a kilogram of wheat flour (probably of 85 per cent extraction), more than 100 times as much in terms of grain.'[129]

Secondly, the state receives a considerable proportion of the product as payment in kind for services rendered by the MTS. As the MTS have a monopoly of the supply of agricultural equipment, they are able to charge high rates for its use.

The following table shows how the grain produced by the kolkhozes was disposed of in 1938 (in percentages):[130]

Obligatory deliveries	15.0
Payment to MTS	16.0
Return of loans	2.0
Sales to government and on the market	5.1
Allocation to seed reserves	18.6
Allocation to fodder reserves	13.6
Reserves for assistance to invalids and children's nurseries	0.8
Distribution to members*	26.9
Miscellaneous allocations	2.5

Not only this, but the state also – again these are 1938 figures – appropriated the following exceedingly large shares:[131]

---

* This includes the remuneration of the administrative apparatus. According to an article by A. Teriaeva, 'Organisational-Economic Strengthening of Unified Kolkhozes,' *Voprosy Ekonomiki, 1950, No. 12,* the payments to the administrative apparatus, taking into account the size of the kolkhoz, made up the following proportions of all *trudodni*: kolkhozes with up to 20,000 *trudodni*, 8 per cent; 20–35 thousand, 7 per cent; 35–55 thousand, 6 per cent; 55–75 thousand, 5 per cent; 75–100 thousand, 4 per cent; over 100 thousand, 3 per cent.

	Obligatory deliveries	Payments in kind to MTS	Together
Sunflower seeds	38.7	16.0	54.7
Sugar beets	82.0	17.8	99.8
Cotton, irrigated	81.0	17.5	98.5
Cotton, unirrigated	90.1	5.0	95.1
Meat (1937)	30.0		30.0
Milk (and dairy products in terms of milk) (1937)	44.0		44.0
Wool (1937)	54.7		54.7

These figures may be compared with the frugal share of the kolkhozniks themselves in the output of their so-called 'collectively-owned' farms (1937):[132]

Grain	35.9	Milk	7.6
Sunflower seed	27.0	Butter	26.6
Linseed	3.7	Meat and fat	48.8
Flax	2.6	Wool	7.7
Hempseed	15.7	Honey	35.1
Hemp	3.4	Eggs	26.6
Potatoes	45.4		

At the same time the kolkhozniks have been compelled to work harder and harder on the collective farms, as is shown by the following figures:[133]

Average number of Trudodni* per household

Year	Number	Index
1932	257	100.0
1933	315	122.5
1934	354	133.4
1935	378	147.1
1936	393	152.8
1937	438	170.7
1938	437	170.0

As far as the *length* of the labour-day in the kolkhoz is

---

* *Trudoden* – literally, a workday but actually used as an abstract unit of kolkhoz labour. One day of the most unskilled labour equals one half a *trudoden*, a day of the most highly skilled labour equals two and a half *trudodni*.

concerned, it is no shorter than it was under the tsars. At that time it was- 14 hours for agricultural workers, whilst for horses it was only 11 hours and for oxen 10 hours.[134]

A government decree of 1 August 1940, lays down that during harvest the work-day in kolkhozes, sovkhozes and MTS should begin at five or six in the morning and end at sunset. Again, a pamphlet describing the work of a kolkhoz chairman in an exemplary kolkhoz stated that in spring and at harvest-time the working day was 15 hours, *exclusive* of meal times.[135] A current Russian textbook cites the following time-tables as models:

(a) 'For spring sowing and harvest periods, work starts at 4 am; break for breakfast from 8 to 9 am, break for dinner from 1 to 3 pm; work till . . . 10 pm.[136]

(b) 'For harvest, work is from 5.30 am to 9 pm' (breaks not given).[137]

(c) Stablemen looking after horses appear to have to work from 5 am to 9 pm, or possibly midnight in winter, and from 3 am to 10 pm in summer.[138]

(d) Dairymaids . . . start work at 4.30 am and finish at 8 pm all the year round, with two breaks of one and a half hours a day,[139] and even larger spreadovers are cited elsewhere.

(By the way, the norm demands that dairymaids work the full 365 days a year.)[140]

(e) Hours at a pig farm are from 5 am to 8 pm, with two breaks of 2 hours each.[141]

It is interesting to note that in his book, *The Agrarian Question in Russia at the end of the Nineteenth Century* (1908), Lenin wrote:

'The horseless and one-horse peasants [i.e., the very poor peasants] pay in the form of taxes *one-seventh and one-tenth* respectively of their *gross* expenditure. It is doubtful whether serf dues were as high as that . . .'[142] The agricultural toilers in the 'Socialist Fatherland' pay much more than that!

Collectivisation not only transformed those who came into industry into proletarians, but also those who remained in agriculture. The overwhelming majority of agriculturists are in reality, if not in theory, people who do not own means of production; indeed, we should have less justification in calling the Russian agriculturists of today owners of means of production, than the serfs of the nineteenth century.

Collectivisation has resulted in the freeing of agricultural products for the needs of industrial development, the 'freeing' of the peasantry from its means of production, the transformation of a section of them into reserves of labour power for industry, and the transformation of the rest into part-workers, part-peasants, part-serfs in the kolkhozes.

Similar general results, although different in some important particulars, were achieved by the English bourgeoisie in the sixteenth and seventeenth centuries through the eviction of the peasantry from the land. Marx called this process 'primitive accumulation.'* He wrote: 'The history of this . . . is written in the annals of mankind in letters of blood and fire.'[143]

Much more blood flowed during the primitive accumulation in Russia than in Britain. Stalin accomplished in a few hundred days what Britain took a few hundred years to do. The scale on which he did it and the success with which he carried it out completely dwarf the actions of the Duchess of Sutherland. They bear stern witness to the superiority of a modern industrial economy concentrated in the hands of the state, under the direction of a ruthless bureaucracy.

Engels' prognosis about the future of primitive accumula-

---

* In one fundamental point the process connected with collectivisation is dissimilar to the process which took place in Britain. In Britain the eviction of the peasants created a surplus of agricultural products which was *sold* in the towns. In Russia the overwhelming majority of the surplus of agricultural products is appropriated by the government as taxes without anything being given in exchange.

tion in Russia has been fully realised, although in circumstances different from what he imagined. In a letter to Danielson, dated 24 February 1893, he wrote:

> the circumstances of Russia being the *last* country seized upon by the capitalist *grande industrie*, and at the same time the country with by far the *largest peasant population*, are such as must render the *bouleversement* (upheaval) caused by this economic change more acute than it has been anywhere else. The process of replacing some 500,000 *pomeshchiki* (landowners) and some eighty million peasants by a new class of *bourgeois* landed proprietors cannot be carried out but under fearful sufferings and convulsions. But history is about the most cruel of all goddesses, and she leads her triumphal car over heaps of corpses, not only in war, but also in 'peaceful' economic development.[144]

The turnover tax

Since 1930 the main contribution to capital investment and defence has been from the turnover tax. As M.Dobb writes: 'Indeed we can trace a fairly close correlation, as one might expect, between the mounting curve of expenditure on investment and defence over the decade and the mounting revenue from the turnover tax. In 1932 revenue from this tax, as we have seen, was just over 17 milliard. The combined figure for expenditure out of the budget for defence and for financing the national economy was 25 milliard. In 1934 the two figures were respectively 37 and 37; in 1938 they were 80 and 75; in 1939 they were 92 and 100; in 1940 they were 106 and 113; and in the 1941 estimates they were 124 and 144 (the widened gap in this year being approximately covered by an increase in taxed profits)'.[145]

The turnover tax is the most important single source of Russian state revenue. It makes up the following proportions of the total government income (excluding loans):

1931 46.2% 1932 51.5% 1933 58.2% 1934 64.3%
1935 69.5% 1936 69.7% 1937 69.4% 1938 63.1%
1939 62.1% 1940 58.7% 1942 44.8% 1944 35.3%
1945 40.8% 1946 58.7% 1947 62.1% 1948 60.6%
1949 58.8% 1950 55.9% 1951 57.8%[146]

The turnover tax is similar to the British purchase tax, being levied upon commodities at the time of fabrication and upon government obligatory purchase of agricultural products from the peasants. It is included in the price of the commodity, and so paid to the full by the consumer. The tax is imposed almost solely on agricultural products and on the consumers goods' industries, as can be seen from the following table regarding the proportion of different industries in total output and in government revenue from turnover tax 1939:[147]

Commissariat	Per cent of total gross output	Per cent of turnover tax revenue
Petroleum industry	3.1	8.0
Meat and dairy industry	4.5	7.3
Food industry	11.7	29.7
Textile industry	10.2	13.0
Light industry	7.9	2.6
Agricultural requisitions	2.5	34.4
Other commissariats (chiefly for heavy industry)	60.1	5.0

Thus we find that in 1939 almost 90 per cent of the turnover tax revenue came from impositions on food and consumer goods.

Since the turnover tax is not added to the selling price but is included in it in advance, a turnover tax of, say, 50 per cent actually increases the price of the commodity by 100 per cent; a turnover tax of 75 per cent raises the prices by 300 per cent, and a 90 per cent tax results in a tenfold increase in the acutual price. This must be borne in mind when examining the following figures regarding the rate of turnover tax:[148]

Commodity	Rate %	Date effective
Grain, Ukraine (roubles per quintal):		
Wheat, soft	73.00	
Wheat, hard	74.00	
Rye	60.00	
Barley	46.00	1 April 1940
Oats	25.00	
Buckwheat	289.50	
potatoes (per cent of retail price):	48—62	24 January 1940
Meat (per cent of retail price):		
Beef	67—71	
Veal, pork, mutton	62—67	24 January 1940
Poultry	20—43	
Sausage, frankfurters, smoked meat	50—69	
Fish (per cent of retail price):		
Fish, other than herring	39—53	
Herring, Caspian	35—50	10 April 1940
Caviare	40	
Canned fish, according to kind	5—50	
Salt (per cent of wholesale price):		
Bulk	70—80	1 May 1940
Wrapped, small packages	35—42	
Beverages (per cent of retail price):		
Vodka	84	1 January 1940
Other liquors	55—78	
Soft drinks	20	10 April 1940
Tobacco (per cent of retail price):		
Cigarettes	75—88	1 June 1937
Makhorka	70	
Cotton goods (per cent of wholesale price):		
Calico	55	1 January 1938
Other goods	62—65	

The retrogressive nature of this tax is shown by the fact that while it falls lightly on cars (a mere 2 per cent), radio sets (25 per cent) and caviare (40 per cent), it bears down heavily on wheat (73–74 per cent), salt (70–80 per cent), sugar (73 per cent), laundry soap (61–71 per cent) and cigarettes (75–88 per cent). In the light of these facts it is rather surprising to read the following statement of M.Dobb, in which he talks of the turnover tax: 'it was a means of ensuring that the bulk of the price-rise should be concentrated on luxuries or non-essentials and as little as possible on necessities. This was done by rating the tax on turnover differently for different commodities, the differences ranging from 1 or 2 per cent up to nearly 100 per cent.' ... 'the tax has the effect of a progressive general expenditure tax – a progressive tax on income when it is *spent*.'[149] And again: 'The higher rates of tax are apt to be on luxury goods, since these tend to be in particularly scarce supply. The general effect of the differential rating apparently is, therefore, to cause the price structure to discriminate against non-essentials (and hence to make *real* differences of income smaller than an inspection of *money* differences would lead one at first sight to suppose.'[150]

To gauge the real burden imposed by the turnover tax upon consumers it will be useful to examine simultaneously the total amount of turnover tax and the corresponding net retail turnover:[151]

Year	Gross retail turnover	Turnover tax	Net retail turnover	Rate of tax per cent
	All figures in million roubles			
1931	27,465	11,643	15,822	73.6
1932	40,357	19,514	20,843	93.6
1933	49,789	26,983	22,806	118.3
1934	61,815	37,615	24,200	155.4
1935	81,712	52,026	29,686	175.3
1936	106,761	65,841	40,920	160.9
1937	125,943	75,911	50,032	151.7
1938	138,574	80,411	58,163	138.2
1939	163,456	96,800	66,656	145.2
1940	174,500	105,849	68,651	154.2
1950 (plan)	275,000	187,100	87,900	212.9

The turnover tax, being an indirect, retrogressive tax, openly contradicts the original programme of the Bolshevik Party. Even the Minimum Programme of the Bolsheviks, that is, a programme that could be realised under capitalism, called for the '*abolition of all indirect taxation, and the estab-*

lishment of a progressive tax on incomes and inheritance.'[125]
The Eleventh Party Congress (1922) declared that: 'Taxation policy must aim at regulating the process of accumulating resources by means of direct taxation on property, incomes, etc. Taxation policy is the principal instrument of the revolutionary policy of the proletariat in a transitional epoch.'[153] To solve the contradiction between precept and practice, the authorities have ceased to call the turnover taxes taxes at all. Jasny has pointed out that the 1935 year-book listed the turnover taxes among taxes,[154] but in the next edition of the same year-book the turnover taxes were detached from the item 'income from taxes'[155]. This change in terminology enabled the Minister of Finance of USSR to declare before the Supreme Soviet: 'It is known that the overwhelming part of the revenues of the Soviet budget is composed of payments by the national economy. The share of all taxes from the population is negligible. In 1939 the total sum of taxes from the population amounted to 6.5 milliard roubles, which made up only 4.2 per cent of all budgetary incomes.'[156]

The subordination of man to property

Article 6 of the Soviet Constitution states that: 'The land, its deposits, waters, forests, mills, factories, mines, railways, water and air transport, means of communication, large state-organised farm enterprises (state farms, machine-tractor stations, etc.) and also the basic housing facilities in cities and industrial localities are state property, that is, the wealth of the whole people.'

It is odd that although the people thus, through the state, own the country's wealth, the Russian state should go to

*On pages 86-88, we deal with the present income and inheritance taxes in Russia.

such extraordinary lengths to defend this wealth from them!

Under a law of 7 August 1932, 'On the Protection of the Property of State Enterprises, Collective Farms and Co-operatives and Institutions of Socialist Property', the theft of property belonging to the state, kolkhozes and co-operatives and theft on the railways or waterways, became punishable by death by shooting, accompanied by the confiscation of all property. If there were extenuating circumstances, the penalty incurred was imprisonment for not less than ten years and confiscation of all property.[157] Stalin christened this law 'the foundation of revolutionary legality.'[158]

In point of fact this law was seldom applied in cases of minor theft. Therefore, when the Presidium of the Supreme Soviet of the USSR passed a decree on 4 June 1947, on 'Protection of Citizens' Private Property', the first article of which reads:[159] 'Theft – that is, covert or open appropriation of the private property of citizens – is punishable by confinement in a reformatory labour camp for a period of five to six years. Theft committed by a gang of thieves or for a second time is punishable by confinement at a reformatory labour camp for a period of six to ten years'[160], any mitigation of severity in dealing with crimes against property was more apparent than real.

On the same day the Presidium also passed a decree on 'Embezzlement of State and Public Property', which included the following articles:

1. Theft, appropriation, defalcation or other embezzlement of state property is punishable by confinement in a reformatory labour camp for seven to ten years, with or without confiscation of property.

2. Embezzlement of state property for a second time, as well as when committed by an organised group or on a large scale, is punishable by confinement in a reformatory labour camp for ten to twenty-five years, with confiscation of property.

3. Theft, appropriation, defalcation or other embezzlement of

collective farm, co-operative or other public property is punishable by confinement in a reformatory labour camp for five to eight years, with or without confiscation of property.

4. Embezzlement of collective farm, co-operative or other public property for a second time, as well as that committed by an organised group or gang or on a large scale, is punishable by confinement in a reformatory labour camp for eight to twenty years, with confiscation of property.[161]

A month later the Public Prosecutor's Office gave ten examples of how the decrees were being carried out:

1. In the city of Saratov, V.F.Yudin, who had been previously convicted for theft ... stole fish from a smoke factory. On 24 June 1947 ... Yudin was sentenced to fifteen years' imprisonment in corrective-labour camps.

2. On 11 June 1947, an electrician on the power lines of the Moscow-Riazan railroad, D.A.Kiselov, stole fur goods from a railroad car ... On 24 June 1947, the war tribunal of the Moscow-Riazan railroad sentenced D.A.Kiselov to ten years' imprisonment in the corrective-labour camps.

3. In the town of Pavlov-Posad, in the Moscow region, L.N. Markelov ... stole clothing from the Pavlov-Posad textile factory. On 20 June 1947 ... Markelov was sentenced to eight years' imprisonment in corrective-labour camps.

4. In the Rodnikov district of the Ivanov region, Y.V.Smirnov and V.V.Smirnov ... stole 375 pounds of oats from a kolkhoz. On 26 June 1947 ... both were sentenced to eight years' imprisonment in corrective-labour camps.

5. In the Kirov district of Moscow, E.K.Smirnov, a chauffeur, was arrested for stealing 22 pounds of bread from a bakery. The people's court ... sentenced E.K.Smirnov to seven years' imprisonment in corrective-labour camps.

6. In Saratov, E.I.Gordeyev ... stole various products from a warehouse. On 21 June 1947 ... Gordeyev was sentenced to seven years' imprisonment in corective-labour camps.

7. In Kuibyshev, E.T.Poluboyarov stole a wallet from a train traveller ... On 4 July he was sentenced to five years' imprisonment in corrective-labour camps.

8. On 7 June 1947, in Kazan, at the kolkhoz market, V.E.Bukin snatched money from the hand of Citizeness Pustinsky ... On 20

June 1947 . . . Bukin was sentenced to eight years' imprisonment in corrective-labour camps.

9. On 6 June 1947, in the village of Subovka in the Kutuzovsk district of the Kuibyshev region, A.A.Chubarkin and V.G.Morozov stole from a cellar 88 pounds of potatoes belonging to Citizeness Presnyakov. On 17 June 1947 . . . both were sentenced to five years' imprisonment in corrective-labour camps.

10. On 5 June 1947, in Moscow . . . K.V.Greenwald, who had been previously convicted for theft, took advantage of the absence of his neighbour, entered the room of Citizeness Kovalev and stole various household articles . . . Greenwald was sentenced . . . to ten years' imprisonment in corrective-labour camps.[168]

That the severity of this branch of Soviet law is in marked contrast to the relative leniency with which murder, kidnapping, and other violent forms of crime, are dealt with, is highly significant. It becomes clear that, in Stalinist Russia, the individual is rated much lower than property.

Thus the Criminal Law of RSFSR lays it down that:

Art. 136. Premeditated murder, if committed: (a) for mercenary motives, for jealousy (unless covered by Art. 138) or from any other base incentive, (b) by a person who has already been tried for premediated murder or for inflicting grievous bodily harm, and has undergone the measure of social defence imposed by the court, (c) in a manner endangering the life of many people or causing extreme suffering to the victim, (d) with the aim of facilitating or concealing some other serious crime, (e) by a person who had a particular responsibility for the victim's welfare, (f) by taking advantage of the helpless condition of the victim, entails – deprivation of liberty for a period of up to ten years.

Art. 137. Premeditated murder, if not committed in any of the circumstances described in Art. 136, entails – deprivation of liberty for a period of up to eight years.

Art. 138. Premeditated murder committed under the sudden impulse of strong emotional excitement aroused by violence or gross insult on the part of the deceased, entails – deprivation of liberty for a period of up to five years, or forced labour for a period of up to one year.[169]

Some other punishments laid down for violent crimes against persons are:

Art. 147. Unlawfully depriving any person of liberty by the use of force, entails – deprivation of liberty or forced labour for a period of up to one year.

Depriving any person of liberty by any method endangering the life or health of the victim or causing him physical suffering entails – deprivation of liberty for a period of up to two years.

Art. 148. Placing a person known to be of sound mind in an asylum for mercenary or other personal motives, entails – deprivation of liberty for a period of up to three years.

Art. 149. Kidnapping, concealment or exchanging of another person's child for mercenary motives, out of revenge, or with any other personal object, entails – deprivation of liberty for a period up to three years.[144]

This religion of property-worship subjects even the weakest members of the community – children – to it. As we have seen, the maximum punishment of kidnapping a child, is a mere three years' imprisonment, whereas the punishment meted out to a child for stealing is much greater. Although Stalinist law, in its dealings with juvenile delinquents, accounts children of twelve to be mature and fully responsible of their offences, in civil affairs they are rated as only children. For instance, the *Code of Laws on Marriage, Family and Guardianship of R.S.F.S.R.*, declares: 'Guardians shall be appointed for minors who have not reached the age of fourteen years.'[145] And again: 'Curators shall be appointed over minors who are between the ages of fourteen and eighteen years.'[146]

And yet, on 7 April 1935, a law was promulgated which abolished juvenile courts. 'With the aim of the quickest liquidation of criminality amongst minors,' it stated that 'the Central Executive Committee and the Council of People's Commissars decree: (1) Young people from twelve years of age caught at theft, violence, infliction of bodily injury, mutilation, homicide, or attempts at homicide, are to be brought before the criminal law courts and punished in accordance with all measures of the Criminal Code.'[167] (Apparently capital punishment was still prohibited for those under eighteen, since Article 22 of the Code, which covered this point, was not cancelled.)

This law was soon put into effect, as witnesses *Izvestia*, which on 29 May 1935, made it known that in a little more than two weeks a special tribunal had already distributed many years of imprisonment to sixty 'young bandits.'[168] In some cases the hand of the law was even heavier, imposing the death sentence on youths. Thus, two weeks after the promulgation of the terrible law against juvenile delinquents, a Moscow court sentenced a youth convicted of robbery in a train to death.[169]

The official apologia for using such harsh measures, namely, the doubling of the number of cases of juvenile delinquency in Moscow between 1931 and 1934,[170] is no justification, and certainly belies the legend about the 'victory of socialism,' and the 'prosperous and happy life of the people'.

In 1940, the law of 1935 was extended to include children of twelve or over who commit acts endangering railway traffic, such as loosening rails, placing objects on the rails, and so on. The decree of 31 May 1941,[171] expressly states that the law of 1935 applies not only to deliberate offences, but to offences due to negligence as well.

On 15 June 1943, the government ordered the establishment of special reformatory colonies under the NKVD for *confinement without juridical procedure of children from 11 to 16 years of age*, who are vagrants, have committed larceny, and such-like minor offences.[172] There is evidence that children are also to be found among the grown-up inmates of slave camps. Dallin writes that 'the Zakamensk Camp in Eastern

Siberia has a considerable number of children from the Moscow region among its internees, boys and girls sentenced for criminal offences. They work in mines and near-by industrial plants.'[173]

All that has been said above serves as a new illustration of the statement of Marx: 'Law as well as crime, i.e., the struggle of the isolated individual against dominant relationships has an origin which is not purely arbitrary. On the contrary, crime is rooted in the same conditions, as the governing power existing at the time.'[174] In Stalin's Russia the concept of the nature of crime, and the punishments meted out to the offenders, are rooted in the subordination of humanity to property, of labour to capital, that is, in the basic contradiction propelling the bureaucratic state capitalist order.

Changes in the relations of distribution

In his 'April Theses' Lenin stated that the Party's policy was, 'To pay all officials, who are to be elected and subject to recall at any time, not more than the pay of a good worker.'[175] In his *State and Revolution* (August-September 1917) he posed the question of the mode of payment of wages and salaries immediately after the socialist revolution, in a society which 'is ... in every respect economically, morally and intellectually still stamped with the birthmarks of the society from whose womb it emerges.'[176] In these circumstances the following is attained: 'Equality for all members of society in relation to the ownership of the means of production, that is, equality of labour and equality of wages.'[177]

'*All* citizens are transformed into the salaried employees of the state, which consists of the armed workers. *All* citizens become employees and workers of a *single* national state "syndicate". All that is required is that they should work equally – do their proper share of work – and get paid equally.'[178] 'The whole of society will have become a single office and a single factory, with equality of work and equality of pay.'[179] Hence Lenin posed as 'an immediate objective' of the Bolsheviks the following: 'technicians, managers and bookkeepers, as well as *all* officials, shall receive salaries no higher than a "workman's wages".'[180]

A few months after the revolution (in March 1918) Lenin again declared his support 'for the gradual equalisation of *all* wages and salaries in *all* professions and categories'.[181] He accepted the necessity of certain exceptions to equality in the case of specialists, as he well knew that in the face of their scarcity, and their hostility to the workers' state, such an aim could not be achieved, but he insisted that the income differences should right away be much lower than under tsarism, that the *tendency* in future should be towards increasing equalitarianism, and above all he did not shrink from calling any inequality imposed by backwardness on the Soviet government a retreat from socialism, and a concession to capitalism. Thus he wrote: 'In this transition period we must grant them [the specialists] the best possible conditions of life ... When we discussed the question of rates of pay with the Commissar of Labour, Comrade Schmidt, he mentioned facts like these. He said that in the matter of equalising wages we have done more than has been done anywhere and more than any bourgeois state can do in scores of years. Take the pre-war rates of pay: a manual labourer used to get 1 rouble a day – 25 roubles a month – while a specialist got 500 roubles a month ... The expert received twenty times more than the worker. Our present rates of pay vary from six hundred roubles to three thousand roubles – a difference of only five times. We have done a great deal in the matter of equalisation.'[182] The high payment to specialists was 'payment according to bourgeois relationships,' 'a step backward,' a 'concession' to capitalism imposed by the objective reality on the Soviet government.[183]

In 1919 the Russian Communist Party stated its wages policy in these terms: 'While aspiring to equality of reward for all kinds of labour and to complete communism, the Soviet government cannot consider as its task the immediate realisation of this equality at the present moment, when only the first steps are being made towards the transition from capitalism to communism.'[184] The Tenth Party Congress in 1921 decided that while 'for a variety of reasons differences in money wages corresponding to qualifications must temporarily be maintained, nevertheless the wage-rate policy must be built, upon the greatest possible equality between wage rates.'[185]

At the same congress it was declared necessary 'to work out completely adequate measures to destroy inequality in the conditions of life, in wages, etc., between the specialists and the responsible workers on the one hand, and the toiling masses on the other, as this inequality undermines democracy and is a source of corruption to the Party and lowers the authority of the communists.'[186] Yet under the regime of War Communism there was practically complete equality of wages and salaries. According to data given by the Soviet statistician, Strumilin, the wages of the most highly paid workers were, in 1917, 232 per cent of those of the lowest paid, and by the first part of 1921 were only 102 per cent, or practically equal.[187] (On the other hand, the conditions of scarcity which prevailed under War Communism frequently gave officials the opportunity of abusing their control over the sources of supply and distribution).

The virtual equality in wages ended with the introduction of the New Economic Policy. A unified scale of wages was introduced in 1921–22, which contained seventeen grades ranging from apprentices to the top specialists, and which gave the most highly-skilled worker three and a half times as much as the lowest-paid unskilled worker. Specialists could earn a maximum of eight times as much as the unskilled worker. (This did not apply to Party members, who had a special scale of maximum wages, much below that of non-Party specialists).

The income differences were very much smaller than those existing prior to the revolution. The wages and salaries of railway employees before and after the revolution will illustrate this. In 1902, the income of signalmen was 10–20 roubles a month, of machinists, 30–60 roubles, while that of heads of a railway service was 500–750 roubles, and of the director-in-chief, 1,000–1,500 roubles.[188] In March 1924, the differences ranged between 13.27 gold roubles a month for line-workers and 26.80 roubles for administrative staff.[189]

In industry, the average wage of workers in March 1926, was 58.64 chervonets roubles, while a factory manager received 187.90 chervonets roubles if he was a Party member, and 309.50 chervonets roubles if he was not a Party member.[190]

There were some factors, however, which mitigated these differences until the introduction of the First Five-Year Plan. First of all, no member of the Communist Party was allowed to earn more than a skilled worker. This provision was of great importance, as the majority of the directors of enterprises, departments of industry, etc., were Party members. In 1928, 71.4 per cent of the personnel of the managing boards of the trusts were Party members, as were 84.4 per cent on the boards of the syndicates, and 89.3 per cent on those of individual enterprises.

An additional factor, which made the differences much smaller in fact than they would seem from the unified scale of wages, was that the *total* number of specialists (a section of whom were Party members who thus did not earn more than skilled workers) was very small. In 1928 they constituted only 2.27 per cent of all those engaged in industry.

A general picture of the income differentiation in Russia was given in the *Statistical Handbook of USSR 1926* (Russian), according to which the annual average income of manual workers in pre-war roubles was 465 in 1926–27. At the same time the maximum allowed to specialists was 1,811. Excluding the bourgeoisie, the NEP men and the kulaks, there were only 114,000 people who earned this maximum. They made up 0.3 per cent of all earners, and their income made up only 1 per cent of the national income.[191]

With the inauguration of the Five-Year Plans under the banner of 'Victorious Socialism', all the Bolshevik traditions of egalitarianism were overthrown. Stalin led the attack declaring: '*Uravnilovka* [a term of abuse for egalitarianism] has as its origin the peasant outlook, the psychology of equal division of all goods, the psychology of primitive peasant "communism". *Uravnilovka* has nothing in common with Marxian Socialism.'[192] Woe betide anyone who would now dare to oppose income differences in Russia, no matter how great they were. Molotov went as far as to declare at the Seventh Congress of Soviets of USSR: 'Bolshevik policy demands a resolute struggle against egalitarians as accomplices of the class enemy, as elements hostile to socialism.'[193]

The rule limiting the income of Party members was modified in 1929 and later* abolished altogether. The law by which people who held two posts – as many specialists do – could get only one-and-a-half times the maximum salary in force, was abolished. The 'general law of wages' of 17 June

---

* This rule was repealed in such secrecy that it is not known exactly when it happened, but it became evident from news in the Russian press that it was not in existence in 1934.

1920[194], which laid down that anyone exceeding the norm in piece-work was not to receive more than 100 per cent above the normal rate was also repealed. On the other hand the law prohibiting the payment to any worker on piece-work of less than two-thirds of the norm was abrogated.[195]

No further restrictions on inequality of incomes remained, and they grew at an alarming rate.

After 1934 the Russian statisticians ceased to publish figures relating to the division of workers and employees by income, and published only the average income of all workers and employees, a figure arrived at by averaging the incomes of charwomen, unskilled labourers, skilled workers, specialists, chief engineers, managers, and so on.*

In spite of this lack of information, certain facts can be adduced, particularly that there was a sharp rise in the level of salaries taken by the bureaucrats, and a sharp drop in working class wage levels.

For instance, in 1937, when plant engineers were earning 1,500 roubles a month, directors 2,000 roubles – unless the government gave special permission for more to be earned – and skilled workers 200–300 roubles, the Soviet government introduced a minimum wage of 110 roubles per month for piece-workers and 115 roubles for time-workers. That many workers earned only the bare minimum is clearly established by the fact that the law fixing these minima led to a budget grant of 600 million roubles for 1938.[196] By comparison with such wages as these, 2,000 roubles a month was no mean salary. Not only this, but in addition to fixed salary, directors and plant engineers received bonuses, the size of which depend upon the extent to which their enterprise exceeds

---

* It is interesting to note that a Soviet book on economic statistics criticises US statistics for its custom of including in the wages and salaries bill the salaries of company directors thus raising the average wage and salary. (*Dictionary Handbook of Social-Economic Statistics* (Russian), Moscow 1948, p. 12.) What is sauce for the goose is apparently not sauce for the gander!

production quotas laid down in the economic plan. For instance, in 1948, it was reported that the rates of bonuses paid to managements of automotive transport enterprises for the fulfilment and overfulfilment of the plan were:[197]

Bonus and percentage of basic salary

	For fulfilment of plan	For each per cent of overfulfilment of plan
Senior management (director, chief engineer)	up to 30%	up to 4%
Intermediate management (chiefs of departments)	up to 25%	up to 3%
Junior management (shop chiefs, etc.)	up to 20%	up to 3%

And so a director of a plant that overfulfils the plan by only 10 per cent gets a bonus of up to 70 per cent of his basic salary; a 20 per cent overfulfilment is rewarded by a bonus of 110 per cent; 30 per cent overfulfilment by a bonus of 150 per cent; 50 per cent overfulfilment by a bonus of 230 per cent.

Yet another source of income is the Director's Fund, an institution which was established on 19 April 1936.[198]

According to the law, 4 per cent of the planned profit and 50 per cent of all profits above this, were to be put in the Director's Fund. One Russian economist has given figures for 1937 which show the sums involved:[199]

	Realisation of plan in %	Actual cost as % of planned cost	Director's fund in million roubles	Director's fund per worker (roubles)
Petroleum industry	104.1	103.8	21.7	344.92
Meat industry	118.6	104.1	51.9	752.69
Spirit industry	108.8	103.0	86.0	1,175.00

Since the average wage of all workers and employees in 1937 was only 254 roubles per month,[200] these figures show that by exceeding the plan by only a small percentage, the year's Director's Fund averaged out per worker amounted to more than one average monthly wage in the petroleum industry, in the meat industry three, and in the spirit industry more than four-and-a-half. According to another Soviet economist: 'In the five industrial Commissariats the Director's Fund per worker was 6.3 per cent of the average annual wage. However, in several branches, this percentage is considerably higher and reaches 21.5 per cent in woodworking, about 25 per cent in the fur and leather footwear industries, and up to 55 per cent in the spirits, macaroni and food industries.'[201] It is obvious, therefore, that huge sums are concentrated in the hands of directors of industries employing thousands of workers.

The Director's Fund's ostensible aim is to build houses for workers and employees, clubs, canteens, crêches, kindergartens, to give bonuses for outstanding achievements at work, etc.

We have no statistical data on how the Director's Funds are distributed. The only indication we have is given by the paper *Za Industrializatsiya* of 29 April 1937, which published figures concerning the distribution of the Director's Fund in the Porchen plant in Kharkov:

Of the 60,000 roubles constituting the Director's Fund, the Director appropriated 22,000 for himself, the secretary of the Party Committee 10,000, the chief of the production office 8,000, the chief accountant 6,000, the president of the trade union committee 4,000, the head of the workshop 5,000.[202]

Other sections of the privileged classes also enjoy exceptionally high incomes. A letter to *Pravda* from the writer, Aleksei Tolstoy, and the playwright, V.Vishnevsky, which aimed at dispelling 'the misunderstanding on the exceptionally high earnings of authors on the fantastic royalties,'[203] gave the following figures of authors' earnings:

Monthly earnings in 1936	No. of persons
More than 10,000 roubles	14
6,000–10,000 roubles	11
2,000–5,000 roubles	39
1,000–2,000 roubles	114
500–1,000 roubles	137
Up to 500 roubles	about 4,000

When it is recalled that, in that same year of 1936, the average income of all Soviet workers and employees was 2,776 roubles, or 231 roubles a month,[204] comment becomes superfluous.

Today, government officials who, according to Lenin, should not earn more than the average skilled worker, have widely varying incomes. By a decision of the Supreme Soviet of the USSR of 17 January 1938, the Presidents and Vice-Presidents of the Council of the Union and Council of Nationalities have salaries of 300,000 roubles a year, and each deputy of the Supreme Soviet 12,000 roubles a year, plus 150 roubles per day of session.[205] The President of the Supreme Soviet of the RSFSR and his deputies receive 150,000 roubles a year.[206] Presumably the presidents and vice-presidents of the other Federated Republics have the same salaries. A Soviet Army private got 10 roubles a month during the war, a lieutenant 1,000 and a colonel 2,400. In the US army, which can by no stretch of the imagination be called a socialist army, the monthly rate of pay of a private was 50 dollars, of a lieutenant 150 dollars, and of a colonel 333 dollars.[207]

Bureaucrats have yet another possible source of income from various state prizes. The original decree announcing the establishment of the Stalin Prizes in honour of the leader's sixtieth birthday limited their value to a maximum of 100,000 roubles each.[208] The maximum has since been raised to 300,000 roubles, and each year as many as a thousand

Stalin Prizes are awarded, ranging from 50,000 to 300,000 roubles each, all tax-free.

Another clear pointer to the tremendous income differences in Russia is the income tax rates. The income tax rates of 4 April 1940, listed a range of incomes that stretched from less than 1,800 roubles a year to more than 300,000 roubles.[209]

A senior government official, a director or a successful author, has a house in Moscow, a summer house in the Crimea, one or two cars, a number of servants, and so on, as a matter of course.

Even during the war, when in the face of the emergency, all efforts were made to get the maximum production out of the workers, there existed extreme differences in the conditions of the different classes. A maid with two children, one of ten and another of three, told Alexander Werth in 1942: 'The children live chiefly on bread and tea; the little one receives substitute milk – what can you do? – stuff made of soya beans, without taste and of little nutritive value. With my meat coupons this month I only got a little fish. Sometimes I get a little soup left over at the restaurant – and that's about all.'[210]

At the same time, Alexander Werth could write in his diary: 'That lunch at the National today was a very sumptuous affair, for, in spite of the food shortage in Moscow, there always seems to be enough of the best possible food whenever there is reason for any kind of big feed, with official persons as guests. For *zakuski* there was the best fresh caviare, and plenty of butter, and smoked salmon; then sturgeon and, after the sturgeon, chicken cutlets *à la Maréchal*, then ice and coffee with brandy and liqueurs; and all down the table there was the usual array of bottles.'[211]

The differentiation of Russian society into privileged and pariahs was shown very graphically in the rationing system during the war. A differential rationing system was introduced, a thing that no-one would have dared to suggest in the democratic capitalist states of the West. It is true that this was shocking even to the Soviet people, so much so that neither *Pravda* nor *Izvestia* mentioned the subject at all and the rationing system as a whole was shrouded in mystery.[212]

In point of fact, the luxuries of the rich are relatively much cheaper than the necessities of the poor. This will be clearly perceived if we repeat a few figures of the turnover tax rate:[213]

Wheat, 73-74%
Salt in bulk, 70-80%
Meat (beef) 67-71%
Caviare 40%
Radio sets 25%
Automobiles 2%

As a result: 'In mid-1948, the equivalent of the car *Moskvich* [costing 9,000 roubles] was 310 pounds of butter [butter cost 62–66 roubles a pound], while in the United States a somewhat better car was worth about as much as 1,750 pounds of butter.'[214]

Income differences lead to large variations in inherited property. In the early days of the Revolution, by the decree of 27 April 1918, all inheritances of more than 10,000 roubles were confiscated.[215] This was in the spirit of the *Communist Manifesto* which put forward as one of the demands of the transition from capitalism to socialism the abolition of all right of inheritance. A few years later the law changed radically, and by 1929 there was already in existence a table of inheritance tax ranging from 1,000 roubles and less to 500,000 roubles and above.[216] At present, the inheritance tax does not go beyond 10 per cent. This is very low, even in comparison with the inheritance taxes in capitalist Britain and United States.

During the last war a spate of reports emanating from the

Russian press told of people who gave loans to the government of a million or more roubles. The 'Friends of the Soviet Union' explained this in the following manner: 'In the Soviet Union the millionaire has acquired his roubles by his own toil and by services to the Soviet State and people.'[217]

If we examine this statement, we find that, as late as 1940, the average income of workers and employees being only 4,000 roubles, to collect a million roubles would have taken an average worker 250 years – provided he spent no money on himself at all. The Soviet millionaire gets, in interest alone, 50,000 roubles for every million, which is many times more than the income of any worker.

But the clearest expression of the differentiation of Russian society into the privileged and the pariahs is the government pensions scheme. If an army private, who was a worker or employee before his call-up, dies, his family receives a pension of between 52.5 roubles and 240 roubles a month. If he was not a worker or employee, his family receives 40, 70 or 90 roubles, according to whether he had one, two, three or more dependents unable to work. People in rural areas get only 80 per cent of these rates. As against this, the family of a deceased colonel receives 1,920 roubles per month.[218] Dependents of a worker killed through accident at work receive a maximum of 200 roubles per month (except in some rare instances in which they get 300).[219] As against this, some privileged people receive large sums on the death of the head of the family. When M.F.Vladimirsky, deputy of the Supreme Soviet, died, his widow was granted a lump sum of 50,000 roubles and a life pension of 2,000 roubles a month, while his sister got a life pension of 750 roubles a month.[220] When Colonel-General V.A.Yuskevich died, his widow was granted a lump sum of 50,000 roubles and a life pension of 2,000 roubles a month.[221] The press is full of other such instances.

Part and parcel of the antagonistic relations of distribution is the ladder of education.

Article 121 of the Stalin Constitution of 1936 declared: 'Citizens of the USSR have the right to education. This right is ensured by universal, compulsory, elementary education, by education, including higher education, being free of charge,' etc., etc. But even when all education is free, there is no real equality of opportunity for study between the children of the poor and the rich, because the former have to start earning as soon as possible, and because many parents cannot afford to maintain their children while they study. It is therefore not surprising that the proportion of children in the USSR benefiting from education decreases as education becomes more advanced. In the school-year 1939–40, for instance, the total number of students attending all education institutes was:[222]

	Number (000s)
Elementary school (classes I-IV)	20,471
Junior secondary schools (classes V-VII)	9,715
Full secondary schools (classes VII-X)	1,870
Secondary technical and factory schools	945
Universities and higher technical schools	620

If we knew the number of children of different ages in the country, it would be possible to calculate what proportions of children of different ages attended school. But even without this information, on the basis of the above figures, the disparity between educational opportunities of children of different ages is obvious. Assuming that all children aged 7 to 11 attend school, less than half that number were lucky enough to stay for more than four years. Only one in ten had more than seven years' schooling; and less than one in twenty finished the ten-year course (as against ten years' compulsory schooling in capitalist Britain).

Even prior to the establishment of fees for universities,

technical colleges and other high schools many of the pupils who succeeded in reaching the universities and higher technical schools had to leave before finishing their studies because of financial difficulties. Between 1928 and 1938, the total number of people admitted to engineering colleges training for industry and transport was 609,200, while only 242,300 graduated. The number admitted to technical colleges was 1,062,000, and the number of graduates only 362,700.[223]

In 1938, 42.3 per cent of all students in higher schools were children of the intelligentsia.[224] Since then no statistics of the social composition of students have been published, but no doubt the percentage of students from 'good' homes has increased, because of the imposition of fees from 1940 onwards.

Article 146 of the Stalin Constitution states: 'The Constitution of the USSR may be amended only by the decision of the Supreme Soviet of the USSR adopted by a majority of not less than two-thirds of the votes cast in each of its chambers.' This did not prevent the government from imposing fees for higher secondary and university education without even convening the Supreme Soviet to amend Article 21 of the Constitution, cited above, which decreed that education should be free. The decree of the Council of People's Commissars, published on 2 October 1940,[225] imposed a fee of 150–200 roubles a year for the higher classes of secondary school (VIIIth, IXth and Xth grades of school), and 300–500 roubles a year for colleges. The size of these sums can be appreciated by comparing them with the average wage and salary of the period – 335 roubles a month, and with the wage of many workers actually standing at a mere 150 roubles a month. It is obvious that the imposition of fees is an effective barrier to higher education, especially in families where there are three or four children.

To make matters worse, the Soviet government had the temerity to declare that the imposition of these fees was a sign of the growing prosperity of the people. The preamble to the decree declared: 'Taking into consideration the higher level of material well-being of the toilers and the great expenses of the Soviet state for the building up, maintenance and equipment of the constantly growing net of secondary and high schools, the Council of People's Commissars recognises the necessity of imposing a part of the expense of education in secondary and high schools of the USSR on the toilers themselves, and therefore resolves ...' The same brand of logic leads to the conclusion that a really prosperous country is one in which even elementary education has to be paid for!

It must have been obvious to the students that the need to pay fees was no evidence of prosperous circumstances. Between the school year 1940–41, during which fees were introduced, and 1942–43, some 20 per cent left high schools in the RSFSR due to 'the sifting out in connection with the introduction of fees for tuition and the changes in the methods of allotting stipends.'[226]

Another decree issued the same day, 2 October 1940, on 'State Labour Reserves of USSR' authorised the annual draft of 800,000 to 1,000,000 boys between fourteen and seventeen years of age (the age of classes VIII to X) into compulsory vocational education. The quota of children to be supplied by each area is stipulated, and the responsibility for carrying out the order was to be that of the district and town Soviets.[227] Commissions were set up consisting of the Chairman of the town or district Soviet, a trade union representative, and the local secretary of the Komsomol, which instruct each school to provide a certain quota of children to be selected by the teacher. As pupils of the VIIIth to Xth classes are exempt, this regulation falls almost exclusively on pupils from poor families. (The harshness of the discipline imposed on youths recruited to vocational schools is clear from the fact that for leaving without permission and other violations of discipline, they are subject to punishment of up to one year's confinement in a reformatory.)[228] To widen the net, the Presidium of the Supreme Soviet decreed on 19 June 1947, that the age limits for Labour Reserve should be raised: in a number of industries it was raised to nineteen years of age.[229]

Looking at the two decrees issued on 2 October 1940, one cannot but be reminded of the circular issued in 1887 by Delianov, Tsar Alexander III's Minister of Education. 'The Minister, desirous of improving the quality of pupils in the secondary schools' decided that 'the children of coach-men, servants, cooks, laundresses, small shopkeepers and such-like persons should not be encouraged to rise above the environment to which they belong.'

In conclusion, it is clear from what has been said above that the difference between income differentiation before the Five-Year Plan and that after its introduction necessarily leaves the realm of quantity alone and becomes a qualitative difference also. If a specialist or factory manager receives between four and eight times more than an unskilled worker, it does not necessarily mean that there is a relation of exploitation between the two. A skilled worker, specialist or manager produces more values than an unskilled worker per hour of work.

Even if the specialist receives more than the difference in the values that they produce, it still does not prove that he exploits the unskilled worker. This can be simply demonstrated. Let us assume that in a workers' state an unskilled worker produces his necessities in six hours a day, and that he works eight hours, the other two hours being devoted to the production of social services, to increasing the amount of means of production in the hands of society, etc. As these two hours of work are not labour for someone else, but for himself, it would be wrong to call it surplus labour. But to avoid introducing a new term, and to distinguish the two hours from the first six hours, let us call it 'surplus labour,' while the six hours we shall call 'necessary labour'. For the sake of simplicity let us say that an hour of unskilled labour produces the value embodied in 1 shilling. The unskilled worker thus produces 8s. and receives 6s. Let us assume that the specialist produces 5 units of value, or 5s., in an hour of his labour. If the specialist earned five times more than the unskilled worker, i.e., 30s., there would clearly be no relation of exploitation between them. Even if he earned six times more than the unskilled worker, while he produced only five times more, there still would not exist a relation of exploitation, as the specialist would be earning 36 shillings a day, while he produces 40s. But if the specialist earned 100s. or 200s., the situation would be fundamentally changed. In such a case a large part of his income would *necessarily* come from the labour of others.

The statistics at our disposal show conclusively that although the bureaucracy enjoyed a privileged position in the period preceding the Five-Year Plan, it can on no account be said that in the majority of cases it received surplus value from the labour of others. It can just as conclusively be said that since the introduction of the Five-Year Plans, the bureaucracy's income consisted to a large extent of surplus value.

Bureaucratic mismanagement

Under capitalism based upon private ownership of the means of production, the capitalist uses for his financial compass the automatism of the market, with its blind determination of the prices of factors of production as well as of the commodity produced. He must operate an accurate accounting system. His punishment for miscalculation is a financial loss; for a grave mistake, bankruptcy. Under a statified economy, where most of the prices are determined administratively, and where the income of the plant manager has no direct correlation to the real economic situation of his plant, accurate accounting becomes even more vitally necessary, as the manager of a plant can conceal the defects of the enterprise for a long time should it become necessary; he is not subject to the market law alone. Without accurate accountancy any distortion in one enterprise can be assimilated as an element in the calculations of other enterprises, and so on cumulatively. The Kremlin can punish the manager who fails, but the failure comes to light only after the damage is done. Again, the administrative and extremely harsh nature of the impending punishment (demotion, imprisonment, etc.) merely gives an added urgency and encouragement to the dissembling manager,·and provides greater incentive for such managers to plot with other officials of the administration. Further, the same ruthless quality of retribution engenders a high degree of circumspection, not to say timidity, in any manager faced with the need to take a risk or to make a decision. Hence a marked tendency throughout the managerial side of Russian industry to 'pass the buck' and to increase, *ad nauseam*, the number of unproductive officials. Yet again, such managers are sharply conscious of the implacably administrative nature of the sanctions hanging over them, and, therefore, of the great extent to which their own fate depends upon arbitrary decisions derived automatically from a current general policy which can be and is frequently superseded overnight by one of an entirely different character.

Finally, it is a commonplace that the high complexity and diversification of any modern industrial economy necessitates a maximum degree of local autonomous initiative and the widest field of managerial discretion. But this is a state of things in direct conflict with the extreme bureaucratic rule in Russia.

The Stalinist industrialisation drive is planned, if by planning we understand central direction. Under private capitalism the economy operates blindly, so that at any given moment it represents the sum total of many private and autonomous decisions.* In Russia, however, the government decides almost everything. If, however, by the term 'planned economy,' we understand an economy in which all component elements are adjusted and regulated into a single rhythm, in which frictions are at a minimum, and, above all, in which foresight prevails in the making of economic decisions – then the Russian economy is anything but planned. The First Five-Year Plan was launched upon the assumption that agriculture would remain mainly in private peasant hands (the kolkhozes were to produce only 11.5 per cent of the total grain output of the country during the last year of the Plan).[230] It ended with 70 per cent of agriculture in kolkhozes and sovkhozes. It forecast the following increase in livestock: horses, 6.1 million; cattle, 14.5 million; pigs, 12.2 million; sheep and goats, 28.8 million; altogether 61.6 million[231]; in fact the number of horses declined by 13.9 million, cattle by 30.2 million, pigs by 14.4 million, sheep and goats by 94.6 million, altogether a decline of 153.1 million.[232] The Plan also assumed that the relations between all branches of the economy would be based upon market-exchange – and yet

---

* It is beyond the province of the present essay to investigate the interesting subject of the centrally directed plan within existing private capitalism, especially as a manifestation of war-time expediency.

the period actually ended with total rationing. Another assumption was that the number of workers employed in state economy would increase by 33 per cent[233] – but in point of fact it rose by 96.6 per cent.[234] Standards of living were supposed to rise, instead they declined. It can be assumed that production targets of different goods are mutually linked, yet the rate of fulfilment of the different targets differed over a very wide range. The Plan assumed that the rural population would grow by 9.0 per cent, the urban population by 24.4 per cent, and the total population by 11.8 per cent, but actually the corresponding figures were 1.1, 40.2 and 8.1 per cent. The same is true for the later Plans too. Inflation (a rise of no less than 1,500 per cent, in the price level during the two decades of the Plan era), the terrible famine of 1932–33, the harsh administrative measures against peasants and workers – these are some of the symptoms of the bureaucracy's lack of foresight in running the economy, and of the disharmony between the different interdependent elements of the economy.

There is a great lack of co-ordination between different plants. To give an example: according to the chief engineer of the Stalingrad tractor factory, Demianovich, there were 753 tractors worth 18 million roubles piled up in the yards of the factory in October 1940, because parts to be bought from small plants to the value of 100,000 roubles were missing. This led to a serious interruption of production.[235]

The great dislocations in the economy are revealed also in a phenomenon that is strangely peculiar to Russia in such an extreme form: different enterprises producing the same product show tremendous differences in costs of production. Thus the annual output of pig iron and steel per worker in various plants in 1939 was:[236]

Plant	Pig iron	Steel
	tons	tons
Magnitogorsk Combine	2,840	1,168
Kuznetsk Combine	2,324	1,389
Krivoy Rog Plant	1,733	
'Zaporozhstal'	1,679	1,074
'Azovstal'	1,642	664
Kirov Plant	2,102	523
Dzerzhinsky Plant	785	529
Petrovsky Plant	799	299
Kramatorsk Plant	725	293
Ordzhonikidze Plant	707	400
Frunze Plant	636	403

In the book from which the above table is quoted it is made quite clear that the basic reason for these large variations in the productivity of labour does not lie in differences in the natural conditions of production, but in the technical equipment of the enterprises.[237] In many cases, even where there are no big differences in the technical equipment of the plants concerned, the production costs vary a lot. Thus, *Izvestia* wrote: 'Often two enterprises under the same Ministry and with the same equipment show very different costs of production, in one case administrative costs being two or three times as great as in the other ... Hundreds of thousands of superfluous workers can be released and the cost of production can be considerably reduced if order is established with regard to shop personnel.'[238]

Another cause of cost differences is the big variation in the proportion of defective goods. In his report to the Supreme Soviet on the State Budget of 1947, the Minister of Finance, Zverev, said of two factories producing electric bulbs that in one the cost of production was *five times* higher than in the other. The reason he gave was that in the one 47.3 per cent of the output was defective, while in the other only 7.3 was.[239] It is obvious that such differences in production costs could not exist under conditions of capitalism based on private property. The backward enterprise would early have been driven out of production. Obviously preserving these plants without equalising or nearly equalising their costs of production involves, from a general economic standpoint, immense wastage.

This lack of co-ordination among different industries and the inconsistency of their development is shown in the spasmodic rise and fall of prices and in the absence of harmonious relations between them. Dr Jasny has illustrated this very clearly. One of the examples he gives is this:

> The development of the prices of timber and lumber during the Plan era was fantastically inconsistent. After a small decline in 1927–28, the lumber prices were raised by more than 100 per cent, effective 1 April 1936. They remained unchanged, thereafter, for almost 13 years in spite of inflation, the extreme shortage of timber, and the cutting of forests far in excess of what was economically reasonable. The lumber prices were raised almost three-fold, effective 1 January 1949, to become about 7 times as high as in 1926–27.
>
> Round timber, large quantities of which are used directly in construction in the USSR, declined in price 14.7 per cent from 1926–27 to 1927–28 and then was raised only moderately in 1936. Timber prices were raised slightly again in 1944, but even after this they still were only moderately above prices of 1926–27. Then, to make up for all such arrears, timber prices were boosted in one stroke more than 4.5-fold in 1949. Roughly the timber prices were close to 50 per cent of those of lumber (sawn timber) in 1926–27; in 1936 they became little more than 20 per cent of the latter; the percentage was raised to about 30 in 1944 and exceeded 40 in 1949.
>
> The prices of railway ties, a simple timber product, showed yet another course: doubled in 1936 and again more than doubled in 1943. Again they were more than doubled in 1949, with the result that the prices effective 1 January 1949, were almost 10-fold their 1927 level.[140]

In another book Jasny gives yet another example of the lack of tie-ins between the prices of competing goods or between the prices of raw materials and finished products:

'In 1933,' he writes, 'the price of kerosene for technical purposes, f.o.b. destination, was raised about 10-fold, to a level about 45-fold that of good Donbass boiler coal, f.o.b. mine. In 1949, the same kerosene cost not quite six times as much as coal. There is no justification – there cannot even be any explanation – for such shifting ground. The varying rates between kerosene and coal prices are an extreme case, but the number of unjustified large shifts in price and rate relationships is almost infinite. In 1949, important types of rolled steel cost about 5–6 times as much as coal; in the second half of 1950 the relation was only about three to one.'[241] And again: 'It was a great blunder to raise machinery prices 30–35 per cent in one year (1949) and then to eliminate the entire increase and more the next year (1950); or to raise railway freight rates on short distances much less than on long distances (rate revision of 1939) and to do exactly the opposite in the next revision (1949).[242]

The crowning example of the crude methods employed in adjusting prices and the absence of tie-in between them was given by Stalin himself:

  our business executives and planners, with few exceptions, are poorly acquainted with the operations of the law of value, do not study them, and are unable to take account of them in their computations. This, in fact, explains the confusion that still reigns in the sphere of price-fixing policy. Here is one of many examples. Some time ago it was decided to adjust the prices of cotton and grain in the interests of cotton growing, to establish more accurate prices for grain sold to the cotton growers, and to raise the price of cotton delivered to the state. Our business executives and planners submitted a proposal on this score which could not but astound the members of the Central Committee, since it suggested fixing the price of a ton of grain at practically the same level as a ton of cotton, and, moreover, the price of a ton of grain was taken as equivalent to that of a ton of baked bread. In reply to the remarks of members of the Central Committee that the price of a ton of bread must be higher than that of a ton of grain because of the additional expense of milling and baking, and that cotton was generally much dearer than grain, as was also borne out by the prices in the world market, the authors of the proposal could find nothing coherent to say. The Central Committee was therefore obliged to take the matter into its own hands and to lower the prices of grain and raise the prices of cotton.[243]

What a muddle! And in the very highest quarters of the land.

One other peculiar phenomenon that reveals the lack of integration between individual plants, is the rise of a group of middlemen who make a living by finding out plants with surpluses and deficits and arranging barter agreements between them, violating the prices fixed by the authorities. *Planovoe Khoziaistvo* reported a case in which a heavy machinery factory promised a building organisation, in exchange for 2.5 million bricks, not only the official price of the bricks, but also the following extras: 800 tons of coal, 250 tons of timber, 11 tons of kerosene and various amounts of a number of other commodities.[244] All this is illegal, but nevertheless very widespread: the bureaucratic government that prohibits this, is, after all, the cause of its appearance.

Another example of the same species is the kolkhoz market, particularly flourishing during the war, with its food rationing, and which in all but name was a 'black market'.

Hence, also, the appearance of the *tolkach* – the supply expeditor – who, quite illegally, takes an enormous commission for acquiring materials, machines, etc. Hence also the great importance of *blat*, or personal influence, for acquiring materials, machines, etc., to which the factory director is not entitled. Russian publications give ample testimony that it is a major phenomenon there.

The vast extent of the conflicts between enterprises, trusts, glavks, ministries, etc., is revealed in the exceptionally large number of law-suits between them. In 1938, for instance, over 330,000 cases were litigated in *Gosarbitrazh* (State

Board of Arbitration, a special system of courts for disputes between economic organs).[245] This figure does not include the disputes between economic units – glavks and plants within an individual ministry – which are dealt with by departmental arbitration boards. Berman writes: 'The types of disputes that come before *Gosarbitrazh* are amazingly diverse. Many arise over the quality of the goods supplied under the contract. A large number involve the question of prices, for despite the fact that prices are fixed, many devices exist for avoiding or evading the established prices.'[246]

One of the most important elements in bureaucratic mis-management is the swift, arbitrary changing of decisions by the central government itself. A few examples will be given.

For a number of years it had been an act of faith to believe that the bigger the enterprise the better it was irrespective of optimal technical levels of efficiency. Thus, for instance, Stalin declared: 'All the arguments of "science" against the possibility and expediency of creating large grain factories of 50,000 to 100,000 hectares each have collapsed and crumbled into dust.'[247]

In 1930, a kolkhoz was organised, consisting of 50 villages and 84,000 hectares; another encompassed 29 villages and 33,553 hectares.[248] However, after terrible losses, the govern-ment beat a retreat; in 1938 the average kolkhoz had an area of 484 hectares of arable land. For nine years (1928–37) the enthusiasm for gigantic enterprises held sway before a reaction set in, after which 'gigantomania' was declared the result of the pernicious activities of 'Trotskyist-Fascists'.

At other times targets of production were put at a ridiculously high level, leading to adventuristic tempos, at a formidable cost in wreckage, wear and tear of machinery, and wastage of material and labour. Thus, for instance, G.K. Ordzhonikidze, Commissar of Heavy Industry, stated at the Seventeenth Party Conference (30 January 1932) that the task for 1932 was this: 'In the course of one year we must more than double the capacity of the metal factories, raising it to 13.5–14 million tons [of pig-iron] ... What does fulfilling the production programme of the iron and metal industry in 1932 mean? ... It means to yield in one year an increase of 4 million tons ... How much time did it take the countries of capitalism to achieve the same thing? ... England took 35 years to accomplish this ... It took Germany ten years ... the United States eight years. The USSR must cover the same ground in one year.'[249] Actually, it took not one year but six to seven.

The organ of *Gosplan* adopted an even more absurd position when drafting targets for the Second Five-Year Plan. It announced that in 1937 USSR would produce: 450–550 million tons of coal, 150 million tons of crude oil, 60 million tons of pig iron, 150 million kilowatt hours of electrical energy. This plan had to be slashed by more than half at the Seventeenth Party Conference (January 1932), and by still more at the Seventeenth Party Congress (January 1934) which passed the final draft. A simple comparison of the targets shows how arbitrary and adventuristic is the planning of the government:[250]

Production plan for 1937

	Gosplan Plan	17th Party Conference	17th Party Congress	Actual fulfilment
	(1931)	(1932)	(1934)	(1937)
Coal (million tons)	450–550	250	152.5	128.0
Crude oil (million tons)	150	80–90	46.8	30.5
Pig iron (million tons)	60	22	17.4	14.5
Electricity (million kwh.)	150	100	38.0	25.4

Another curious yet typical incident. In 1931 an important member of the Supreme Council of National Economy was so bold as to say that he did not believe that it would be possible to produce 60 million poods of cotton, but only 30 million.[251]

He was brought to court, and the prosecutor declared: 'Just the two figures are enough to show the practical harm of Sokolovsky's work.' Sokolovsky 'confessed,' and said that actually 60 million poods could be achieved. (The 'confession' did not save him, and he had to pay for his former scepticism with ten years' imprisonment). Four years later, in 1935, at a conference of cotton growers, the Commissar of Light Industry, Lubimov, and the Commissar of Agriculture, Chernov, informed Stalin that great successes in the cotton programme would render it possible to produce in that year ... 32 million poods of cotton! Stalin considered it unattainable and sceptically questioned: 'Are you not carried away by enthusiasm?'[252]

In summing up, it may be said that, in Russia, instead of a real plan, strict methods of government dictation are evolved for filling the gaps made in the economy by the decisions and activities of this very government. Therefore, instead of speaking about a Soviet planned economy, it would be much more exact to speak of a bureaucratically directed economy. Actually the totalitarian, bureaucratic political dictatorship helps to overcome the results of bad planning, which at the same time, has its origin in this self-same bureaucratic set-up.

One should, however, avoid the mistake of assuming that the mismanagement corroding Russia's national economy precludes very substantial, nay, stupendous, achievements. Actually, between the bureaucratic mismanagement and the great upward sweep of Russia's industry, there is a tight, dialectical unity. Only the backwardness of the productive forces of the country, the great drive towards their rapid expansion (together with a whole series of factors connected with this) and, above all, the subordination of consumption to capital accumulation, can explain the rise of bureaucratic state capitalism.

Russia - an industrial giant

The efforts and self-sacrifice of the people, have raised Russia, despite bureaucratic mismanagement and waste, to the position of a great industrial power, from being, in terms of industrial output, fourth in Europe and fifth in the world to being first in Europe and second in the world. She has stepped out of her sleepy backwardness to become a modern, powerful, industrially advanced country. The bureaucracy has thus earned as much tribute as Marx and Engels paid to the bourgeoisie. 'It has been the first to show what man's activity can bring about. It has accomplished wonders far surpassing Egyptian pyramids, Roman aqueducts and Gothic cathedrals . . . The bourgeoisie . . . draws all . . . nations into civilisation . . . It has created enormous cities . . . and has thus rescued a considerable part of the population from the idiocy of rural life. The bourgeoisie, during its rule of scarce one hundred years, has created more massive and more colossal productive forces than have all preceding generations to-gether.'[253]

The price paid for these achievements has, of course, been human misery on a scale impossible to estimate.

From a socialist standpoint, however, the decisive criterion is not the growth of production *per se*, but the social relations accompanying this tremendous development of the productive forces. Is it or is it not accompanied by an improvement in the economic position of the workers, by an increase in their political power, by a strengthening of democracy, a reduction of economic and social inequality, and a decline of state coercion? Is the industrial development planned, and if so, planned by whom, and in whose interests? These are the basic socialist criteria for economic advance.

Marx visualised that the development of the productive forces under capitalism would drive humanity towards a crisis out of which there were only two ways: the one, a socialist reorganisation of society, the other, a decline into barbarism. The threat of barbarism takes the form, before our very eyes, of hitching the productive forces of humanity, of industry and science, to the chariot of war and destruction. The place of Magnitogorsk and Oak Ridge in man's history will be decided not by their tremendous material achievements, but by the social and political relations underlying them.

Chapter 2: State and party in Stalinist Russia

**Marx and Engels on the nature of a workers' state ·
The Russian army · The Soviets · Elections · The
party · Withering away of state and law**

In the last chapter the main facets of the social and economic
relations in Russia were described. In this chapter we shall
deal with the political aspects – the state and the party.

Marx and Engels on the nature of a workers' state

Marx and Engels used that rather ominous sounding and
widely misunderstood term, 'dictatorship of the proletariat,'
to denote the *content*, not the *form*, of the state which would
replace the capitalist state, that is to say, to define the ruling
class. To them, in this context, dictatorship simply meant
class rule, and, therefore, the Athenian city state, the Roman
Empire, Napoleon's rule, British parliamentary government,
Bismarck's Germany and the Paris Commune were all dictatorships because, in all of them, a class or a number of
classes, were under the rule of another class. In Marx and
Engels' writings the form of the dictatorship of the proletariat is conceived of as a very full democracy. For instance,
in the *Communist Manifesto* it is stated that: 'the first step
in the revolution by the working class is to raise the proletariat
to the position of ruling class, to win the battle of democracy.'[1]
More than forty years later, Engels wrote: 'If one thing is
certain it is that our Party and the working class can only
come to power under the form of the democratic republic.
This is even the specific form for the dictatorship of the

proletariat, as the great French revolution has already shown.'[2]

The ideas of Marx and Engels regarding the democratic form of the dictatorship of the proletariat were realised in the Paris Commune of 1871. The latter wrote: 'Look at the Paris Commune. That was the Dictatorship of the Proletariat.'[3] And Marx pointed out that: 'The first decree of the Commune ... was the suppression of the standing army, and the substitution for it of the armed people.' And then: 'The Commune was formed of the municipal councillors, chosen by universal suffrage in various wards of the town, responsible and revocable at short terms. The majority of its members were naturally working men, or acknowledged representatives of the working class ... Instead of continuing to be the agent of the Central Government, the police were at once stripped of their political attributes, and turned into the responsible and at all times revocable agents of the Commune. So were the officials of all other branches of the Administration. From the members of the Commune downwards, the public service had to be done at *workmen's wages*. The vested interests and the representation allowances of the high dignitaries of State disappeared along with the high dignitaries themselves ... The judicial functionaries were to be divested of sham independence ... Like the rest of the public servants, magistrates and judges were to be elective, responsible and revocable.'[4]

To quote Engels once more: 'Against this transformation of the State and the organs of the State from servants of Society into masters of Society – a process which had been inevitable in all previous States – the Commune made use of two infallible expedients. In the first place, it filled all posts – administrative, judicial and educational – by election on the basis of universal suffrage of all concerned, with the right of these electors to recall their delegate at any time. And in the second place, all officials, high or low, were paid only the wages received by other workers. The highest salary paid by the Commune to anyone was 6,000 francs. In this way an effective barrier to place-hunting and careerism was set up, even apart from the imperative mandates to delegates to representative bodies which were also added in profusion.'[5]

Marx declared that with its universal suffrage, the right of recall of every civil servant, workmen's wages for all officials, maximum local self-government, and the absence of armed forces elevated above the people and oppressing them, the Paris Commune constituted complete democracy.

The antithesis of the workers' state was the monstrous bureaucracy and army of the capitalist states, which, in Engel's words, 'threaten to devour the whole of society.'[6]

This, briefly, is Marx' and Engels' conception of a workers' state, a consistent, extreme democracy.

To this conception, let us now counterpose the reality of the Russian Stalinist state.

The Russian army

The main factor in the state is the armed forces. To use Lenin's formulation, the state 'consists of special bodies of armed men which have prisons, etc., at their disposal.'[7] Therefore, the starting point of any analysis of the present Russian state apparatus, especially from the standpoint of marxism, must be the structure of the armed forces. As Trotsky so aptly wrote: 'The army is a copy of society and suffers from all its diseases, usually at a higher temperature.'[8]

The formation of a people's militia was traditionally demanded by socialist parties.* Accordingly, one of the first

---

* See, for instance, Article 12 of the 1903 programme of the Russian Social Democratic Workers' Party.'[9]

acts of the Bolshevik leaders, on taking power, was to issue a decree which included the following clauses:

2. Full power within any army unit and combination of units is to be in the hands of its soldier's committees and soviets.

4. The elective principle for army commanders is hereby introduced. All commanders up to the regimental commander are to be elected by a general vote of [the different units] ... Commanders higher than regimental commanders, including the commander-in-chief, are to be elected by a congress ... of committees of the army units [for which the commander is being elected].[10]

Next day a further decree added:

In fulfilment of the will of the revolutionary people which is concerned with the immediate and decisive eradication of every inequality, the Council of People's Commissars hereby decrees:

1. To abolish all ranks and title from the rank of corporal to that of general ...

2. To abolish all privileges and the external marks formerly connected with the different ranks and titles;

3. To abolish all saluting;

4. To abolish all decorations and other signs of distinction;

5. To abolish all officer's organisations ...

6. To abolish the institution of batmen in the army.[11]

But the Bolsheviks' desire for a real democratisation of the army, for its transformation into a people's militia, met with disaster on the rocks of objective reality.

In the early days, after the October Revolution, the revolutionary armed forces consisted of small groups of volunteers. The masses of the people were sick and tired of war and were not ready to volunteer for the new revolutionary armed forces. In order to meet the challenge of the White Armies which were backed by powerful foreign powers, the Bolsheviks were *forced* to replace voluntary principle by conscription. In addition, lacking experienced commanders, they were forced to recruit tens of thousands of officers of the former Tsarist army. This clearly made it necessary to abandon the elective principle in the choice of army commanders: one could hardly expect the peasants and workers in uniform to elect to their command those officers whom they so hated as representatives of the old regime. The needs of battle also made it imperative to abandon the ideal of an army built on a territorial basis – of arming the people – and to return it to the barracks.

The Bolshevik leaders never denied for a moment that these measures constituted a deviation from the socialist pro-gramme. (See, for instance, the resolution of the Eighth Party Congress, March, 1919.[12]) Moreover, they strongly opposed any attempt to render them permanent. Thus, for instance, when a former general of the Tsarist army, who fought with the Bolsheviks during the civil war, stated that the army of a socialist country should not be based on a militia, but on the old, established barrack system, the People's Commissar of War, Trotsky, sternly replied: 'the Communist Party did not come to power in order to replace the tricolour barracks by red ones.'[13] The Bolsheviks fre-quently reiterated their intention to introduce the militia system as early as possible. Thus, for instance, at the Seventh Congress of the Soviets, held in December 1919, Trotsky declared: 'It is necessary to begin a transition to the realisa-tion of the *militia system* of arming the Soviet Republic.'[14]

The Ninth Party Congress decided to concretise this intention by building units of a workers' militia side by side with the regular army, and it was hoped to develop these gradually until they should replace the latter entirely.[15]

But this resolution was never carried out. Any plan to introduce a people's militia was inhibited by objective realities – Russia's backward productive forces, the low cultural level of the people, the fact that the proletariat was a small minority of the population. This was explained clearly by I.Smilga, a leading Bolshevik in the army, who said in 1921:

> The militia system, whose basic characteristic is the territorial principle, is faced with an insuperable political obstacle in the path of its introduction in Russia. Given the numerically weak proletariat in Russia, we *are not able* to ensure proletarian guidance in the territorial militia units ... Even greater difficulties in the path of the introduction of the militia system arise from the viewpoint of strategy. With the weakness of our railroad system, we should not be able, in case of war, to concentrate forces in the threatened directions ... Furthermore, the experience of the Civil War has incontrovertibly shown that territorial formations *were entirely unsuitable*, the soldiers deserting and not wishing to leave their villages during offensive as well as retreat. Therefore, the return to this form of organisation would be a crude, wholly unjustifiable error.[16]

The backwardness of the productive forces, and, connected with it, the peasant nature of the country, were the two decisive factors in making the Red Army a regular army and not a militia (although many elements of democracy and equalitarianism not normally associated with regular armed forces were built into the structure of the Red Army). The economic level of a given country is, after all, the decisive historical factor. As Marx said: 'Our theory that the organisation of labour is conditioned by the means of production, is, it seems, nowhere as brilliantly corroborated as in the "human slaughter industry".'[17]

The material and cultural backwardness of Russia revealed itself also in the relations between soldiers and officers.

From the beginning the Bolsheviks found it an unavoidable necessity to appoint ex-Tsarist officers, notwithstanding their previous agitation for the substitution of all appointed officers by those elected by the soldiers. It was impossible to wage the war against the White Armies without tried commanders, and if the choice were left to the soldiers they would not have elected ex-Tsarist officers.

From the beginning there was a struggle between the political commissars on the one hand, and the Party collectives in the army on the other. This conflict converged with another between centralist and decentralist tendencies. Out of these two struggles the political commissars emerged victorious over the Party collectives, and the Centre overcame the guerrilla tendencies. The convergence of these two struggles reflected a strengthening bureaucratic tendency in the army.

It was not long before the ex-Tsarist officers began to influence the new commanders of proletarian origin. The Bolshevik, Petrovsky, stated: 'Within the walls of the military school we encountered the old regime view of the peasant about the role of the officer with respect to the mass of the private soldiers. We had also noticed a certain trend to the upper class traditions of the cadets of the czarist military schools ... Professionalism is the scourge which lashed morally officers of all times and in all countries ... They [the Red Army Commanders] became members of the new officers' group, and no agitation whatsoever, nor beautiful speeches about the necessity of contact with the masses, would be of any avail. The conditions of existence are stronger than kind wishes.'[18]

The commanders, the political commissars, and others with authority in the Red Army, began to use their positions to gain advantage for themselves. Trotsky took them severely to task for this, such as on the occasion (31 October 1920) when he wrote to the Revolutionary Military Councils of Fronts and Armies condemning the use of government cars by those in authority for 'gay parties right before the eyes of the tired Red Army soldiers.' He spoke angrily of 'commanders [who] dress with extreme elegance while the fighters go half-naked,' and attacked the drinking bouts indulged in by commanders and political commissars. And he concluded: 'such facts cannot but provoke exasperation and discontent among the Red Army soldiers.' In the same letter he expounds his aim: 'Without setting the impossible goal of immediate elimination of all and sundry privileges in the army, to endeavour to reduce these systematically to the actually necessary minimum.'[19] His realistic revolutionary conception clearly reveals the immense difficulties of the situation.

In spite of these abuses, however, the existence of the Bolshevik Party with cells throughout the army, together with the revolutionary enthusiasm and self-sacrifice of the common soldiers and the presence of Trotsky at its head, ensured the maintenance of the proletarian character of the Red Army during the civil war.

With the partial victory of the bureaucracy in 1923, arrogance and a dictatorial attitude towards their troops became the rule among the officers rather than the exception. The key positions in the Party cells within the army were gradually taken over by the commanders themselves until, in 1926, it was noted by the Political Department of the army that two-thirds of all positions in the Party apparatus in the army were in the hands of commanders.[20] In other words, the officers became the political leaders who were supposed to defend the soldiers against the officers!

Even so, this was still not a *completely independent* officer caste. For one thing, the living conditions of the commanders were hard and not very different from those of the soldiers. According to White: 'In 1925 only 30 per cent of the commanding personnel were housed in a manner regarded by Frunze [People's Commissar of War] at all as tolerable. Seventy per cent had housing facilities below that level. Frunze spoke of various localities where several commanders with their families had only one room among them. In other words, each family had only a part of a room at its disposal. The reserve commanders, when called for re-training outside of the ranks of the army, were remunerated for the work on a basis which would not look attractive to a Chinese coolie. Those employed or belonging to the peasantry were paid five kopeks per hour, while the unemployed among them were paid nine kopeks per hour, for the time they were engaged in their studies.'[21]

Wollenberg, who was himself a commander in the Red Army, gives these facts:

In 1924 the pay of a corps-commander was 150 roubles a month, corresponding roughly to that earned by a well-paid metal worker. It was thus 25 roubles a month below the 'Party maximum,' i.e., the largest monthly salary that a Party member was allowed to accept in those days ... There was at that time no special officers' mess. The meals of officers and men were prepared in the same kitchens. Communist officers seldom wore the badges of their rank when off duty, and frequently dispensed with them even when on duty. At that time the Red Army acknowledged a relationship of superior and subordinate only during the performance of a military duty, and in any case every soldier knew his commanding officer with or without badges of rank.

Officers' servants were abolished.[22]

Furthermore, soldiers were allowed to, and did in fact, complain about their officers to the Military Prosecutor's Office. There were on the average 1,892 complaints per month during 1925, 1,923 monthly during 1926, and 2,082 monthly during 1927. Until 1931–33 'natural and easy relations between officers and men'[23] existed.

White puts the turning point to the consolidation of the officer caste a little earlier – the Army Statutes of 1928, which he describes as 'the real dividing line', and what followed as 'the development of a trend already well established.'[24] By these statutes a life career was opened to army officers, and White describes them, with ample justification, as the

114 · *State Capitalism in Russia*

'Magna Carta of the commanding personnel,' as 'something closely akin to the Petrine Table of Ranks.'[25]

In 1929 the 'gradual transformation of Red Army Houses into Officers' Clubs'[26] began. Although soldiers' pay remained very low, officers' salaries began to rise, as the following table shows:[27]

Increase in officers' monthly allowances

	1934 roubles	1939 roubles	Increase per cent
Platoon commander	260	625	240
Company commander	285	750	263
Battalion commander	335	850	254
Regimental commander	400	1,200	300
Divisional commander	475	1,600	337
Corps commander	550	2,000	364

It has been estimated that in 1937 the average annual pay of privates and non-commissioned officers taken together amounted to 150 roubles, and of officers to 8,000 roubles.[28] During the second world war, privates in the Soviet Army received an allowance of 10 roubles a month, lieutenants, 1,000, and colonels, 2,400. In sharp contrast to this wide differentiation – we do not quote this approvingly but only for comparison – privates in the United States Army received 50 dollars a month, lieutenants, 150, and colonels, 333 dollars.[29]

Although the value of the rouble declined very sharply during the last two or three decades, this has affected officers much less than civilians, for they have been able to take advantage of the *Voentorg*, an exclusive co-operative organisation which runs shops, restaurants, laundries, and tailoring and boot-making establishments. Special houses with all conveniences are built for them. They and their families travel free on railways, buses, ships, etc. (The ordinary soldiers get none of these advantages; the only concession

State and party in Stalinist Russia • 115

made to them is free postage for their outgoing letters and for their families' letters coming to them.)[30]

A decree of 22 September 1935, introduced the following ranks into the army and air force: lieutenant, senior lieutenant, captain, major, colonel, brigadier, commander of division, commander of army corps, army commander of the second rank, army commander of the first rank, and, lastly, marshal of the Soviet Union.[31] Similar ranks were introduced into the navy. Additional ones were given to the military technical services.[32] On 7 May 1940, more ranks were introduced into the army and air forces: major-general, lieutenant-general, colonel-general, general of the army; and into the navy: rear-admiral, vice-admiral, admiral, admiral of the fleet.[33] Finally, on 26 June 1945, the rank of generalissimo of the Soviet Union was introduced.[34]

On 3 September 1940, badges of rank on the old Tsarist pattern, such as gold braid epaulettes, and gold, platinum and diamond star emblems (worn by Marshals) were restored.[35] This was a far cry from the days of the civil war when the Whites were dubbed 'gold braid epauletters'. A volume of the *Small Soviet Encyclopaedia* published in 1930 stated that epaulettes 'were abolished by the November, 1917, Revolution as symbols of class oppression in the army.'[36] In sharp contrast to this, the Red Army paper wrote in 1943, after the introduction of the epaulettes: 'The introduction of the traditional soldiers' and officers' epaulettes ... emphasises and symbolises the continuity of the glory of Russian arms throughout the history of Russia right down to our times.'[37]

Fraternisation between officers and soldiers was prohibited.[38] Even reservists are divided into the same ranks as the army and they have the right to wear their military uniforms at any time.

'Nowadays,' wrote John Gibbons, the *Daily Worker* correspondent in Moscow, 'privates, and NCOs travelling in a bus, tube or train, must give up their seats to men of superior rank, should they be standing.'[39]

In order to keep up the appearance of superior breeding, officers are not permitted to carry large parcels in the street, nor to wear felt boots when visiting a theatre. High officers are not allowed to travel by underground or tramcar.[40] There are special officers' messes and officers' clubs. Even on leave, an officer is not allowed to sit at table with other ranks in public. Every officer has his permanent batman. Special schools have been established for officers' children, from kindergarten onwards. A former count and officer of the Tsarist bodyguard, lieutenant-general Aleksei Ignatiev, has in effect become the director of manners and etiquette in Stalin's army. Dancing lessons are compulsory at the Military College.

It is doubtful whether the officers of any other army in history dispose of greater disciplinary powers than do the Russian officers. Statutes introduced on 12 October 1940, stated that: 'In case of insubordination, the commander has the right to apply all measures of coercion up to and including the application of force and firearms. The commander bears no responsibility for the consequence in case he finds it necessary to apply force and firearms in order to compel an insubordinate to fulfil a command and to restore discipline and order ... The commander who does not in such instances apply all necessary measures to fulfil an order is remitted to trial before court martial.'[41]

V.Ulrich, who presided over the Moscow Trials, comments on these statutes thus: 'The disciplinary statutes considerably extend the right of commanders as regards the use of force and firearms ... Comradely relations between soldiers and officers are no more ... The hail-fellow-well-met spirit in the relationships between a commander and a subordinate can have no place in the Red Army. Discussion of any kind is absolutely prohibited among subordinates.'[42]

An article in *Pravda* of the same period sheds light on yet another aspect of these statutes: 'Grievances may be introduced only personally and individually. Submission of group grievances for others is prohibited. No more group declarations, no more joint discussions – whether concerning an order, bad food, or any other topic – all this comes under the heading of "insubordination" and for it a soldier may be shot on the spot without so much as a court-martial, hearing or investigation, if a superior officer solely and personally so decides.'[43]

Thus the officers have developed into as clearly defined a military hierarchy as ever existed in any society in history.

The Soviets

Officially, the institutions in which sovereignty resides in the USSR are the Soviets, headed by the Supreme Soviet (until 1937, by the Congress of Soviets). There are numerous indications that for many years these bodies have been little else but rubber-stamping organs, real power resting elsewhere.

In the early days, things were different. In 1918, for example, Congress met five times. Between 1919 and 1922, it met once a year, but since then the intervals between meetings have lengthened considerably. In 1923 other units joined the Russian Soviet Federated Socialist Republic (RSFSR) constituting the Union of Soviet Socialist Republics (USSR). The first Congress of Soviets of USSR took place in December 1922; the second in January-February 1924; the third in May 1925, and then once every two years until 1931. The seventh Congress took place in January–February 1935, four years after the previous one. There has been no improvement since (although the war emergencies doubtless serves as an excuse, albeit a feeble one, to postpone sessions). This Soviet 'parliament' sat for only 104 days in the years 1917–36, or less than six days a year.[44] The figure for later years is even lower, and it is significant that no congress at all was convoked during 1931–35, the period of the greatest and quickest transformation of Russia. Many major steps, such as the Five-Year Plan, collectivisation and industrialisation were decided upon without consulting the 'highest authority' in the land.

During the period 1917–36 the power of making laws was formally vested in the hands of the Congress of Soviets and its elected Central Executive Committee. Since the victory of Stalin, however, meetings of the Central Executive Committee have averaged not more than ten days a year.

Russia has travelled far since the time when the Chairman of the Central Executive Committee could say: 'The Central Executive Committee, as the supreme organ of the Soviet Republic ... lays down the policy ... for the Soviet of People's Commissars to carry out.'[45]

As regards the Presidium of the Supreme Soviet, it is not known when it is convened, nor what is discussed at its sessions, for no reports of its proceedings ever appear.

Since the end of the twenties every decision made by the Congress of Soviets and afterwards, by the Supreme Soviet, has been carried unanimously. Not only has no vote ever been cast against any proposal put forward but there has never been a single abstention, nor a proposal for amendment, nor even a speech in opposition.

The merely ceremonial nature of the Supreme Soviet is clearly shown up by the character of its deliberations. Thus, for instance, when that major switch in foreign policy took place, from alliance with France and England to collaboration with Hitler, the Supreme Soviet decided that there was no need to discuss the problem 'because of the clarity and consistency of the foreign policy of the Soviet Government.'[46]

The annual budget is sometimes brought to the notice of the Supreme Soviet many months *after* its measures are already operating. Thus, for instance, the annual budget of 1952, effective from 1 January of that year, was announced by the Minister of Finance, Zverev, only on 6 March 1952.[47] The budget for 1954 was 'deliberated' on 11 April.[48] Similarly one finds that while the First Five-Year Plan came into operation on 1 October 1928, it was approved only in April 1929. The Second Five-Year Plan came into operation on 1 January 1933, but was not officially approved until twenty-two months later, on 17 November 1934. The corresponding dates for the Third Five-Year Plan were 1 January 1939 and March 1939; for the Fourth, 1 January 1946, and March 1946; and for the Fifth, 1 January 1951, and October 1952.

In the light of these facts, the following statement by the Dean of Canterbury, Dr Hewlett Johnson, can only be called preposterous nonsense: 'the Executive [is] subordinate to the Supreme Soviet ... All actions of the Executive must be ratified by the Supreme Soviet: "The highest organ of the state", runs Article 30, "is the Supreme Soviet." The significance of the enforcement of this law will be apparent at once to those who see with alarm precisely the opposite tendency here, as for example, when the British Cabinet takes action without consulting Parliament or without seeking immediate and speedy ratification of its action by Parliament. More significant still is the determination that the Supreme Soviet shall control the Budget. Those who hold the purse-strings hold the ultimate power.'[49] The chapter heading in which this passage occurs is entitled: 'The Most Democratic Constitution in the World'!

Elections

On the eve of the 1937 general elections, Stalin declared: 'Never before – no, really never – has the world ever seen elections so completely free, and so truly democratic! History has recorded no other example of the kind.'[50] And one enthusiastic American supporter of Stalin's regime states: 'with secret balloting, without fear or favour, he [the Soviet citizen] can vote for the person or policy that he really wants.'[51]

Yet in these 'completely free, and so truly democratic' elections there is *never* more than one candidate for the electors to choose in each constituency. Also, never in any single one of the hundreds of constituencies has the percentage of voters ever been less than 98 per cent. The poll has nearly always been 99.9 per cent, and one candidate actually polled *more* than 100 per cent! It was Stalin who polled 2,122 votes in the elections to the local Soviets that took place on 21 December 1947, despite the fact that the constituency that 'elected' him had only 1,617 voters! The sheer idiocy of this incident is only exceeded by the outrageous explanation offered by *Pravda* next day. It reads: 'The extra ballot papers were put into the urns by citizens of neighbouring constituencies anxious to seize the opportunity to express their gratitude to their leaders.'[52]

Usually, of course, matters are arranged with more care, and, consequently, very little evidence of the jerrymandering exists. Nevertheless there are other cases on record. Such a one was the referendum in Lithuania, on 12 July 1940, to settle the matter of the proposed amalgamation of Lithuania with the USSR. The Tass agency in Moscow was not informed that the local authorities had decided to extend the referendum over two days, and so Moscow announced the results after the first day of the referendum, although the votes were not actually counted till the next day. By 'accident', the results turned out to be exactly as forecast: 'It was an unfortunate slip by which a London newspaper published the official results from a Russian news agency twenty-four hours before the polls were officially closed.'[53]

The *Election Regulations* stipulated that any interference with the electoral rights of citizens will be punished. Yet, for example, between the nomination of candidates and the actual elections to the Supreme Soviet in December 1937, thirty-seven candidates – among them two members of the Political Bureau, Kossior and Chubar – disappeared and were replaced by others. No explanation was offered to the electors, and no-one, it would seem, considered it healthy to enquire into the matter.

Fifteen days before the same elections, the Moscow correspondent of the *New York Times* cabled to his paper a forecast as to the composition and personnel of the next Supreme Soviet. He stated that it would consist of 246 high Party officials, 365 civil and military officials, 78 representatives of the intelligentsia, 131 workmen and 223 kolkhoz members, and gave their names.[54] Except for the 37 arrested at the last minute, his forecast exactly corresponded to the results in every detail. How could that conceivably happen in any election that was not rigged?

The party

Since the Communist Party of the Soviet Union is a state party, analysis of its structure, composition and functioning must be also an analysis of the state machine.

Before analysing the working of the Party from the time Stalin came to the helm, it is important to counterpose to its present monolithic and totalitarian character the actual democratic working of the Party in the period prior to the rise of the bureaucracy.

The Bolshevik Party had never been a monolithic or totalitarian party. Far from it. Internal democracy had always been of the utmost importance in Party life, but for one reason or another, this factor has been glossed over in most of the literature dealing with the subject.

It will therefore be worth while to digress somewhat and devote some space to setting out a number of cases which illustrate inner Party democracy in the pre-Stalinist years.

We shall begin with a few examples from the period prior to the October Revolution.

In 1907, after the final defeat of the revolution, the Party suffered a crisis over the question of what attitude to take to the elections to the Tsarist Duma. At the Third Conference of the Russian Social Democratic Workers' Party (held in July 1907), in which Bolsheviks as well as Menshevik were represented, a curious situation arose: all the Bolshevik delegates, with the sole exception of Lenin, voted in favour of boycotting the elections to the Duma; Lenin voted with the Mensheviks.[55] Three years later, a plenum of the Central Committee of the Bolsheviks passed a resolution calling for unity with the Mensheviks; again the only dissentient voice was Lenin's.[56]

When the 1914–18 war broke out, not one of the Party's branches adopted the revolutionary defeatist position which Lenin advocated,[57] and at a trial of some Bolshevik leaders in 1915, Kamenev and two Bolshevik Duma deputies repudiated Lenin's revolutionary defeatist position.[58]

After the February revolution one finds that the large majority of the Party leaders were not for a revolutionary Soviet government, but for support of the coalition provisional government. The Bolshevik faction had forty members in the Petrograd Soviet on 2 March 1917, but when the resolution to transfer power to the bourgeois coalition government was put to the vote, only nineteen voted against.[59] At a meeting of the Petrograd Committee of the Party (5 March 1917), a resolution for a revolutionary Soviet government received only one vote.[60] *Pravda*, edited by Stalin at that time, had a position which can in no way be called revolutionary. It decisively declared its support for the Provisional Government 'in so far as it struggles against reaction or counter-revolution.'[61]

Again, when Lenin came to Russia on 3 April 1917, and issued his famous 'April Theses' – a light guiding the Party to the October Revolution – he was for a time in a small minority in his own Party. *Pravda*'s comment on the 'April Theses' was that it was 'Lenin's personal opinion,' and quite 'unacceptable'.[62] At a meeting of the Petrograd Committee of the Party, held on 8 April 1917, the 'Theses' received only two votes, while thirteen voted against it and one abstained.[63] However, at the Conference of the Party held 14–22 April the 'Theses' gained a majority: 71 for, 39 against and 8 abstentions.[64] The same conference defeated Lenin on another important question, viz., whether the Party should participate in the proposed Stockholm Conference of the Socialist Parties. Against his views, it decided in favour of full participation.[65]

Again, on 14 September, Kerensky convened a 'Democratic Conference' and Lenin spoke strongly in favour of boycotting it. The Central Committee decided by 9 votes to 8 to boycott it, but as the vote was so nearly equal, the final decision was left to the Party conference, which was to be constituted out of the Bolshevik faction in the 'Democratic Conference'. This meeting decided by 77 votes to 50 not to boycott it.[66]

When the most important question of all, the question of the October insurrection, was on the order of the day, the leadership again was found to be sharply divided: a strong faction led by Zinoviev, Kamenev, Rykov, Piatakov, Miliutin and Nogin, opposed the uprising. Nevertheless, when the Political Bureau was elected by the Central Committee, neither Zinoviev nor Kamenev were excluded.

After taking power, the differences in the Party leadership continued to be as sharp as before. A few days after the revolution, a number of Party leaders came out with a demand for a coalition with other socialist parties. Those insisting on this included Rykov, the People's Commissar of the Interior, Miliutin, the People's Commissar of Agriculture, Nogin, the People's Commissar of Industry and Trade, Lunacharsky, the People's Commissar of Education, Shliapnikov, the People's Commissar of Labour, Kamenev, the President of the Republic, and Zinoviev. They went as far as resigning from the government, thus compelling Lenin and his supporters to open negotiations with the other parties.[67] (The negotiations broke down because the Mensheviks insisted on the exclusion of Lenin and Trotsky from the coalition government).[68]

Again, on the question of holding or postponing the elections to the Constituent Assembly (in December 1917), Lenin found himself in a minority in the Central Committee, and against his advice, the elections were held.[69] A little later he was again defeated on the question of the peace negotiations with Germany at Brest-Litovsk. He was for an immediate peace. But at a meeting of the Central Committee and active workers, held on 21 January 1918, his motion received only 15 votes against Bukharin's motion for 'revolutionary war', which received 32 votes, and Trotsky's, for 'neither peace nor war', which received 16.[70] At a session of the Central Committee next day, Lenin was again defeated. But at last he succeeded, under the pressure of events, in convincing the majority of members of the Central Committee of his point of view, and at its session on 24 February, his motion for peace gained 7 votes, while 4 voted against and another 4 abstained.[71]

The atmosphere of monolithism which has been imputed so assiduously to the Bolshevik party both before and immediately after the Revolution, lifts when faced with the facts. This atmosphere, however, became a reality later.

For a long time the most important body in the Party was the Congress. Lenin, for instance, declared: 'The Congress ... [is] the most responsible assembly of the Party and the Republic.'[72] But with the rise of power of the bureaucracy, it progressively lost its importance. The 1919, 1922 and 1925 Party Rules (Rules 20, 20, 21 respectively) stipulated that Congresses were to be held annually,[73] and until the Fourteenth Congress (in 1925) this was adhered to. But after that they were held more and more infrequently. The next Congress took place two years later; between that one and the Sixteenth Congress (in 1930), two-and-a-half years elapsed, and between the Sixteenth and Seventeenth (in 1934), three-and-a-half years. This latter Congress promulgated new rules by which Congress was to be convened 'not less than once in three years' (Rule 27).[74]

But even this was not observed. Five years elapsed between the Seventeenth and the Eighteenth Congress (1939), and then, between the Eighteenth and Nineteenth Congress (1952), there was a long gap of over thirteen years.

According to the Party Rules, the Central Committee must convene Party Conferences between Congresses, and, under the regulations adopted at the Eighteenth Congress and still officially in force these must be held 'not less than once a year'. Since 1919, Conferences have been held in 1919, 1920, 1921 (twice), 1923, 1924, 1925, 1926, 1929, 1932, 1934, and most recently in 1941.

Congress elects the Central Committee, the leading body of the Party. Formally the Central Committee is accountable to the Party Congress, but, when the latter is not convened for more than thirteen years, this provision can hardly be other than a dead letter.

Formally the Central Committee elects the Political Bureau, and therefore the latter should be accountable to the former. In actual fact, however, the Central Committee is entirely subordinate to the Political Bureau.

If the Central Committee *really* exercised supreme authority in the Party, it would have been impossible for a *majority* – over three-quarters in fact – of its members to have been expelled and persecuted as 'enemies of the people,' as happened between the Seventeenth and Eighteenth Congresses. Only 16 out of the 71 members of the Central Committee elected in 1934 reappeared in the list of Central Committee members elected five years later, and of the 68 candidate members only 8 reappeared in the list.

The Political Bureau, which has thirteen or fourteen members, selects the Secretariat, the head of which is the General Secretary. For thirty years this post has been held by Stalin. Since the death of Stalin the administrative set-up has become more complicated. Although to all appearances, Georgii M. Malenkov is Stalin's heir, the job of General Secretary was given to someone else – Nikita S.Khrushchev. It is now clear that Khrushshev has the upper hand.

The predominance of the bureaucracy is illustrated by the fact that the General Secretary who was, originally, merely an executor of the will of the Central Committee,[75] is, under Stalin's rule, omnipotent, wielding greater power than any Tsar dared dream of.

Lenin, for example, was never a member of the Party Secretariat. In his day, it never included the most celebrated leaders of the Party. For instance, immediately before Stalin's inclusion (1922), the Secretariat was composed of Molotov, Yaroslavsky and Mikhailov, none of whom could conceivably be placed in the top flight of Bolshevik leaders. Only with the entrenchment of the bureaucracy and the construction of a Party hierarchy controlled from above did the post of General Secretary become all-important.

It is impossible to trace exactly the changes in the social composition of the Party since 1930. Since that year, the practice of publishing such information has ceased. (The omission is in itself highly significant). Nevertheless, it is possible to gain some indication of the social composition of the Party from the educational level of the members.

In Russia, only one in twenty children finishes secondary school, not to speak of the university.* Yet, of the 1,588,852 Party members in 1939, 127,000 had received a university education, compared with only 9,000 in 1934, and 8,396 in 1927; and 335,000 had received a secondary education, compared with only 110,000 in 1934, and 84,111 in 1927.[76] At the 1924 Party Congress, 6.5 per cent of the voting delegates had received a university education; at the 1930 Congress, 7.2 per cent; in 1934, about 10 per cent; in 1939, 31.5 per cent, and at the 1941 Party Conference, 41.8 per cent. The percentage of delegates who had received a secondary education were: in 1924, 17.9 per cent; in 1930, 15.7 per cent; in 1934 about 31 per cent; in 1939, 22.5 per cent; and in 1941, 29.1 per cent (including those with an incomplete university education).[77] Thus (adding the two together), the proportion of delegates who could be classified as belonging to the 'Soviet intelligentsia', was: in 1924, 24.4 per cent; in 1930, 22.9 per cent; in 1939, 54 per cent; and in 1941, 70.9 per cent. At the 1934 Congress, when 41 per cent of voting delegates had received secondary and higher education, only 9.3 per cent were industrial and agricultural workers. The percentage must have been far smaller in 1939 and 1941.

---

*See page 89.

As regards the Komsomol, its secretary, N.A.Mikhailov, stated: 'At the present time more than half the secretaries of provincial, territorial and central committees of the Union Republics have a higher or incomplete higher education. The remaining secretaries have a secondary education. Amongst the secretaries of the district committees of the Komsomol, 67 per cent have a secondary or higher education.' (*Pravda*, 30 March 1949).

Moreover, of the manual workers at Party Congresses, a considerable number were Stakhanovites. During the war, when the number of Party members increased from two-and-a-half million to six million, 47 per cent of all the candidates accepted had received a high school or university education.[78] On 1 January 1947, of six million members and candidates, 400,000 had had a university education, 1,300,000 had completed a course at high school, and 1,500,000 had an incomplete high school education.[79]

Local information on the social status of new entrants to the Party shows the same trend. For example, during 1941 and the first two months of 1942, in the province of Cheliabinsk, of those admitted to probationary membership, 600 were workers, 289 kolkhoz members, and 2,035 'white-collar workers'. Of those who completed their term of probation during that period and became full members, 909 were workers, 399 kolkhoz members, and 3,515 'white-collar workers'. Thus, more than 70 per cent of new candidates and new members were of the latter category.[80]

In 1923 only 29 per cent of the factory directors were in the Party. By 1925, with the partial victory of Stalin's faction, 73.7 per cent of the members of the managing boards of trusts, 81.5 per cent of those on the boards of syndicates, and 95 per cent of the directors of large enterprises were Party members; by 1927 the corresponding figures were 75.1 per cent, 82.9 per cent, and 96.9 per cent.[81] In 1936 between

97.5 per cent and 99.1 per cent of this type of personnel belonged to the Party, and the figure for the chiefs of trusts was 100 per cent.[82]

As for Red Army Commanders, whereas in 1920 only 10.5 per cent belonged to the Party, the figure had reached 30.6 per cent in 1924 and 51.1 per cent in 1929,[83] and, if we include those belonging to the Komsomol, it had soared to 71.8 per cent by 1933.[84] Today there is no doubt that they *all* belong.

If we consider that in January 1937, managerial personnel numbered 1,751,000,[85] and that at least nine-tenths of these belonged to the Party, it is obvious that relatively few people outside this class could possibly have belonged, for the total number of Party members and candidates was only about two-and-a-half million. There is no exact figure available for 1937, but the figures for 1934 and 1939 were 2,807,000 and 2,477,000.

This conjecture is borne out by examples such as that of the Presnia Machine-Building Factory in Moscow. Of the 1,300 employees in that factory, members of the Party numbered 119, of whom more than a hundred were salaried employees and only about a dozen were manual workers.[86] These proportions would, no doubt, be similar in most other factories.

Parallel with the change in the social composition of Party membership came the elimination of the old guard of the Party. Of the 1,588,852 Party members on 1 March 1939, only 1.3 per cent had belonged since the 1917 Revolution, and 8.3 per cent since 1920, that is, since the end of the civil war.[87] At the end of the Eighteenth Congress it was, in fact, emphasised that 70 per cent of the Party members had joined only since 1929. On the eve of the February Revolution the Party had 23,600 members; in August 1917, 200,000; and in March 1921, 730,000.[88] It is, therefore, obvious that only about one-fourteenth of the 1917 members and about one-sixth of the 1920 members were still in the Party in 1939.

This large-scale disappearance of the old guard cannot be explained by natural causes, because the great majority of Party members in 1917 and 1920 were very young. Even in 1927, 53.8 per cent of the Party members were below 29 years old, 32.0 per cent were between 30 and 39, 11.4 per cent were between 40 and 49, and only 2.8 per cent were older than 50.[89]

A few additional facts will suffice to show how far Stalin went in the physical liquidation of the old leaders of the Bolshevik Party.

The first Political Bureau of 10 October 1917 (it did not yet bear that name) consisted of Lenin, Trotsky, Zinoviev, Kamenev, Sokolnikov, Bubnov and Stalin.[90] In 1918 Bukharin was added. In 1920 Preobrazhensky and Serebriakov were added, but a year later they were replaced by Zinoviev and Tomsky. In 1923 Rykov took Bukharin's place.[91]

Throughout the civil war the Bureau was composed of Lenin, Trotsky, Kamenev, Bukharin and Stalin. Of all these leading figures, only two, Lenin and Stalin, have died a natural death. Zinoviev, Kamenev, Bukharin, Rykov and Serebriakov were executed, each after a show trial; Trotsky was murdered in Mexico by a GPU agent; Tomsky committed suicide on the eve of his arrest, and, after his death, was denigrated as an 'enemy of the people' and a 'fascist'; Sokolnikov was condemned to a long term of imprisonment; and Preobrazhensky and Bubnov disappeared during the 'Great Purge'.

In the document known as his 'Testament', Lenin singles out six people for particular mention. Of these six, four were shot by Stalin's order after a 'trial'; these were Piatakov, Bukharin (of these two Lenin wrote: 'in my opinion, the most able forces among the youngest'), Zinoviev and Kamenev. Trotsky was murdered. The only one of the six of whom

Lenin spoke scathingly was the executioner – of the other five!

Of the fifteen members of the first Bolshevik government ever to be organised (the Council of People's Commissars of October, 1917), only one, Stalin, survived the 'purge'. Four members died a natural death: Lenin, Nogin, Skvortsov-Stepanov and Lunacharsky. The other ten – Trotsky, Rykov, Shliapnikov, Krylenko, Dybenko, Antonov-Ovsenko, Lomov-Oppokov, Miliutin, Glebov-Avilov and Teodorovich – were either executed by Stalin's order or died in his prisons.

All the highest officials of the various Commissariats have been 'purged' repeatedly. Thus, for instance, one Commissar of Labour after another has been removed and then executed or held in prison. The first to hold this position was Shliapnikov, then V.Smirnov, later Mikhail Uglanov, and, finally, V.V.Schmidt.

Among those purged as 'fascist dogs', Trotsky had been so prominent in the Party that both during and after the civil war, the Party was called the 'Party of Lenin-Trotsky', and the government was similarly known; Rykov had replaced Lenin, after his death, as Chairman of the Council of People's Commissars (or roughly Premier); Zinoviev was Chairman of the Presidium of the Executive Committee (or President) of the Communist International; and Tomsky was the President of the Trade Union Congress. Others purged included the army chiefs. One Deputy-Commissar of Defence, M.N.Tukhachevsky, was executed, and another, Jan Gamarnik, committed suicide when faced with arrest (according to an official announcement); another, Marshal Egorov, 'disappeared' a little later, and so did the Commissar of the Navy, Smirnov. Of the fifteen commanders of armies appointed in 1935, only one continued to enjoy his high position after the purges. One had died a natural death, but all the others had been branded as 'traitors' and 'purg-ed.'[92] Nearly all the ambassadors of the USSR were also 'purged', as were two chiefs of the political police: Yagoda, who had himself prepared the Zinoviev-Kamenev frame-up, and Yezhov, who prepared the other, later trials, in one of which Yagoda became a defendant.

If all those liquidated by Stalin had really been 'fascists' and 'traitors', it is a complete mystery how they, comprising as they did at least nine-tenths of the leadership of the Party and the State throughout the October Revolution and the civil war, came to lead a socialist revolution. Thus by their sheer magnitude the 'purges' proved their sham nature.

To add a grim touch of mockery to the tragedy of the 'purges', Stalin placed the responsibility for their enormous extent upon their first victims, the Trotskyites, who, he claimed, wished thereby 'artificially to sow discontent and bitterness'; thus 'the Trotskyite double-dealers can artfully hook . . . the embittered comrades and skilfully drag them into the bog of Trotskyite wrecking.'[93] Zhdanov, in a speech to the Eighteenth Party Congress, rounded out this fantastic allegation with a claim that by extending the 'purge' the Trotskyites had aimed 'to destroy the Party apparatus'. By the same logic the Inquisition could have accused their victims of responsibility for the *auto-da-fé*! The following incident, cited by Zhdanov in the same speech, indicates with cruel irony, the vast scope of the 'purge'. He said: 'Certain Party members have resorted to the aid of medical institutions in the effort to insure themselves [from being "purged"]. Here is a medical certificate issued to one of these citizens: "Owing to his state of health and mind Comrade (so and so) is not fit to be used as a tool by any class enemy. District Psychiatrist, October District, City of Kiev (Signature)".'[94]

Withering away of state and law

Marx postulated that with the establishment of socialism and the abolition of social classes, the state would cease to exist. The absence of conflicts between classes or other social groups would make superfluous any permanent apparatus of coercion in the form of army, police and prisons. Law, too, would cease to exist, since 'law is nothing without an apparatus capable of enforcing the observance of law.'[95] Under socialism all conflicts would be between individuals. For the suppression of such individual wrongdoing as would continue to manifest itself after the abolition of poverty – the chief cause of 'crime' in present-day society – no special repressive organisations would be needed. The 'General Will' – to use Rousseau's term – would prevail and deal with such problems. As Stalin once said, long ago, in 1927: 'Socialist society [is a] society without classes, society without a state'.[96]

These ideas found expression in the Constitution of the RSFSR, issued on 10 July 1918. It stated: 'The fundamental object of the Constitution of the Russian Socialist Federal Soviet Republic, a Constitution designed to serve the present period of transition, is the establishment, in the form of a strong All-Russian Soviet authority, of the dictatorship of the urban and rural proletariat together with the peasant poor, to secure the complete suppression of the bourgeoisie, the abolition of the exploitation of man by man, and the realisation of *Socialism, under which neither class divisions nor state authority will any longer exist.*'[97]

After the victory of Stalin, however, the line changed entirely. Stalinist spokesmen have stopped speaking of the 'withering away of the state', and, indeed, have gone to quite the other extreme, claiming that 'socialism in one country' and even 'communism in one country' goes hand in hand with the strengthening of the state. Thus P.F.Yudin wrote in 1948: 'The Soviet State is the main force, the main instrument of the construction of socialism and the realisation of the construction of communist society. That is why the task of strengthening the Soviet state by all means is the main task of present as well as of future activity in the construction of a communist society.'[98] Again: 'The consolidation of the Soviet state by every means has been the *necessary condition* for the building of socialism, and now, of communism; this is equally one of the most important laws of the development of Soviet society.'[99] Another Soviet theoretician said: 'communism pre-supposes the existence of a perfect apparatus administering the economy and culture. The apparatus develops gradually and finds its form in the conditions of the transition from socialism to communism ... That is why the rise of communism will be in accordance with the degree of perfectibility of our state and economic apparatus.'[100]

The strengthening of the Russian state, its increasing totalitarianism, can only be the result of profound class antagonisms and not of the victory of socialism.

Chapter 3: The economy of a workers' state

The transformation of capitalist relations of production into Socialist relations of production · The division of labour and the division into classes · Workers and technicians · Labour discipline · The workers and the means of production · The relations of distribution in the transition period · Peasants and workers · In conclusion

Before considering the fundamental features of the economy of a workers' state, it is necessary to mention one very important factor. Marx and Engels expected the revolution to begin in the developed countries. They thus assumed that the new society from its inception would be materially and culturally more developed than the most advanced capitalist countries. Every prognosis, however, is conditional. History did not unfold exactly as Marx and Engels had expected. It was in Russia, one of the most backward of capitalist countries, that the revolution first broke out and the workers took power, while the revolutions which followed in the more developed countries failed.

The transformation of capitalist relations of production into socialist relations of production

There are two sorts of productive forces: the means of production and labour power. The development of these productive forces under capitalism — the centralisation of capital on the one hand and the socialisation of the labour process on the other – creates the material conditions necessary for socialism.

Of all the relations of production which prevail under capitalism – relations between capitalists and capitalists, between capitalists and workers, between the workers themselves, between technicians and workers, technicians and capitalists, etc. – only one section is carried over into the socialist society, namely the relations obtaining between the workers in the process of production; the workers united through social production become the basis for new relations of production. Some elements in the relations of production existing under capitalism are abolished altogether by socialism through the abolition of the capitalists, while others, such as the 'new middle class' (technicians, accountants, etc.) will be fitted into a new context.

This 'new middle class' constitutes part of the productive forces, and as such is a necessary element of production. However, its position in the hierarchy of capitalist society is a transitory one, as transitory as capitalism. Socialism will do away entirely with this hierarchical position in the process of production above that of the proletariat. A new relationship will be created between the different elements necessary for the socialist mode of production, between mental and manual labour. The new relationship (to be dealt with more fully later on) begins to take shape with the transition period.

The working class, which constitutes a part of the productive forces and a part of the capitalist relations of production at one and the same time, becomes the *basis* for the new relations of production and the point of departure for the development of the productive forces on the foundation of these relations. In the words of Marx,

Of all the instruments of production, the greatest productive power is the revolutionary class itself. The organisation of the revolutionary elements as a class pre-supposes the existence of the productive forces which could be engendered in the bosom of the old society.[1]

The division of labour and the division into classes

Engels writes:

In every society in which production has developed spontaneously – and our present society is of this type – it is not the producers who control the means of production, but the means of production which control the producers. In such a society each new lever of production is necessarily transformed into a new means for the subjection of the producers to the means of production. This is most of all true of that lever of production which, prior to the introduction of large-scale industry, was by far the most powerful – the division of labour.[2]

The division of labour, expressed in the separation of manual from mental labour, is of an historically transitory character; it has its roots in the separation of the workers from the means of production, and in the resultant antagonism of these two elements to each other. In the words of Marx:

Intelligence in production expands in one direction because it vanishes in many others. What is lost by the detail labourers, is concentrated in the capital that employs them. It is a result of the division of labour in manufactures, that the labourer is brought face to face with the intellectual potencies of the material process of production, as the property of another, and as a ruling power. This separation begins in simple co-operation, where the capitalist represents to the single workman, the oneness and the will of the associated labour. It is developed in manufacture which cuts down the labourer into a detail labourer. It is completed in modern industry, which makes science a productive force distinct from labour and presses it into the service of capital.[3]

The complete victory of socialism means the complete abolition of the separation of mental and manual labour. Clearly it would be impossible to abolish this separation immediately after the socialist revolution, but *workers' control over production will become an immediate bridge between mental and manual labour, and the point of departure for their future synthesis, the total abolition of classes.*

Here we come to a problem which is fundamental from the standpoint of the transformation of the relations of production, of the bridge between mental and manual labour.

Workers and technicians

Technicians constitute a necessary element in the process of production, an important part of the productive forces of society, whether capitalist or communist. At the same time, as we have already said, under capitalism they form a layer in the hierarchy of production. They come into being as part and parcel of this hierarchy. Their monopolist position as regards the 'mental means of production' (as Bukharin terms it) is the result of the separation of the workers from the means of production on the one hand, and the socialisation of labour on the other. Socialism will abolish this hierarchy. In the transition period it will continue to exist in one sense, but in another, be abolished. Insofar as mental labour remains the privilege of the few, the hierarchical relations will continue to exist in the factories, railways, etc., even after the proletarian revolution. But *seeing that the place of the capitalist in the hierarchy will be taken by the workers' state, i.e., by the workers as a collective, the technicians being subordinated to the workers, the mental hierarchy in this sense will be abolished. Workers' control over technicians means the subordination of capitalist elements to socialist ones. The more efficient workers' control, the higher the material and cultural level of the masses, the more will the monopolist position of mental workers be undermined, till it is completely abolished and a full synthesis of mental and manual labour achieved.*

The economy of a workers' state · 139

Because of the double role of technicians in their relation to workers in the process of production, the founders of marxism pointed out that the subordination of the technicians to the interests of society as a whole will be one of the greatest difficulties experienced by the new society. Thus Engels wrote: 'If . . . a war brings us to power prematurely, the technicians will be our chief enemies; they will deceive and betray us wherever they can and we shall have to use terror against them but shall get cheated all the same.'[4]

Labour discipline

Every form of social production needs the co-ordination of the different people participating in it; in other words, every form of social production needs discipline. Under capitalism this discipline confronts the worker as an external coercive power, as the power which capital has over him. Under socialism discipline will be the result of consciousness, it will become the habit of a free people. In the transition period it will be the outcome of the unity of the two elements – consciousness and coercion. The state institutions will be the organisation of the masses as a conscious factor. Collective ownership of the means of production by the workers, i.e., the ownership by the workers' state of the means of production, will be the basis for the conscious element in labour discipline. At the same time the working class as a collective, through its institutions – soviets, trade unions, etc. – will appear as a coercive power as regards the disciplining of the individual workers in production. Individualistic consumption, the 'bourgeois right' as regards distribution, will serve as a weapon of coercive discipline.

The technicians, supervisors, etc., have a special place in labour discipline. Under capitalism, the supervisor is the transmission belt through which capitalist coercion of the worker is exercised. Under communism a supervisor will not fulfil any coercive function. His relations with the workers will be analogous to those between a conductor and his orchestra, as labour discipline will be based on consciousness and habit. In the transition period, whereas the workers, as regards themselves, will be both a disciplining and a disciplined factor, a subject and an object, the technicians will serve in reality only as a transmission belt, this time of the workers' state, even though they remain formally discipliners of the workers.

The worker and the means of production

The Communist Manifesto says:

In bourgeois society, living labour is but a means to increase accumulated labour. In communist society, accumulated labour is but a means to widen, to enrich, to promote the existence of the labourer.

In bourgeois society, therefore, the past dominates the present; in communist society, the present dominates the past. In bourgeois society capital is independent and has no individuality.*

In communist society accumulation will be conditioned by the needs of consumption of the people. In capitalist society accumulation determines the extent of employment and the rate of wages – i.e., the rate of consumption of the working people. Even as regards the capitalist himself the factor that makes him a capitalist is not consumption but accumulation. As Marx said:

Accumulation for accumulation's sake, production for production's sake: by this formula classical economy expressed the historical mission of the bourgeoisie, and did not for a single instant deceive itself over the birth-throes of wealth.*

Because the worker is dominated by the product of his labour, the process of capitalist accumulation determines, limits, and undermines consumption. Because the labourer will dominate his product, communist consumption will determine the accumulation of means of production.

In every society, whatever form the relations of production take, rationalisation of production generally involves a more round-about way of production, i.e., an increase in the portion of the total social labour devoted to the production of means of production. This means an increase in the rate of 'accumulation' relatively to rate of consumption. Under communism, this increase in the rate of 'accumulation' as against the rate of consumption would at the same time mean a large absolute increase in the consumption of the workers. Under capitalism, however, because of the antagonistic way of distribution, the rate of surplus value increases, and thus also the rate of accumulation, while the rate of consumption of the masses is subordinated to them.

Accumulation for accumulation's sake under capitalism is the result of two factors: one, the separation of the workers from the means of production, the other, the existence of competition between the capitalists, whether individual monopolistic or state capitalists. Socialism abolishes both these aspects of the relations of production. Workers' control over production and the abolition of national boundaries – these are the two conditions for the full subordination of accumulation to consumption. Under such conditions society will accumulate in order to consume.

This subordination of accumulation to consumption, by raising the material and cultural conditions of the masses will at the same time undermine the monopoly of the technicians over the 'mental means of production', and thus strengthen the workers' control over production.

The relations of distribution in the transition period

The most exact and concise analysis of this question was given by Marx in his *Critique of the Gotha Programme*:

What we have to deal with here is a communist society, not as it has *developed* on its own foundation, but, on the contrary, as it *emerges* from capitalist society; which is thus in every respect, economically, morally and intellectually, still stamped with the birth-marks of the old society from whose womb it emerges. Accordingly the individual producer receives back from society – after the deductions have been made [deductions in the interests of society as a whole] – exactly what he gives to it. What he has given to it is his individual amount of labour. For example, the social working day consists of the sum of the individual labour hours; the individual labour time of the individual producer is the part of the social labour day contributed by him, his share in it. He receives a certificate from society that he has furnished such and such an amount of labour (after deducting his labour for the common fund) and with this certificate he draws from the social stock of means of consumption as much as costs the same amount of labour. The same amount of labour which he has given to society in one form, he receives back in another.

Here obviously the same principle avails as that which regulated the exchange of commodities, as far as this is exchange of equal values. Content and form are changed, because under the altered circumstances no one can give anything except his labour, and because, on the other hand, nothing can pass into the ownership of individuals except individual means of consumption. But, as far as the distribution of the latter among the individual producers is concerned, the same principle prevails as in the exchange of commodity-equivalents, so much labour in one form is exchanged for an equal amount of labour in another form.

Hence, *equal right* here is still in principle – *bourgeois right*, although principle and practice are no longer in conflict, while the exchange of equivalents in commodity exchange only exists on the *average* and not in the individual case.

In spite of this advance, this *equal right* is still stigmatised by a bourgeois limitation. The right of the producers is *proportional* to the labour they supply; the equality consists in the fact that measurement is made with an *equal standard*, labour.

But one man is superior to another physically or mentally and so supplies more labour in the same time, or can labour for a longer time; and labour, to serve as a measure, must be defined by its duration or intensity, otherwise it ceases to be a standard of measurement. This *equal* right is an unequal right for unequal labour. It recognises no class differences, because everyone is only a worker like everyone else; but it tacitly recognises unequal individual endowment and thus productive capacity as natural privileges. *It is therefore a right of inequality in its content like every right.* Right by its very nature can only consist in the application of an equal standard; but unequal individuals (and they would not be different individuals if they were not unequal) are only measurable by an equal standard in so far as they are brought under an equal point of view, are taken from one *definite* side only, e.g., in the present case are regarded *only as workers*, and nothing more seen in them, everything else being ignored. Further, one worker is married, another not; one has more children than another and so on and so forth. Thus with an equal capacity to work, and hence an equal share in the social consumption fund, one will in fact receive more than another, one will be richer than another, and so on. To avoid all these defects, right instead of being equal would have to be unequal.

But these defects are inevitable in the first phase of communist society as it is when it has just emerged after prolonged birth pangs from capitalist society. Right can never be higher than the economic structure of society and the cultural development thereby determined.

In a higher phase of communist society, after the enslaving subordination of individuals under division of labour, and therewith also the antithesis between mental and physical labour, has vanished, after labour has become not merely a means to live but has become itself the primary necessity of life, after the productive forces have also increased with the all-round development of the individual, and all the springs of co-operative wealth flow more abundantly – only then can the narrow horizon of bourgeois right be fully left behind and society inscribe on its banners: from each according to his ability, to each according to his needs.'

Even though the workers differ from one another in skill, in their needs and those of their families, etc., in one thing they must be *absolutely equal* in order that the same amount of labour which every worker gives to society in one form be received back in another: in the ownership of the means of production. The growth of production, the increase of the amount of means of production belonging to society, i.e., owned equally by all the workers, will progressively undermine equal rights in the distribution of the products. This in turn will progressively increase equality among the people. And thus does the bourgeois right of the transition period include its own negation.

Bourgeois right in the transition period, while it lays down that every worker will receive means of consumption from society according to the labour he gives it, is based on social equality as regards the means of production, and thereby will wither away of itself.

Peasants and workers

The October Revolution was the fusion of two revolutions: that of the socialist working class, the product of mature capitalism, and that of the peasants, the product of the conflict between rising capitalism and the old feudal institutions. As at all times, the peasants were ready enough to expropriate the private property of the large estate owners, but they wanted their own small *private* properties. Whilst they were prepared to revolt against feudalism, they were not for that reason in favour of socialism. French history shows the same attitude on the part of the French peasantry. After 1789, they always supported reactionary governments against the 'red menace' of the Parisian working class. It was they who formed the solid backing for Bonaparte, and later, for his nephew, Napoleon III, for Cavaignac and for Thiers. In Western Europe (excluding Spain and Italy), where large estates have been abolished, the villages rarely return a socialist or communist member of parliament. Hence it is not surprising that the victorious alliance of the workers and peasants in the October revolution was immediately followed by very strained relations. Once the White armies, and with them the danger of the restoration of landlordism, had been overcome, very little remained of the peasants' loyalty toward the workers. It had been one thing for the peasant to support a government which distributed land, but it was quite another matter when the same government began to requisition his produce to feed the hungry populations of the cities. This duality in the attitude of the peasants towards the Soviet government was expressed by a number of provincial delegates to the Twelfth Congress of the Communist Party, in April 1923. Their reports showed that the peasants thought of the Bolsheviks and the Communists as quite different people: the former gave them land, the latter imposed the yoke of the state upon them. (This misunderstanding was facilitated by the fact that it was only at the Seventh Congress of the Party – 1918 – that the name Communist Party was adopted).

Socialist workers stand for socialised labour, state ownership and socialist planning; the peasantry for individual small-scale production, private property and freedom to trade. It is impossible to avoid permanent conflict between the two systems of production. 'Small-scale production gives birth to capitalism and the bourgeoisie, constantly, daily, hourly, elementally and in vast proportions.'[8] Backwardness of agricultural production and its individual character are a serious impediment to the development of planned industrial production. To paraphrase Abraham Lincoln: 'You cannot have your house half based on collectivist, planned, labour, and the other half anarchic and individualistic.'

The conservatism of the Russian peasantry was accentuated after the October revolution by the fact that the agrarian revolution not only took the revolutionary wind from the peasantry by abolishing feudal land ownership, but also by the fact that it also greatly diminished the class differences within the peasantry itself. The number of proletarian and semi-proletarian agriculturists, the natural allies of the urban working class, was drastically reduced by the agrarian revolution, which was more consistently democratic and went much further in Russia than it had done in France, in 1789. In the French Revolution the large estates were generally sold and so fell into the hands of people who had money – the urban and rural rich. In Russia not only the large estates, but many of the rich peasant farms too, were seized by the peasants and the land freely distributed.

It is an extremely difficult matter to apply social methods of production to agriculture. Unlike industry, agriculture, even in the most advanced countries, is based predominantly on small-scale production units. Many industrial plants employ hundreds of thousands of workers, but even in the United States the small farm is predominant. Thus of all labour engaged in US agriculture in 1944, 77 per cent was family labour.[9]

That the survival of the small farm may in many cases be due to the fact that the small farmer, who is worker, capitalist and land-owner combined, is prepared to work very hard indeed – harder than the industrial worker – renouncing rent and profit, and even then getting an income below that of the urban worker, is irrelevant to our argument.

The decisive factor is that the technical superiority of large-scale over small-scale production is incomparably smaller in agriculture than in industry. This applies even more to intensive mixed farming than to grain production. (And, by the way, we must not forget that, as the population in the towns increases and the standard of living rises, the importance of cereal production declines relatively to that of intensive agriculture – the production of milk, vegetables, fruit, meat and so on.) In many countries, large farms came into existence less as the result of small farmers being outdone in the course of free competition, than as the result of extra-economic factors – enclosures, as survivals of the feudal estates, and the like.

Engels' view of the attitude to be adopted towards the peasants after the socialist revolution was as follows:

> it is ... clear to us that if we were in possession of state power, we would not think of forcefully expropriating the small peasant (with compensation or without is immaterial) ... Our aim in regard to the small peasant consists first of all in leading his small-scale production and private enterprise into co-operative lines, though not by force, but by example and granting public assistance for that purpose. And, of course, we shall have ample means of showing the small peasant all the advantages connected with such a transformation ...
>
> We stand decisively on the side of the small peasant: we will do everything possible to make his lot more tolerable and facilitate his transition to the co-operative, if he decides to take this step. If he cannot as yet bring himself to this decision, we will give him plenty of time to ponder over it on his holding.[10]

He believed that it would take *generations* for the peasantry of Western and Central Europe to decide voluntarily to join co-operative farms. Obviously, in a country where the vast majority of the population are engaged in agriculture and where industry is much less able to supply the needs of the peasants and thus attract them to collective production – as in Russia, in 1917 – the obstacles to the *voluntary* enlistment of the peasants in producers' co-operatives are even greater. Voluntary co-operation demands a highly mechanised agriculture, good prices for agricultural products, paid by the state, a plentiful supply of cheap industrial goods for the peasantry and very low taxes for them. In short, general plenty.

Soon after the revolution, it became clear to a number of Bolshevik theoreticians – and primarily to the economist Evgeni Preobrazhensky – that the surplus produced in industry would not by itself be enough for capital accumulation, especially as 'from the moment of its victory the working class ... cannot treat its own labour power, its health and working conditions in the same way as the capitalist did. This is a decisive impediment to the tempo of socialist accumulation, an impediment which capitalist industry did not know in the first period of its development.'[11] In opposition to 'socialist accumulation' (defined as an addition to the functioning means of production as a result of the surplus product produced in the socialist economy itself) Preobrazhensky postulated the 'primitive socialist accumulation',* which he defined as 'the accumulation in the hands of the state of material resources obtained chiefly from sources lying outside the state economic system.' 'This accumulation will, necessarily, in a backward agrarian country, play a colossal role ... Primitive accumulation will predominate during the period of industrialisation ... We must, therefore, term this whole stage as the period of primitive or preparatory socialist accumulation.'[13] This 'source lying outside the state economic system' was agriculture. Just as in the mercantilist period in Western Europe, early merchant-capitalists amassed wealth by colonial exploitation, so the socialist industry would draw on internal 'colonies' (to use a term Preobrazhensky vehemently opposed) – small individualistic agriculture. Preobrazhensky did not advocate following the mercantilist merchants in the use of violence against the peasants nor raising any class – in this case the working class – to the position of an exploiting class. He propounded measures which were far milder than those used by the mercantilist

* The first to coin this term seems to have been the Bolshevik economist V.M.Smirnov.[12]

bourgeoisie. He proposed the partial suppression of the law of value by changing the terms of exchange between industry and agriculture in favour of the former and against the latter, so that a unit of labour in state industry would be exchanged for more than a unit of labour in agriculture. He assumed that these terms of exchange would soon lead to such a quick rise in the general level of production in society, that not only would the income of society as a whole rise, but also the income, in absolute terms, of the peasantry.

Actually the implementation of Preobrazhensky's 'socialist primitive accumulation' would logically have led to a very different state of affairs from that which he visualised. Any attempt to 'squeeze' the peasants would be likely to be met by a deliberate reduction in production, so that if the 'terms of trade' between agriculture and industry were in favour of the latter, the amount of trade would fall. There would be only one way to deal with such a 'strike', and that would be to use violence against the peasants, to expropriate them, and to concentrate them on such large farms that it would be possible for the state to control their work and output. If the state used these methods, it would also be faced with serious opposition from the workers, many of whom, in a backward country such as is under consideration, being newly recruited to industry, would, naturally, still have close family ties with the villages. Moreover, if the state, imposing a 'primitive socialist accumulation', resorted to oppression, what would there be to stop it from doing the same as regards 'socialist accumulation' proper, as regards the extortion of surplus value from the workers in state industry itself?

One solution to the conflict between state industry and individualist agriculture in a backward country would have been to make the rate of development of industry depend upon the rate at which agricultural surpluses increased. As a result of the agrarian revolution there was a great decline in the surpluses of agriculture coming on to the market, because the large landowners and the kulaks had been the main contributors of those surpluses. The distribution of the land, by increasing the share of the middle peasant, who worked mainly for subsistence, reduced the sources of marketable agricultural produce.

Larger surpluses could certainly have been obtained by increasing the proportion of land held by the rich peasants, termed in Russia *kulaks*. But to make the development of state industry dependent upon that of kulak agriculture it would have been necessary to have held the tempo of industrial development down to a snail's pace, and thus to have weakened the industrial working class in relation to the kulaks. It would inevitably have led to a victory of private capitalism throughout the economy.

Alternatively, the conflict between industry and agriculture might have been resolved by rapid industrialisation based on 'primitive accumulation' – by expropriating the peasants and forcing them into large mechanised farms, thus releasing labour power for industry and making agricultural surpluses available for the urban population. Such a method of 'primitive accumulation' must also, ultimately, lead to the subordination of the industrial workers to the needs of capital accumulation. It is the path of the submersion of individual agricultural production in a state capitalist economy.

In both cases it is ridiculous to expect socialist democracy to flourish. On the contrary, in the first case, the state must necessarily come under increasing pressure from the kulaks and therefore must become more and more divorced from the workers. In the second case, the state must become omnipotent, and, it follows, its officials will become autocratic in their relations with both workers and peasants.

(These two methods of dealing with the problem were actually tried out, the first during the period of the 'New

Economic Policy' (NEP) – 1921–28 – and the second with the Five-Year Plans.)

In conclusion

The economy of a workers' state and a capitalist economy have many common characteristics. The workers' state – a transition stage between capitalism and communism – inevitably includes some of the features of the society from whose ruins it rises, and some of the nuclei of the future society. These antagonistic elements are, however, bound together in the transition period, the former being subordinated to the latter, the past to the future. Common to both a workers' state and capitalism is the division of labour, primarily the division between mental and manual labour. The distinguishing feature is the existence or non-existence of workers' control over production. Worker's control forms the bridge, albeit a narrow bridge, to the abolition of the separation of manual and mental labour, which will be completely realised with the establishment of communist society. Common to both a workers' state and capitalism is the fact that the technicians form a hierarchy above the workers (although in a workers' state it is not in *essence* a hierarchy). The distinguishing feature lies in the fact that in a workers' state the technicians are not subordinated to capital, but to the will of the workers' state, to the collective of producers. This is the point of departure to the abolition of any social hierarchy in production. Elements of coercion in labour discipline will exist in a workers' state, as they do in capitalism. But in a workers' state, as opposed to what obtains under capitalism, they will not be the only elements, and they will be more and more subordinated to elements of consciousness until such time as social solidarity, harmonious relations between people and education will render coercion in the process of production completely superfluous. In a workers' state as well as in the capitalist commodity economy, equivalents are exchanged, a product containing a certain quantity of socially necessary labour is exchanged for another product containing an equivalent amount. But in a workers' state this result is achieved firstly through the conscious direction of the economy and not through the action of blind forces, and secondly – and this is of fundamental importance – the exchange of equivalents is based on the existence of the equality of rights of all direct producers as regards the ownership of the means of production. Bourgeois right under the bourgeoisie means exploitation; the bourgeois right of distribution in a workers' state 'tacitly recognizes unequal individual endowment and thus productive capacity as natural privileges,' but at the same time it declares the equality of producers with regard to the means of production. The prerequisites for the bourgeois right of distribution in a workers' state are the absence of any exploitation whatsoever, and the development towards the complete abolition of all economic inequality, including that resulting from natural individual endowment.

Chapter 4: The material heritage of pre-October society

The material heritage of the Tsarist period · The rule of the working class where the material conditions for the abolition of capitalist relations of production do not exist · Socialist relations of production · Capitalist function · Why the Five-Year Plan signifies the transformation of the bureaucracy into a ruling class

In the introduction to *The Critique of Political Economy* Marx formulates concisely the main conclusions of historical materialism. He writes:

> No social order ever disappears before all the productive forces, for which there is room in it, have been developed; and new, higher relations of production never appear before the material conditions of their existence have matured in the womb of the old society.

The Mensheviks quoted this sentence in order to prove that capitalism in Russia was not yet ripe for the socialist revolution, and that it was assured a long future until it would reach such a stage. This simple conclusion, however, neglects a whole series of factors which determine, limit or extend the possibilities of development of the productive forces.

What determined the development in Tsarist Russia was, on the one hand, the relation of forces between classes within Russia itself, and, on the other, Russia's dependence vis-à-vis world capitalism. These two factors are dialectically knit together. If not for the unity of the world, the uneven, combined development of the different countries could not be explained: why the class struggle should take the deepest and most extreme form in such a backward country as Russia, how it was that the Russian proletariat under Tsarism was more concentrated in gigantic enterprises even than the proletariat of the USA. These phenomena are evidence of the high level of social production which the *world economy* had reached, and the maturity of the *world* for the substitution of socialist relations of production for capitalist ones. The First World War which accelerated the downfall of Tsarism was no proof of the high level of productive forces in *each* of the belligerent countries, but it did show that the material conditions were ripe for the socialist revolution on a world scale. The series of military defeats, in which the Russian army suffered disastrous losses, showed clearly the industrial and military backwardness of Russia within the advanced world. The fact that marxism – the fruit of the synthesis of French socialism, English economic theory and German philosophy – was imported to Russia when the workers' movement was still in its cradle, is evidence of the spiritual unity of the world. On the other hand, the fact that opportunism and revisionism struck much weaker roots in the Russian labour movement than in the countries of the West reveals the backwardness of Russia in a world ripe for socialism: the low standard of living of the workers, kept low by the stream of peasant migration into the towns; the fact that the Russian bourgeoisie had no overseas investments and could thus not use part of the resulting superprofits to bribe a layer of workers and improve temporarily the conditions of the masses as a whole for a period of time, as was done in the West; the concentration of the workers in gigantic enterprises; the fact that the country was perched precariously on the powder-barrel of the agrarian revolution.

The fact that the productive forces develop within a framework of national and international social relations, and not, as they would have it, in a vacuum, entirely invalidated the Mensheviks' dream of the tremendous possibilities of development open to Russian capitalism. On the contrary, the continued existence of Russian capitalism in the concrete national and international relations then extant would have conserved the burden of feudalism. It would have involved the country in wars which might well have resulted in transferring backward Russia into a colony or semi-colony of the Western Powers. It would have meant that the development of the national minorities, which made up about half the population of Russia, would have continued to be hindered.

The above quotation from *The Critique of Political Economy* applies to the world system, not to a country in isolation. The very fact that the first proletarian revolution broke out in a backward country affirms this; it is the best witness to the ripeness of the world for the socialist revolution.

One of the fundamental causes of the insoluble crisis in the modern world, is the fact that, with the international division of labour, national boundaries have become too narrow a framework for the development of productive forces. For a country like Russia, the existence of national frontiers not only places serious obstacles in the way of getting material help from the more advanced industrial countries, but imposes the heavy burden of an armaments race with other national states.

Until Lenin's death, no-one in the Bolshevik Party suggested that Russia could build socialism by her own unaided efforts. Lenin himself repeatedly emphasised the opposite. 'The Russian revolution,' he wrote, on 4 June 1918, 'was due not to the special merits of the Russian proletariat, but to the course of historic events, and this proletariat was placed temporarily in the leading position by the will of history and made for a time the vanguard of the world revolution.'[1]

'We always staked our play upon an international revolution

and this was unconditionally right ... we always emphasised
... *the fact that in one country it is impossible to accomplish
such a work as a socialist revolution.*'*

Even after Lenin's death, Stalin, who later propounded the
idea of 'socialism in one country', said: 'But to overthrow the
power of the bourgeoisie and establish that of the proletariat
in a single country is still not to assure the complete victory of
Socialism. The chief task, the organisation of Socialist production, is still to be accomplished. Can we succeed and
secure the definitive victory of Socialism in one country
without the combined efforts of the proletarians of several
advanced countries? Most certainly not. The efforts of a
single country are enough to overthrow the bourgeoisie: this
is what the history of our revolution proves. But for the
definitive triumph of Socialism, the organisation of Socialist
production, the efforts of one country alone are not enough,
particularly of an essentially rural country like Russia; the
efforts of the proletarians of several advanced countries are
needed.'†

It need hardly be mentioned that Trotsky expressed the
same internationalist idea on many occasions.

The Russian revolution can be explained by the law of
uneven development, which is one facet of the unity of world
development. But this law allows two possibilities of development: firstly, that the Russian revolution, being evidence of
the maturity of the world for socialism, would be the prelude

---

* 6 November 1920. Lenin, *Works* (Russian) 3rd ed., vol. XXV, pp. 473–4.
My emphasis; these words are struck out of the fourth edition of Lenin's *Works*
(Russian). See vol. XXXI, p. 370.

† Stalin, *The Theory and Practice of Leninism*, Communist Party of Great
Britain, 1925, pp. 45–6. In the second Russian edition of this book, which appeared in December 1924, the above section is omitted, and instead one reads:
'Having consolidated its power, and taking the lead of the peasantry, the proletariat of the victorious country can and must build a socialist society ... Such
in general are the characteristic features of the Leninist theory of the proletarian
revolution.' (Stalin, *Works* (Russian) vol. VI pp. 107–8; also Stalin, *Problems of
Leninism*, pp. 27–8).

to a series of new revolutions which would break out immediately or after a certain interval; secondly – and this is a reformulation of the first possibility – because of the unevenness, that this 'certain interval' would lengthen into years, and leave the Russian revolution isolated in a hostile capitalist world. Before October 1917, it was impossible to determine which path humanity would follow by basing oneself simply on general considerations relating to the universality of world history; the contradictions contained in this universality, i.e. the law of uneven development, must also be considered. Human practice alone can decide which way history will go. Now, we may say in retrospect what human practice, viz., the support the social democratic parties gave capitalism in Western and Central Europe, caused the failure of the revolutions that followed in the wake of the October revolution.

In order that the productive forces be able to develop, the social order that existed under the Tsar had to disappear. But what social order was to take its place? Seeing that the destruction of the social order of Tsarist Russia was an expression of the maturity of the world for socialism, there is no doubt that, had the revolution spread, the social order that would have taken its place would have been the first stage of communist society. But as the October revolution did not spread, what social order *could* appear in Russia?

The first step to take in answering this question is to analyse the material heritage handed down from the social order that existed before October.

Men do not build themselves a new world with 'earthly goods' as vulgar superstition believes, but with the historical achievements of the old world which is about to go under. In the course of evolution they must begin entirely by themselves to produce the material conditions for a new society, and no effort of the human mind or will can release them from this fate.[1]

The material heritage of the Tsarist period

In 1913, 80 per cent of the population of Russia earned their livelihood from agriculture; only 10 per cent from industry, mining and transport. These figures alone are sufficient to show up the backwardness of Russia. Of all the countries of Europe only Yugoslavia, Turkey, Rumania and Bulgaria show a similar occupational distribution of the population.

As far back as the middle of the nineteenth century the countries of Western and Central Europe and the USA showed a much higher percentage of their population occupied in industry, mining and transport and a much lower percentage in agriculture than did Russia in 1913. Thus in Britain in 1841 the percentage of population occupied in agriculture, fishing and forestry was 22.7, that occupied in manufacture, building, mining and transport 47.3. France, which lagged a long way behind Britain, had, in 1837, 63 per cent occupied in agriculture; in 1866 it had 43 per cent occupied in agriculture and 38 per cent in industry. Germany in 1800 had nearly two-thirds of the population occupied in agriculture; in 1852 it had 44.4 per cent occupied in agriculture and 40.9 per cent occupied in industry and handicrafts. The USA, originally a country of agricultural settlement in the main, had 72.3 per cent occupied in agriculture, forestry and fishing, and 12.3 per cent occupied in manufacture, building and mining in 1880; in 1850 it had 64.8 per cent and 17.8 per cent respectively.

National income statistics show clearly how poor was the material heritage which the Bolsheviks acquired on taking power; not only in comparison with the contemporary developed capitalist countries, but even with these same countries in the infancy of their capitalist development.

The most complete and accurate – in so far as accuracy is possible in such a vast and complex calculation of the national income in different countries at different periods, was under-taken by Colin Clark in his book *The Conditions of Economic Progress* (London, 1940).

Clark estimates the real income per occupied person in Russia in 1913 to be 306 International Units (IUs).*

As against this the real income per occupied person in some developed countries was:[3]

Great Britain		France		Germany		USA	
Year	I.U.	Year	I.U.	Year	I.U.	Year	I.U.
1688	372	1850–59†	382	1850	420	1850	787
1860–69†	638	1860–69†	469	1877	632	1880	1,032
1904–10†	999	1911	786	1913	881	1900	1,388
1913	1,071					1917	1,562
						1929	1,636

Thus the average income per occupied person in Russia in 1913 was only 80.9 per cent of the corresponding figure for Britain in *1688* – nearly a hundred years before the Industrial Revolution.

The rule of the working class where the material conditions for the abolition of capitalist relations of production do not exist

Marx and Engels deal more than once with the question of what would happen if the working class took power before the historical prerequisites for the substitution of capitalist relations of production by socialist ones were present. They concluded that in such an event the working class would lose power to the bourgeoisie. The working class would be in power only temporarily and would blaze a path for the devel-oping capitalism. Thus, for instance, Marx wrote in 1847:

If it is true that the bourgeoisie politically, that is, through state power, 'maintains the injustice of property relations'

---

* Clark defines the 'International Unit' as 'the amount of goods and services which one dollar would purchase in USA over the average of the period 1925–34'.
† Annual average

[Heinzen's expression], then it is not less true that it does not create them. The 'injustice of property relations' is conditioned by the modern division of labour, the modern form of exchange, competition, concentration, etc., and does not owe its origin in any way to the political domination of the bourgeois class; ... the political domination of the bourgeois class flows from ... the existing relations of production. Therefore, *if the proletariat overthrows the political domination of the bourgeoisie its victory will only be temporary, a point in the process of the bourgeois revolution itself, and will serve its cause as it did in 1794, so long as the 'movement' of history has not created the material conditions which make it necessary to abolish the bourgeois mode of production and therewith definitely overthrow the political domination of the bourgeoisie.* The 'Reign of Terror' in France therefore had to accomplish the cleansing of the surface of France from feudal ruins by its terrible hammer blows. The timid, cautious bourgeoisie would not have managed to complete this task in decades. The bloody acts of the people hence merely served to level the path for the bourgeoisie.'[4]

Engels wrote in similar vein.

The worst thing that can befall a leader of an extreme party, is to be compelled to take over a government in an epoch when the movement is not yet ripe for the domination of the class which he represents and for the realisation of the measures which that domination would imply ... he necessarily finds himself in a dilemma. What he *can* do is in contrast to all his actions as hitherto practised, to all his principles and to the present interests of his party; what he *ought* to do cannot be achieved. In a word, he is compelled to represent not his party nor his class, but the class for whom conditions are ripe for domination. In the interests of the movement itself, he is compelled to defend the interests of an alien class, and to feed his own class with phrases and promises, with the assertion that the interests of that alien class are their own interests. Whoever puts himself in this awkward position is irrevocably lost.'[5]

What Marx and Engels say about a revolution which brings the proletariat to power before the historical premises for the transition from capitalism to socialism exist, does not apply directly to the October revolution. This is so not only because the material historical premises *were* present on an international scale, but also because of the specific conditions obtaining in Russia. Not only was the Russian bourgeoisie overthrown politically, but it was also expropriated economically a few months after October. The rural bourgeoisie that remained did not succeed in overthrowing the proletariat, and its social weight, especially from the time of the Five-Year Plan, was almost negligible. The isolation of October did not make it 'a point in the process' of the development of the Russian bourgeoisie because the Russian bourgeoisie was annihilated. If so, what relations of production could come after October?

Socialist relations of production?

The establishment of socialist relations of production demands a much higher level of productive forces than was the heritage of Tsarism. Engels' explanation of the reason for class division in society, for the division into exploiters and exploited, entirely fitted Russia's conditions *even after October*:

The division of society into an exploiting and an exploited class, a ruling and an oppressed class, was the necessary outcome of the low development of production hitherto. So long as the sum of social labour yielded a product which only slightly exceeded what was necessary for the bare existence of all; *so long, therefore, as all or almost all the time of the great majority of the members of society was absorbed in labour, so long was society necessarily divided into classes.* Alongside of this great majority exclusively absorbed in labour there developed a class, freed from direct productive labour, which managed the general business of society: the direction of labour, affairs of state, justice, science, art and so forth. It is therefore the law of the division of labour which lies at the root of the division into classes. But this does not mean that this division into classes was not established by violence and robbery, by deception and fraud, or that the ruling class, once in the saddle, has ever failed to strengthen its domination at the cost of the working class and to convert its social management into the exploitation of the masses.'

Capitalist function

The historical mission of the bourgeoisie is summed up in Lenin's two postulates: 'Increase in the productive forces of social labour and the socialisation of labour.' On a world scale this task had already been fulfilled. In Russia the revolution got rid of the impediments to the development of the productive forces, put an end to the remnants of feudalism, built up a monopoly of foreign trade which protects the development of the productive forces of the country from the devastating pressure of world capitalism, and also gave a tremendous lever to the development of the productive forces in the form of state ownership of the means of production. Under such conditions, all the impediments to the historical mission of capitalism – the socialisation of labour and concentration of the means of production which are necessary prerequisites for the establishment of socialism and which the bourgeoisie was not able to provide are abolished. *Post-October Russia stood before the fulfilment of the historical mission of the bourgeoisie.*

Even in an advanced country there will be certain bourgeois tasks which a victorious proletarian revolution will have to accomplish. For instance, in certain parts of the USA (mainly agriculture) the development of the productive forces is impeded under the capitalist system, so that social production and the concentration of the means of production is not yet realised. But because the productive forces of the USA as a whole are very well developed, these bourgeois tasks will be only accessories, subordinate to the work of building a socialist society. Thus, for instance, the establishment of social production and the concentration of the means

The material heritage of pre-October society · 163

of production where they do not yet exist, will not be achieved by the creation of a proletariat on the one hand and capital on the other; the labourers from the beginning will not be divorced from the means of production. In contrast to this, the fulfilment of the bourgeois tasks was the *central* problem in post-October Russia with its low level of national income. In the United States the addition of new means of production necessary for the socialisation of labour can be accompanied by a rise in the standard of living of the masses, by a strengthening of the element of conviction in production discipline, by the fortification of workers' control, by the progressive dwindling of the differences in income between manual and mental workers, etc. But can this be achieved in a backward country under conditions of siege? Can labour discipline based mainly on conviction prevail when the level of production is very low? Can a quick tempo of accumulation, necessitated by the backwardness of the country and the pressure of world capitalism, be accomplished without the separation of society into the managers of the general business of society and the managed, the directors of labour and the directed? Could such a separation be ended before those who directed production also directed distribution in their own interests? Can a workers' revolution in a backward country isolated by triumphant international capitalism be anything but 'a point in the process' of the development of capitalism, even if the capitalist class is abolished?

Why the Five-Year Plan signifies the transformation of the bureaucracy into a ruling class

In Chapters 1 and 2 we have seen that the inauguration of the Five-Year Plan marked the turning point in the development of the relations of distribution, in the relations between accumulation and consumption, between the productivity of labour and the standard of living of the workers, in the control over production, in the legal rights of the workers, in the institution of forced labour, in the relation of agriculturists to the means of production, in the tremendous swelling of the turnover tax, and finally, in the structure and organisation of the state machine. The reality of industrialisation and collectivisation turned out to be in absolute contradiction to the hopes the masses placed in them, and even to the illusions held by the bureaucracy itself. They thought the Five-Year Plans would take Russia far in the direction of socialism. However, this is not the first time in history that the results of human actions are in outright contradiction to the wishes and hopes of the actors themselves.

How can we answer the question: Why was the First Five-Year Plan such a turning point?

It was now, for the first time, that the bureaucracy sought to create a proletariat and to accumulate capital rapidly. In other words, it was now that the bureaucracy sought to realise the historical mission of the bourgeoisie as quickly as possible. A quick accumulation of capital on the basis of a low level of production, of a small national income per capita, must put a burdensome pressure on the consumption of the masses, on their standard of living. Under such conditions, the bureaucracy, transformed into a personification of capital, for whom the accumulation of capital is the be-all and end-all here, must get rid of all remnants of workers' control, must substitute conviction in the labour process by coercion, must atomise the working class, must force all social-political life into a totalitarian mould. It is obvious that the bureaucracy, which became necessary in the process of capital accumulation, and which became the oppressor of the workers, would not be tardy in making use of its social supremacy in the relations of production in order to gain advantages for itself in the relations of distribution. Thus

The material heritage of pre-October society · 165

industrialisation and technical revolution in agriculture ('collectivisation') in a backward country under conditions of siege transforms the bureaucracy from a layer which is under the direct and indirect pressure and control of the proletariat, into a ruling class, into a manager of 'the general business of society: the direction of labour, affairs of state, justice, science, art and so forth'.

Dialectical historical development, full of contradictions and surprises, brought it about that the first step the bureaucracy took with the subjective intention of hastening the building of 'socialism in one country' became the foundation of the building of state capitalism.

Chapter 5: The common and different features of state capitalism and a workers' state
State capitalism - a partial negation of capitalism
State capitalism - a transition to socialism

None of the Marxist theoreticians doubted that if the concentration of capital could reach such a stage that one capitalist, a collective of capitalists or the state, concentrated the total national capital in its hands while competition on the world market continued, such an economy would still be a capitalist economy. At the same time, *all* the marxist theoreticians emphasised that long before the concentration of capital could reach such a level, either the antagonism between the proletariat and the bourgeoisie would bring about a victorious socialist revolution, or the antagonisms between the capitalist states would drive them into such a destructive imperialist war, that society would totally decline.

While state capitalism is possible *theoretically* it is indubitable that individual capitalism through evolutionary development will in practice never arrive at the concentration of the entire social capital in one hand. Trotsky clearly explained why this would not happen.

Theoretically, to be sure, it is possible to conceive a situation in which the bourgeoisie as a whole constitutes itself a stock company which, by means of its state, administers the whole national economy. The economic laws of such a regime would present no mysteries. A single capitalist, as is well known, receives in the form of profit, not that part of the surplus value which is directly created by the workers of his own enterprise, but a share of combined surplus value created throughout the country proportionate to the amount of his own capital. Under an integral 'state capitalism', this law of the equal rate of profit would be realised, not by devious routes – that is, competition among different capitals – but immediately and directly through state bookkeeping. Such a regime never existed, however, and, because of profound contradictions among the proprietors themselves, never will exist – the more so, since, in its quality of universal repository of capitalist property, the state would be too tempting an object for social revolution.[1]

The last two factors – the 'contradictions among the proprietors themselves' and the fact that if it were the 'universal repository of capitalist property, the state would be too tempting an object for social revolution', explain why it is most improbable that traditional individual capitalism will develop gradually till it reaches 100 per cent state capitalism. But do these two factors exclude the possibility that after a ruling working class is overthrown, not traditional capitalism, but state capitalism, is restored? The revolutionary proletariat has already concentrated the means of production in the hands of one body, and so eliminated the first factor. As regards the second factor, in any case any oppression and exploitation of the workers by the state makes the state a 'tempting . . . object for social revolution'; the political expropriation of the working class is thus identical with its economic expropriation.

The only argument that could be given against the possibility of the existence of state capitalism is that if the states becomes the repository of all capital, the economy ceases to be capitalist; in other words, *theoretically* state capitalism is impossible. This argument, indeed, has been given by Burnham, Dwight MacDonald and others. Thus, for instance, Burnham writes:

The term 'state capitalism' seems to be due to a misunderstanding . . . When the state owns only a part, and a minor part, of the economy, with the rest of the economy remaining capitalist private enterprise, we might correctly speak of 'state capitalism' in connection with that minor state-owned part: since, as we have seen the economy remains in its balance capitalist and even the state-owned part may be directed primarily to the benefit of the capitalist part. But the 'capitalism' in 'state capitalism' is derived not from the state-controlled part. When the latter disappears, or becomes negligible, then the capitalism has disappeared. There is no paradox in saying that 10 times 10% state capitalism, far from equalling 100% capitalism, equals 0% capitalism. The multiplication is of *state*, not of *capitalism*. Though the mathematics would be much more complex, it would be nearer an analogy to say that, just as 10% *state* capitalist economy equals only 90% *capitalist* economy, so 100% (or even 80% or 70%) *state* economy would have eliminated capitalism altogether.[1]

Of course if state capitalism is a contradiction in terms, the name of such a society in which the competition on the world market, commodity production, wage labour, etc., prevail, will be quite arbitrarily chosen. One may call it managerial society, or bureaucratic collectivism, arbitrarily determining its laws. Bruno R. tells us that bureaucratic collectivism leads automatically to communism. Burnham tells us that in managerial society production will rise uninterruptedly (pp. 115–6), that a capitalist crisis of overproduction will not break out (p. 114), that unemployment will never exist, that managerial society will develop the backward countries (pp. 154–5), that it will become more and more democratic (pp. 145–7), and because of all this it receives the enthusiastic support of the masses (p. 160). As against this Shachtman tells us that bureaucratic collectivism is barbarism.

If Adam Smith came to life today, he would have found great difficulty in discovering any similarity between the economy of, let us say, Nazi Germany, with its tremendous monopoly organisations, its state regulation of raw material distribution, state regulation of the labour market, state purchase of more than half the national product, etc., and the manufacture of the nineteenth century based on the employment of a few or at most a few score workers, free competition between enterprises, active participation of capitalists in organising production, non-existence of the capitalist crisis of overproduction, etc. A perusal of the gradual development of capitalism from one stage to the next makes it easier to see what is common to both economies, and that the laws of both are capitalist. The difference between the Russian economy and the Nazi economy is much smaller than the difference between the Nazi economy and the economy of Adam Smith's time. It is only the absence of the gradualness of development through the stage of monopoly capitalism, which makes it difficult to grasp the similarities and differences between the Russian economy and traditional monopoly capitalism, and the dissimilarity of state capitalism and traditional capitalism on the one hand, and a workers' state on the other.

Seeing that state capitalism is the extreme theoretical limit which capitalism can reach, it necessarily is the furthest away from traditional capitalism. It is the negation of capitalism on the basis of capitalism itself. Similarly, seeing that a workers' state is the lowest stage of the new socialist society, it must necessarily have many features in common with state capitalism. What distinguishes between them categorically is the *fundamental*, the *essential* difference between the capitalist system and the socialist system. The comparison of state capitalism with traditional capitalism on the one hand, and with a workers' state on the other, will show that state capitalism is a transition stage to socialism, this side of the socialist revolution, while a workers' state is a transition stage to socialism the other side of the socialist revolution.

State capitalism - a partial negation of capitalism

The regulation of economic activity by the state is, in itself, a partial negation of the law of value,* even if the state is, as yet, not the repository of the means of production.

The law of value assumes the regulation of economic functions in an anarchical way. It determines the exchange relations between the different branches of the economy, and explains how relations between people appear, not as direct, crystal clear relations, but indirectly, lost in mysticism. Now, the law of value holds absolute sway only under conditions of free competition, i.e., when there is free movement of capital, commodities and labour power. Therefore, even the most elementary forms of monopolistic organisation already negate the law of value to a certain extent. Thus when the state regulates the allocation of capital and labour power, the price of commodities, etc., it is most certainly a partial negation of capitalism. This is even more the case when the state becomes an important buyer of products. On this question Lenin said:

> When capitalists work for the defence, i.e., for the government treasury, it is obviously no more 'pure' capitalism, but a special form of national economy. Pure capitalism means commodity production. Commodity production means work for an *unknown* and free market. But the capitalist 'working' for the defence does not 'work' for the market at all. He fills the order of the government, and in most cases for money that had been advanced to him by the treasury.[3]

With the increasing monopolisation of the economy, the partial negation of the law of value becomes progressively more extensive. Banking capital receives a social form long before industrial capital. As Marx noted: 'The banking system . . . presents indeed the form of common bookkeeping

---

* For a fuller explanation of this, see Chapter 7.

and distribution of means of production on a social scale, but only the form.'⁴

This is even more the case when the state becomes the main form of investment for money capital. It reaches its extreme when the capitalist state takes the banking system into its own hands.

Capitalist private property is also partially negated by the monopoly structure. Wherever, under the capitalism of free competition, the capitalist was the absolute owner of his own private property, under monopoly capitalism, and especially under its most extreme form, state capitalism, the individual capitalist no longer has absolute ownership of the means of production. In share companies, capital becomes 'directly endowed with the form of social capital . . . It is the abolition of capital as private property within the boundaries of capitalist production itself'.⁵

This is even more true when the state regulates the flow of capital. In such a case, private property is deprived of its freedom of contract. Private capital disappears, while individual appropriation continues. This reaches its extreme when the state takes the means of production into its own hands. The bondholder as an individual ceases to have any control whatsoever over his part of the social capital.

Furthermore, state capitalism is a partial negation of labour power as a commodity. For labour power to appear as a 'pure' commodity in the market, two conditions are necessary: firstly, the worker must be 'free' of the means of production, and secondly, he must be free of any legal impediments to the selling of his labour power. Under state regulation of the labour market, e.g., under fascism, the worker ceases to be free to sell his labour power. If then the state becomes the actual possessor of the means of production, the choice of employer is entirely abolished, while the choice of place of work is much restricted. And if state capitalism is accompanied by a freezing of wages, compulsory mobilisation, etc., this freedom is even more negated.

Partial negation of the law of value does not, however, free the economy from this law. On the contrary, the economy as a whole is subordinated to it even more. The difference lies only in the *form* in which the law of value expresses itself. When one monopoly increases its rate of profit as against other industries, it simply increases its share in the total surplus value, or it increases the rate of exploitation of its workers by compelling them to produce more surplus value. When one industry receives subsidies from the state, and thus sells its commodities below its cost of production, a part of the total cost of production is simply transferred from one branch to another. When the state regulates prices, the point of departure is always costs of production. Under all these conditions, whatever their specific form, wage labour continues its antagonism to capital, surplus value continues to be produced, and continues to be converted into capital. The total labour time of society and the total labour time directed to the production of the necessities of life of the workers as a whole determine the rate of exploitation, the rate of surplus value. The total labour time allotted to the production of new means of production determines the rate of accumulation. While the price of every commodity does not exactly express its value (this did not happen, except accidentally, even under individual capitalism) the division of the total product of society among the different classes, as also its allotment to accumulation and consumption is dependent on the law of value. Where the state owns all the means of production and the workers are exploited while the *world* economy is as yet disunited and atomised, this dependence receives its purest, most direct and absolute form.

State capitalism - a transition to socialism

Everything that centralises the means of production centralises the working class. State capitalism brings this concentration to the highest stage possible under the capitalist system,
state capitalism brings the working class to its greatest
possible concentration.

The partial negation of capitalism on the basis of capitalist
relations of production, means that the productive forces
which develop in the bosom of the capitalist system so out-
grow it, that the capitalist class is compelled to use 'socialist'
measures, and manipulate them in their own interests. 'In
spite of themselves, the capitalists are dragged, as it were,
into a new social order, a transitional social order from complete free competition to complete socialisation.'[6]

The productive forces are too strong for capitalism, and
'socialist' elements therefore enter into the economy (Engels
called this 'the invading socialist society'). *But they are
subordinated to the interests of the preservation of capitalism.*
Similarly, in a workers' state, because the productive forces
are insufficiently developed for socialism, the working class
is compelled to use capitalist measures (e.g., the capitalist
law applied to distribution) in the interests of building
socialism.

State capitalism and a workers' state are two stages in the
transition period from capitalism to socialism. State capitalism is the extreme opposite of socialism – they are symmetrically opposed, and they are dialectically united with one
another.

Whereas under state capitalism wage labour is partially
negated in that the worker is not free to choose his employer,
under the dictatorship of the proletariat, wage labour is
partially negated in that the workers as a collective cease to
be 'free' of the means of production. At the same time, in a

workers' state, wage labour ceases to be a commodity. The 'sale' of labour power is different from the sale of labour power under capitalism, because under a workers' state the workers as individuals do not sell their labour power but put it at their own service in their role of a collective. Labour power ceases really to be a commodity, as here the exchange takes place between the workers as individuals, and these same workers as a collective, and not between two entities which are totally independent of one another except in their exchange. Whereas state capitalism brings about the fusion of the unions with the state until they are ultimately annulled as unions, the workers' state raises the influence of the trade unions to the maximum. Whereas state capitalism signifies historically the totalitarianism of the state, a workers' state brings the highest degree of democracy society has ever known. State capitalism signifies the extreme subjugation of the working class by a capitalist class in control of the means of production. A workers' state means the suppression of the capitalists by a working class in control of the means of production.

Lenin clearly formulated the relation between state capitalism and socialism in these words:

the measure called 'war socialism' by the German Plekhanovs (Scheidemann, Lensch, and others) is in reality war-time state monopoly capitalism. Or to speak more plainly and clearly, it is military penal labour for the workers, military defence of the capitalists' profits.

But try and substitute for the Junker-capitalist, for the land-owner-capitalist state, a *revolutionary democratic* state, i.e., such as would destroy all privileges in a revolutionary way without being afraid of introducing in a revolutionary way the fullest possible democracy – and you shall see that, in a truly revolutionary democratic state, state monopoly capitalism inevitably and unavoidably means progress towards Socialism.

... For Socialism is nothing but the next step forward from state capitalist monopoly. In other words, Socialism is nothing

State capitalism and a workers' state · 175

but state capitalist monopoly made to *benefit the whole people*; by this token it *ceases* to be capitalist monopoly.'

Bukharin, who dealt extensively with the question of state capitalism, formulated the relation between state capitalism and the dictatorship of the proletariat very clearly:

In the system of state capitalism the economic subject is the *capitalist state*, the collective capitalist. In the dictatorship of the proletariat, the economic subject is the *proletarian* state, the collectively organised working class, 'The proletariat organised as the state power.' Under state capitalism, the production process is that of the production of surplus value which falls into the hands of a capitalist class, which tries to transform this value into surplus product. Under the dictatorship of the proletariat the production process is a means for the planned satisfaction of social needs. The system of state capitalism is the most complete form of exploitation of the masses by a handful of oligarchs. The dictatorship of the proletariat makes any exploitation whatsoever altogether unthinkable, as it transforms collective capitalist property and its private capitalist form into collective-proletarian 'property'! Notwithstanding their formal similarity, these are diametrical opposites in content. This antagonism determines also the antagonism of all the parts of the systems under discussion, even if formally they are similar. Thus, for instance, the general labour duty under state capitalism means the enslavement of the working masses; as against this, under the dictatorship of the proletariat it is nothing but the self-organisation of labour by the masses; in the former case the mobilisation of industry means the strengthening of the power of the bourgeoisie and the strengthening of the capitalist regime, while in the latter it means the strengthening of socialism. Under the state capitalist structure all the forms of state compulsion represent a pressure which will assure, broaden and deepen the process of exploitation, while state compulsion under the dictatorship of the proletariat represents a method of building up communist society. In short, the functional contradiction between the formally similar phenomena is here wholly determined by the functional contradiction between the systems of organisation, by their contradictory class characteristics.'

Much earlier than either Lenin or Bukharin, Engels put forward what were fundamentally the same ideas in *Anti-Dühring*.

> The more productive forces it [the state] takes over, the more it becomes the real collective body of all the capitalists, the more citizens it exploits. The workers remain wage-earners, proletarians. The capitalist relationship is not abolished; it is rather pushed to an extreme. But at this extreme it changes into its opposite. State ownership of the productive forces is not the solution of the conflict, but it contains within itself the formal means, the handle to the solution.[*]

Chapter 6: Further consideration of Stalinist society, economics and politics

The Stalinist bureaucracy is a class · The Stalinist bureaucracy - the extreme and pure personification of capital · The form of appropriation of the bureaucracy is different to that of the bourgeoisie · Relations of production and law · The synthesis of the extremities of development · Economics and politics · Can there be a gradual transition from a workers' state to a capitalist state? · Stalinism - barbarism? · Is the Stalinist regime progressive?

The Stalinist bureaucracy is a class

An examination of the definitions of a social class given by different marxist theoreticians, will show that, according to all of them, the Stalinist bureaucracy qualifies as a class. Thus, for instance, Lenin writes:

> We call classes large groups of people that are distinctive by the place they occupy in a definite historically established system of social production; by their relations towards the means of production (in the majority of cases [*not always*] fixed and formulated in laws); by their role in the social system of labour; and consequently, by their method of obtaining the share of national wealth which they dispose of, and by the size of that share. Classes are such groups of people one of which can appropriate the labour of another owing to the difference in their position in a given system of social economy.[1]

Bukharin gives a very similar definition:

> A social class ... is the aggregate of persons *playing the same part in production, standing in the same relation toward other persons in*

the production process, these relations being also in things (instruments of labour).[1]

If there is any doubt left about whether the Stalinist bureaucracy is a class or not, we need but peruse Engels' analysis of the merchant class which did not even take a *direct* part in the process of production. He writes:

A third division of labour was added by civilization: it created a class that did not take part in production, but occupied itself merely with the exchange of products – the merchants. All former attempts at class formation were exclusively concerned with production. They divided the producers into directors and directed, or into producers on a more or less extensive scale. But here a class appears for the first time that captures the control of production in general and subjugates the producers to its rule, without taking the least part in production. A class that makes itself the indispensable mediator between two producers and exploits them both under the pretext of saving them the trouble and risk of exchange, of extending the markets of their products to distant regions, and of thus becoming the most useful class in society: a class of parasites, genuine social ichneumons, that skim the cream of production at home and abroad as a reward for very insignificant services; that rapidly amass enormous wealth and gain social influence accordingly; that for this reason reap ever new honours and ever greater control of production during the period of civilization, until they at last bring to light a product of their own – periodical crises in industry.[2]

In the light of this definition it is clear why Marx could designate the priests, lawyers, etc., as 'ideological classes', which have a class monopoly over what Bukharin aptly calls the 'means of mental production.'

It would be wrong to call the Stalinist bureaucracy a caste for the following reasons: while a class is a group of people who have a definite place in the process of production, a caste is a judicial-political group; the members of a caste can be members of different classes, or in one class there can be members of different castes; a caste is the outcome of the relative immobility of the economy – a rigid division of labour and immobility of the productive forces – whereas the Stalinist bureaucracy was transformed into a ruling class on the crest of the *dynamism* of the economy.

The Stalinist bureaucracy – the extreme and pure personification of capital

Marx wrote:

> Except as personified capital, the capitalist has no historical value, and no right to that historical existence ... But, so far as he is personified in capital, it is not values in use and the enjoyment of them but exchange value and its augmentation, that spur him into action. Fanatically bent on making value expand itself, he ruthlessly forces the human race to produce for production's sake; ... So far, therefore, as his actions are a mere function of capital – endowed as capital is, in his person, with consciousness and a will – his own private consumption is a robbery, perpetrated on accumulation ... Therefore, save, save, save, i.e., reconvert the greatest possible portion of surplus value, or surplus-product into capital! Accumulation for accumulation's sake, production for production's sake.[4]

The two functions – the extraction of surplus value and its transformation into capital – which are fundamental to capitalism, become separated with the separation of control and management. While the function of management is to extract the surplus value from the workers, control directs its transformation into capital. For the capitalist economy these two functions alone are necessary; the bondholders appear more and more only as consumers of a certain part of the surplus value. Consumption of a part of the surplus product by the exploiters is not specific to capitalism, but existed under all class systems. What *is* specific to capitalism is accumulation for accumulation's sake, with the object of standing up to competition.

In capitalist corporations most of the accumulation is institutional; the corporation finances itself internally, while the greater part of the dividends disbursed among the share-holders is used for consumption. Under a state capitalism which evolved gradually from monopoly capitalism, the bond-holders would appear mainly as consumers while the state would appear as the accumulator.

The more that part of the surplus value devoted to accumulation increases as against the part consumed, the more purely does capitalism reveal itself. The more the relative weight of the factor of *control* increases as against that of bondholding, in other words, the more the dividends are subordinated to internal accumulation by the corporation or the state-owner, the more purely does capitalism reveal itself.

(Everyone knows that those who have the control of capital in their hands, those who are the extreme personification of capital, do not deny themselves the pleasures of this world, but the significance of their spending is much smaller quantitatively and different qualitatively than that of accumulation, and is of no basic historical importance.)

We can therefore say that the *Russian bureaucracy*, 'owning' as it does the state and controlling the process of accumulation, *is the personification of capital in its purest form.*

However, *Russia is different from the norm – the concept of state capitalism evolving gradually from monopoly capitalism.* This divergence from the concept of state capitalism which evolves gradually, organically, from monopoly capitalism, does not render the question of the concept of state capitalism unimportant. Far from it, it is of the greatest significance to find that the Russian economy approaches this concept much more closely than ever could a state capitalism which evolved gradually on a capitalist foundation. The fact that the bureaucracy fulfils the tasks of the capitalist class, and by doing so transforms itself into a class, makes it the purest personification of this class. Although different from the capitalist class, it is at one and the same time the nearest to its historical essence. *The Russian bureaucracy as a partial negation of the traditional capitalist class is at the same time the truest personification of the historical mission of this class.*

To say that a bureaucratic class rules in Russia and stop at that, is to circumvent the cardinal issue – the capitalist relations of production prevailing in Russia. To say that Russia is state capitalist is perfectly correct, but not sufficient; it is also necessary to point out the differences in the juridical relations between the ruling class in Russia and that in a state capitalism which evolved gradually from monopoly capitalism. The most precise name for the Russian society is therefore Bureaucratic State Capitalism.

The form of appropriation of the bureaucracy is different from that of the bourgeoisie

In Russia the state appears as an employer, the bureaucrats as managers only. There is a complete separation between the function of ownership and that of management. This, however, is only formally so. In essence ownership is in the hands of the bureaucrats as a collective; it is vested in the state of the bureaucracy. But the fact that the individual manager appears not to own the means of production, and that the appropriation of his part in the national income is in the form of a salary, may deceive one into believing that he receives only the reward for his labour power in the same way as the worker receives the reward for his labour power. In addition, as the labour of management is necessary for every process of social production, and as such has nothing to do with relations of exploitation, the difference between the function of the worker and that of the manager is befogged because both are included in the social process of production. Antagonistic class relations thus *appear* to be harmonious. The labour of the exploited and the labour of organising exploitation both appear as labour. The state appears to stand above the people, as personified ownership, while the bureaucrats who direct the process of production and are therefore historically the personification of capital in essence, appear as labourers, and as such, producers of values by *their labour itself*.

It is clear, however, that the income of the bureaucracy has a direct ratio to the work of the workers and not to its own work. The size of this income is in itself sufficient to reveal the *qualitative* difference between the income of the bureaucracy and the wages of the workers. If there were no qualitative difference between them, we should have to say, for example, that Lord McGowan, who receives the highest director's salary in Britain, does no more than sell his labour power. Besides this, the state, which is the employer and appears to rise above all the people, is in reality the organisation of the bureaucracy as a collective.

What determines the division of surplus value between the state and the bureaucrats as individuals?

While *the quantitative* division of the total value produced between wages and surplus value is dependent on two elements *qualitatively* different – labour power and capital – the division of the surplus value between the bureaucracy as a collective (the state) and individual bureaucrats cannot be based upon any qualitative difference between them. One cannot therefore speak of *exact*, general laws of the division of the surplus value between the state and the bureaucracy or of the distribution of the share of the bureaucracy between the different bureaucrats. Similarly one cannot speak about exact general laws regulating the distribution of profit between profit of enterprise and interest, or between the owners of different sorts of shares in capitalist countries. (See K. Marx, *Capital*, Vol. III, p. 428.)

It would be wrong, however, to assume that absolute arbitrariness governs this division. The *tendencies* can be generalised. They are dependent on the pressure of world capitalism which demands an acceleration of accumulation, the material level which production has already reached, the tendency of the rate of profit to decline which relatively decreases the sources of accumulation, etc. Taking these circumstances into account, we can see why a constantly increasing part of the surplus value is accumulated. At the same time the bureaucracy which administers the process of accumulation, does not overlook the gratification of its own personal desires, and the quantity of surplus value consumed by it rises absolutely. These two processes are possible only if there is a constant increase in the rate of exploitation of the masses, and if new sources of capital are constantly found. (This explains the process of primitive accumulation in which the Russian peasantry is pillaged, and the plunder of the countries of Eastern Europe.)

Relations of production and law

The overwhelming majority of the means of production in Russia is in the hands of the state. Bonds or other forms of legal claim cover so small a part of the means of production as to be of only minor significance.

Why is this so? Is there no tendency to introduce such a form of private claim on a large scale? Why is there a difference between the law of property prevailing in Russia and that in the rest of the capitalist world? In order to answer these questions we must first analyse the relationship between the relations of production and the law of property.

Law is based on the economy. Property relations are the

juridical expressions of relations of production. But there is no exact and absolute parallel between relations of production and the development of law, in the same way as there is no exact and absolute parallel between the economic basis and the other elements of the superstructure. This is because law does not express the relations of production directly but indirectly. If it reflected the relations of production directly, every gradual change in the relations of production being accompanied by an immediate and parallel change in law, it would have ceased to be law. The function of law is, so to say, to bring harmony between the antagonistic interests of the classes, to fill up the gaps which tend to break in the socio-economic system. In order to achieve this, it must rise above the economy, while basing itself upon it.

From the standpoint of its content, law is the indirect reflection of the material basis on which it is erected, but from the standpoint of its *form*, it is but the assimilation and completion of the law inherited from the past. There is always a time-lag between changes in the relations of production and changes in law. The deeper and quicker the change in the relations of production, the more difficult it is for law to keep pace and still formally preserve continuity with its past development. There are numerous historical examples of the rise of a new class which has been reluctant to publicise its coming to power and has accordingly tried to adapt its existence and rights to the framework presented by the past, even though this framework has stood in absolute contradiction to it. Thus, for a very long time the rising bourgeoisie endeavoured to prove that profit and interest are but some sort of rent – at that time the rent of the landlord was justified in the eyes of the ruling classes. The English capitalist class tried to base its political rights on the Magna Carta, the charter of rights of the feudal class, which is fundamentally in contradiction to bourgeois right from the standpoint of both content and form. The attempt of a ruling class to hide its privileges under the cloak of the law handed down from the past is most strongly made in the case of a counter-revolution which dare not declare its existence.

Revolutionary socialism does not hide its aims, and the law it dictates on taking power is therefore revolutionary both in content and form. Had the armies of intervention been victorious after the October revolution, their bloody rule would have been accompanied by the restoration of most of the old laws scrapped by the October revolution. But, as the bureaucracy in Russia transformed itself gradually into a ruling class, the changes in the relations of production were not expressed immediately in the complete change of the law. For various reasons, the main one being the need Stalinist foreign policy has of pseudo-revolutionary propaganda among the workers all over the world, the Russian bureaucracy did not openly declare that a counter-revolution had taken place.

This alone, however, is insufficient to explain why the bureaucracy does not restore private property in the form of bonds or shares covering the whole economy in such a way that every member of the bureaucracy should be able to bequeath a safe economic position to his son. Other factors must be taken into account. The desires of a class, a caste or a social layer are moulded by its material conditions of life. Not only has each class its own special place in the process of production, but each owning class has a different stronghold in the social wealth. If the simple desire for the maximum material and cultural benefits in the abstract had been the driving force of humanity, then not only would the working class have desired socialism, but also the petty and middle bourgeoisie, and even the big bourgeoisie; the more so as this generation lives under the shadow of atomic warfare. But this is not the case. When people make history, they make it according to the external, objective reality in which they find themselves, and which moulds their desires. The feudal lord thus strives to increase the area of his and his son's domains; the merchant endeavours to give his sons security by bequeathing them a large quantity of money; the physician, the lawyer and the other members of the free professions attempt to pass their privileges on to their sons by giving them 'mental means of production' – education. There being no Chinese wall between the different classes and layers, however, each will, of course, try to bequeath more than its special privileges: professionals will inherit both material and mental means of production; merchants will be provided with a higher education, and so on.

The state bureaucracy, as Marx said in his *Critique of Hegel's Philosophy of Law*, possesses the state as private property. In a state which is the repository of the means of production the state bureaucracy – the ruling class – has forms of passing on its privileges which are different from those of the feudal lords, the bourgeoisie or the free professionals. If co-option is the prevailing mode of selection the directors of enterprises, heads of departments, etc., every bureaucrat will try more to pass on to his son his 'connections' than he would, let us say, a million roubles (even though this has importance). Obviously he will at the same time try to limit the number of competitors for positions in the bureaucracy by restricting the possibilities the masses have of getting a higher education, etc.

The synthesis of the extremities of development

Russia presents us with the synthesis of a form of property born of a proletarian revolution and relations of production resulting from a combination of backward forces of production and the pressure of world capitalism. The *content* of the synthesis shows historical continuity with the pre-revolutionary period; the *form* shows historical continuity with the revolutionary period. In the retreat from the revolution the form does not move right back to its point of departure. Despite its subordination to content, it yet has considerable importance.

History often leaps forward or backward. When it leaps backward, it does not return directly to same position, but goes down a spiral, combining the elements of the two systems from which and to which the society passed. For example, because in the state capitalism which is an organic, gradual continuation of the development of capitalism, a form of private property would prevail in the ownership of shares and bonds, we must not conclude that the same will apply to state capitalism which rose gradually on the ruins of a workers' revolution. Historical continuity in the case of state capitalism which evolves from monopoly capitalism, is shown in the existence of private property (bonds). Historical continuity in the case of state capitalism which evolves from a workers' state that degenerated and died, is shown in the *non-existence of private property*.

This spiral development brings about the synthesis of two extremes of capitalist development in Russia, a synthesis of the highest stage which capitalism can ever reach, and which probably no other country will ever reach; and of such a low stage of development as has yet to demand the preparation of the material prerequisites for socialism. The defeat of the October revolution served as a springboard for Russian capitalism which at the same time lags well behind world capitalism.

This synthesis reveals itself in an extremely high concentration of capital, in an extremely high organic composition of capital; and on the other hand, taking the level of technique into account, in a low productivity of labour, in a low cultural level. It explains the speed of the development of the productive forces in Russia, a speed far outstripping what youthful capitalism experienced, and the very opposite of what capitalism in decay and stagnation experiences.

Youthful capitalism practised inhuman brutality on the toilers, as shown by the struggle against 'vagabonds,' the poor laws, the forcing of women and children to work fifteen to eighteen hours a day, etc.; aged capitalism again commits many of the brutalities of its childhood, with the difference that it is able, as fascism has shown, to carry them out much more effectively. Both periods are characterised by the use of compulsion in addition to the automatic mechanism of the economic laws. The synthesis of state capitalism with the youthful tasks of capitalism gives the Russian bureaucracy an unlimited appetite for surplus value and capacity for inhuman brutality, while enabling it to practise at the same time the highest efficiency in carrying out its oppression.

When Engels said that 'man sprang from the beasts, and had consequently to use barbaric and almost bestial means to extricate himself from barbarism', he certainly was not describing the socialist revolution, when history becomes 'conscious of itself'. But he well described the pre-history of humanity. Peter the Great will go down in history as one of the fighters against barbarism using barbaric methods. Herzen wrote that he 'civilised with a knout in his hand and knout in hand persecuted the light.' Stalin will go down in history as the oppressor of the working class, as the power which could have advanced the productive forces and culture of humanity without the knout, because the *world* was mature enough for it, but which nevertheless advanced them 'knout in hand', simultaneously endangering all humanity with the threat of decline through imperialist wars.

The proletarian revolution swept all the impediments to the development of the productive forces from its path and abolished a lot of the old barbarities. But being isolated, and taking place in a backward country, it was vanquished, leaving the field free for the fight against barbarism by barbaric methods.

Economics and politics

The state is 'special bodies of armed men, prisons, etc.' – a weapon in the hands of one class to oppress another class or other classes. In Russia the state is a weapon in the hands of the bureaucracy for the oppression of the mass of toilers. But this alone does not describe all the functions of the Stalinist state. It answers also to the direct needs of the social division of labour, of the organisation of social production. A similar task was fulfilled, *mutatis mutandis*, by the states of ancient China, Egypt and Babylonia. There, because big irrigation works which could be organised at all only if done on a large scale were so wholly necessary, the state developed not only as a result of the appearance of class divisions, and so *indirectly* as a result of the social division of labour, but also *directly*, as part of the process of production. Interdependence and mutual influence of class divisions and the emergence and strengthening of the state are so intricate as to make any separation of economics and politics impossible. Similarly, in Russia, the Stalinist state did not rise only as a result of the widening abyss between the masses and the bureaucracy and so the growing need for 'special bodies of armed men', but also as a direct answer to the needs of the productive forces themselves, as a necessary element of the mode of production.

One of the Chaldean kings said:

I have mastered the secrets of the rivers for the benefit of man ... I have led the waters of the rivers into the wilderness; I have filled the parched ditches with them ... I have watered the desert plains; I have brought them fertility and abundance, I have formed them into habitations of joy.

Plekhanov, who cites this, remarks: 'For all its boastfulness, this is a fairly accurate description of the role of the oriental state in organising the social process of production.'[5]

Stalin could also claim that he built the industries, drove the productive forces of Russia forward, etc. Although, of course, the tyranny of the Chaldean king was historically necessary and progressive in its time, while that of Stalin is historically superfluous and reactionary.

As in ancient societies, so in Russia today, the double function of the state, as a guardian of the ruling class and as organiser of social production, leads to a total fusion of economics and politics.

This fusion is characteristic of capitalism in its highest stage, as well as of a workers' state. But whereas under a workers' state this fusion means that the workers, being politically dominant, advance ever closer to a situation in which the 'government of persons is replaced by the administration of things and the direction of the process of production',[6] under capitalism in its highest stage it means that political coercion is added to the automatism of the economy and is, indeed, given the major role. 'The . . . special feature of the capitalist order is that all the elements of the future society appear in it in a form in which they do not draw nearer to socialism but draw further away from it.'

Thus, for instance:

as regards the army, development brings general obligatory military service . . . that is, an approach to the people's militia. But it is realised in the form of modern militarism, which brings the domination of the military state over the people and pushes the class character of the state to the extreme.[7]

This fusion proves that our period is so ripe for socialism that capitalism is compelled to absorb more and more elements of socialism. As Engels said, this is the invasion of socialist society into capitalism. However, this absorption does not lighten the burden of exploitation and oppression; on the contrary, it makes it bear down much the more heavily. (In a workers' state the workers are free economically because they are politically free. A workers' state is also a fusion of economics and politics, but with symmetrically opposite results.)

Wherever there is a fusion of economics and politics it is theoretically wrong to distinguish between political and economic revolution, or between political and economic counter-revolution. The bourgeoisie can exist as the bourgeoisie, owning private property, under different forms of government: under a feudal monarchy, a constitutional monarchy, a bourgeois republic, under a bonapartist regime such as that of Napoleon I and III, a fascist dictatorship and for a certain time even under a workers' state (the kulaks and NEP-men existed till 1928). In all these cases there is a direct relation of ownership between the bourgeoisie and the means of production. In all of them the state is independent of the *direct* control of the bourgeoisie, and yet in none of them does the bourgeoisie cease to be a ruling class. Where the state is the repository of the means of production, there is an *absolute* fusion between economics and politics; political expropriation also means economic expropriation. If the Chaldean king quoted above were politically expropriated, he would necessarily also have been economically expropriated. The same applies to the Stalinist bureaucracy, and *mutatis mutandis*, also to a workers' state. Seeing that the workers as individuals are *not* owners of means of production even in a workers' state, and their ownership as a collective is expressed through their ownership of a state which is the repository of the means of production, *if they are politically expropriated they are also economically expropriated.*

Can there be a gradual transition from a workers' state to a capitalist state?

The proletariat cannot take over the bourgeois state machine but must smash it. Does it not follow that the *gradual* transition from the workers' state of Lenin and Trotsky (1917–23) to the capitalist state of Stalin, contradicts the basis of the marxist theory of the state? This is one of the pivots of defence for the theory that Russia today is still a workers' state. Those who hold to this theory quote Trotsky in 1933 (but omit to quote his opposite statement of a later date). He wrote in *The Soviet Union and the Fourth International:*

The Marxian thesis relating to the catastrophic character of the transfer of power from the hands of one class into the hands of another applies not only to revolutionary periods, when history madly sweeps ahead, but also to the period of counter-revolution when society rolls backwards. He who asserts that the Soviet Government has been changed *gradually* from proletarian to bourgeois is only, so to speak, running backwards the film of reformism.

The question at issue is the validity or otherwise of the last sentence.

Capitalist restoration can come about in many ways. Political restoration may precede economic restoration: this would have been the case if the White Guards and armies of intervention had succeeded in overthrowing the Bolsheviks. Or economic restoration, even if not complete, may precede political restoration: this would have been the case if the kulaks and NEP-men who entrenched their economic privileges until 1928 had succeeded in overthrowing the regime. In both cases the transition from a workers' state to a capitalist state would not have been gradual. Indeed, to say that it might have been gradual could justifiably be branded as 'only, so to speak, running backwards the film of reformism'. But where the bureaucracy of a workers' state is transformed into a ruling class, economic and political restoration are indissolubly interwoven. The state becomes gradually further divorced from the workers, the relations between it and the workers become more and more like the relations between a capitalist employer and his workers. In such a case the bureaucratic clique that first appears as a distortion, gradually transforms itself into a class which fulfils the tasks of the bourgeoisie in capitalist relations of production. The gradual evolutionary divorce of the bureaucracy from the control of the masses, which continued until 1928, reached the stage of a revolutionary qualitative change with the First Five-Year Plan.

The question, however, still stands: does this not contradict the marxist theory of the state?

From the standpoint of formal logic it is irrefutable that if the proletariat cannot gradually transform the bourgeois state into a workers' state but must smash the state machine, the bureaucracy on becoming the ruling class also cannot gradually transform the workers' state into a bourgeois state, but must smash the state machine. From the standpoint of dialectics, however, we must pose the problem differently. What are the reasons why the proletariat cannot gradually transform the bourgeois state machine, and do these continue as an immovable impediment to the gradual change of the class character of a workers' state?

Marx and Engels said that only England could bypass the smashing of the state machine as the first step in the proletarian revolution. This did not apply to the Continent of Europe. They said that in England the 'social revolution might be effected entirely by peaceful and legal means'. On this Lenin comments: 'This was natural in 1871, when England was still the model of a purely capitalist country, but without militarism and, to a considerable degree, without a bureaucracy.'[8]

It is, then, the bureaucracy and the standing army that constitute the impediment to the workers' peaceful accession to power. But the workers' state has no bureaucracy or standing army. Thus a peaceful transition can be accomplished from a workers' state where these institutions do not exist, to a state capitalist regime where they do.

Let us now see whether what excludes a gradual social revolution excludes a gradual counter-revolution.

If the soldiers in a hierarchically built army strive for decisive control over the army, they immediately meet with the opposition of the officer caste. There is no way of removing such a caste except by revolutionary violence. As against this, if the officers of a people's militia become less and less dependent on the will of the soldiers, as well they might, seeing that they meet with no institutional bureaucracy, their transformation into an officers' caste independent of the soldiers can be accomplished gradually. The transition from a standing army to a militia cannot but be accompanied by a tremendous outbreak of revolutionary violence; on the other hand, the transition from a militia to a standing army, to the extent that it is the result of tendencies inside the militia itself, can and must be gradual. The opposition of the soldiers to the rising bureaucracy *may* lead the latter to use violence against the soldiers. But this is not essential. What applies to the army applies equally to the state. A state without a bureaucracy, or with a weak bureaucracy dependent on the pressure of the masses may gradually be transformed into a state in which the bureaucracy is free of workers' control.

The Moscow trials were the civil war of the bureaucracy against the masses, a war in which only one side was armed and organised. They witnessed the consummation of the bureaucracy's total liberation from popular control. Trotsky, who thought that the Moscow trials and the 'Constitution' were steps towards the restoration of individual capitalism by legal means, then withdrew the argument that a gradual change from a proletarian to a bourgeois state is 'running backwards the film of reformism'. He wrote:

> In reality, the *new constitution* . . . opens up for the bureaucracy 'legal' roads for the economic counter-revolution, i.e., the restoration of capitalism by means of a 'cold strike'.*

Stalinism - barbarism?

The word 'barbarism' denotes different things. We talk about the barbaric exploitation of the workers, the barbaric oppression of the colonial peoples, the barbaric murder of the Jews by the Nazis, etc. 'Barbaric' here does not denote a stage in the history of humanity, a certain content of social relations, but a certain aspect of the actions of a class, which may even be a rising, progressive class: for instance, we talk about the barbaric eviction of the peasantry in Britain at the time of rising capitalism, or the barbaric looting of the population of South America, etc. 'Barbarism' may, however, denote something which, even though it has some connection with the former meaning, is yet entirely different. It may denote the total destruction of civilisation by the decline of society into an a-historical era. This sees 'barbarism' as a whole stage in the history of humanity. A particular event may indeed be barbaric in both senses. The activity of the ruling classes in a third world war, for instance, would be barbaric in the first sense, and as the cause of the total decline of society it would be barbaric in the second sense also. Essentially, however, the meanings are different and must be kept distinct. Barbarism used in connection with our epoch in the first sense signifies the price humanity is paying for the *belatedness* of the socialist revolution. Used in the second sense it signifies the loss of all hope in a society which has decayed and declined. According to this it would be wrong to define Nazism as barbarism in the second sense, as 're-newed feudalism', as the 'state of the termites', as an a-historical period, etc., as the Nazi system was *based* on the labour of proletarians who are historically its gravediggers and the saviours of humanity. It would be even less justified to designate the Stalinist regime as barbarism in the second sense, as this regime, in the face of Russia's backwardness and fear of annihilation through international competition, is rapidly increasing the numbers of the working class.

This question is not a matter of philological hairsplitting, but of prime importance. To use the word barbarism in its second sense would be as wrong as to use the word slave to designate the Russian workers, if slave is used as something distinct from proletarian. Slavery, like barbarism in its first sense, used to denote one aspect of the condition of the Russian worker under Stalin as well as of the German worker under Hitler – his lack of legal freedom, his partial negation of himself as a worker – would be a correct term. But used as a basic definition of a regime it would be wrong. We must therefore strongly oppose the use of the word barbarism in its second sense to denote the Stalinist regime. We must indeed oppose its use in general to denote the stage society has reached today, and can only condone its use in the first sense, that is, used to describe certain aspects of declining capitalism as a whole, whether American, Russian, British or Japanese. Is Stalinist Russia an example of capitalist barbarism? Yes. An example of that barbarism which is a total negation of capitalism? No.

Is the Stalinist regime progressive?

A social order which is necessary to develop the productive forces and prepare the material conditions for a higher order of society, is progressive. We must emphasise the *material conditions*, because if we include *all* the conditions (class consciousness, the existence of mass revolutionary parties, etc., etc.), then any social order will be progressive, as its very existence proves that *all the conditions* for its overthrow are not there.

It does not follow from this definition that when a social order becomes reactionary, becomes an impediment to the development of the productive forces, that these productive forces cease to advance, or that the rate of advance falls absolutely. There is no doubt that feudalism in Europe became reactionary in the thirteenth to eighteenth centuries, but this did not prevent the productive forces developing at the same rate as before or indeed of developing at an even faster rate. Similarly, while Lenin said that the period of imperialism (beginning with the last decades of the nineteenth century) signified the decline and decay of capitalism he at the same time said:

> It would be a mistake to believe that this tendency to decay precludes the possibility of the rapid growth of capitalism. It does not. In the epoch of imperialism, certain branches of industry, certain strata of the bourgeoisie and certain countries betray, to a more or less degree, one or another of these tendencies. *On the whole, capitalism is growing far more rapidly than before.* But this growth is not only becoming more and more uneven in general; its unevenness also manifests itself, in particular, in the decay of the countries which are richest in capital (such as England).[10]

Lenin spoke of the decay of capitalism, and in the same breath he said that the democratic revolution in Russia, by sweeping away the remnants of feudalism, would give tremendous possibilities of development to Russian capitalism, which would stride forward at an American tempo. And this view he held at the time that he believed that the 'Democratic Dictatorship of the Proletariat and Peasantry' would perform the tasks of the bourgeois revolution in Russia.

Looking at the figures for world industrial production since 1891 we can see that in the period of imperialism the productive forces of the world are far from absolute stagnation:[11]

World industrial production (1913: 100)

1891	33
1900	51
1906	73
1913	100
1920	102
1929	148

As regards the capacity of production, we need but take into account the control of atomic energy to see what strides have been made.

Were the backward countries isolated from the rest of the world, we could certainly say that capitalism would be progressive in them. For instance, if the countries of the West declined and disappeared, Indian capitalism would have no less long and glorious a future than British capitalism had in the nineteenth century. The same is true of Russian state capitalism. Revolutionary marxists, however, take the world as our point of departure, and therefore conclude that capitalism, wherever it exists is reactionary. For the problem humanity must solve today, under pain of annihilation, is not how to develop the production forces, but to what end and under what social relations to utilise them.

This conclusion as regards the reactionary character of Russian state capitalism, *notwithstanding* the rapid development of its productive forces, can be refuted only if one could prove that world capitalism has not prepared the material conditions necessary for the establishment of socialism, or that the Stalinist regime is preparing further conditions necessary for the establishment of socialism than those prepared by the world at large. The former contention leads one to the conclusion that we are not yet in the period of the socialist revolution. The most one can say to the latter is that Stalinist Russia will bequeath to socialism a higher concentration of capital and of the working class than any other country. But this is only a *quantitative* difference: if we compare the economies of the USA and England we find that the concentration of capital and socialisation of labour is much higher in the former than in the latter, but this does not make the present-day capitalism in the USA historically progressive.

One may claim that planning inside Russia is an element which transforms the Russian economy into a progressive one in comparison with the capitalism of other countries. This is totally unsound. So long as the working class has no control over production, the workers are not the subject of planning but its object. This applies just as well to the planning within the gigantic enterprise of Ford as to the whole economy of Russia. And so long as the workers are the object, planning is important to them *only* as an element of the material conditions necessary for socialism: as an aspect of the concentration of capital and workers.

In a factory employing 100,000 workers planning is more elaborate and developed than in a factory employing 100 workers, and still more so is it in state capitalism which employs 10,000,000 workers. This does not make the relations of production in the big enterprise progressive relatively to those in the smaller one. The plan in each is dictated by the blind external force of competition between independent producers.

The very fact of the existence of the Stalinist regime declares its reactionary nature, as without the defeated October revolution the Stalinist regime would not have existed, and without the maturity of the world for socialism the October revolution would not have broken out.

Chapter 7: Russian economy and the Marxian law of value and theory of capitalist crisis (economic determinism in the Stalinist regime)

Introduction

According to Marx and Engels the fundamental law of capitalism, as distinct from all other economic systems, the law from which all the other laws of capitalism derive, is the law of value. 'The value form of products therefore already contain in embryo the whole capitalist form of production, the antagonism between capitalists and wage workers, the industrial reserve army, crises.'[1] The law of value is, therefore, the basic law of marxian political economy.

In the introduction to their text-book of political economy, two leading Soviet economists, Lapidus and Ostrovitianov, asked, 'does political economy study all productive relations between people?' and they answer:

No. Take for example the natural economy of the primitive patriarchal peasant which satisfies all its needs from within and enters into no exchange relations with other peasants. Here we have a peculiar type of relations of production. They consist, let us say, in a collective organisation of labour ... in certain subordination of all to the head of the family ... Notwithstanding the tremendous difference between peasant natural economy and communist economy, they have one common feature: both are organised and directed by conscious human will ... There are, no doubt, certain laws regulating the unorganised relationship of capitalist society. But these laws are spontaneous, independent of the conscious and directed will of the participants in this process of production ... *And it is these elementary, spontaneous laws ... that are the subject of political economy.*[1]

Next they asked: 'In what ways and to what extent do the capitalist laws of political economy influence the Soviet economy? What is the relation between spontaneous activity and planned activity in the economy of the Soviet Union? What is the specific weight of these elements, and what is their tendency of development?'[2] They come to the conclusion that political economy applies only to spontaneous processes and not to a planned economy such as socialism, and that it applied in Russia only to the extent that the Russian economy was not yet socialist but merely in a transition stage towards socialism. All other Soviet economists concurred with this argument at the time.

At that time Soviet economists unanimously replied in the negative to the question of whether the law of value has a place in socialism. Any traces of its existence in the Soviet Union were explained as the outcome of her transitional position, of her not yet having fully arrived at socialism.

Thus Lapidus and Ostrovitianov wrote:

If the question were posed before us: Is Soviet economy capitalist or socialist, we should, of course, reply, that to answer, 'capitalist' or 'socialist' is impossible, since the peculiarity of the Soviet economy consists ... in the very fact that it is of a *transitional* nature, passing from capitalism to socialism. In exactly the same way we should have to answer anyone who demands from us: — either or – whether the law of value operates fully here, or whether it has ceased altogether to operate and has been replaced by conscious regulation. To assert that 'either the one or the other' is correct, is impossible, because neither one postulate nor the other is correct, but a third: *that we are living through a process of transition from the one to the other*. The law of value has not yet withered away but continues to operate in our conditions; but it does not operate in the same form in which it operates in the capitalist system, since it is passing through the *process of withering away.*'

The same argument was used by Preobrazhensky: 'The law of value and the element of planning whose basic attribute is expressed in socialist accumulation, are struggling with one another' in the transition period from capitalism to socialism, and with the victory of the latter 'the law of value will wither away.'⁵

Another economist, Leontiev, wrote: 'The law of value is the *law of motion* of capitalist commodity production', the germs of all the 'contradictions of capitalism are inherent in value.'⁶

The Soviet economists could draw extensively on the works of Marx and Engels in support of their arguments. The extract from *Anti-Dühring*, quoted above, confirms their viewpoint. Elsewhere in the same book, Engels ridicules Dühring's conception that the Marxian law of value applies to socialism: under socialism, he writes, 'people will be able to manage everything very simply, without the intervention of the famous "value".'⁷

It would be sheer absurdity, he argued, 'to set up a society in which at last the producers control their products by the logical application of an economic category [value] which is the most comprehensive expression of the subjection of the producers by their own product.'⁸ Or to quote Marx:

'Value is the expression of the *specifically characteristic nature* of the capitalist process of production.'[9]

On yet another occasion, on criticising A.Wagner's *Allgemeine oder Theoretische Volkswirtschaftslehre*, Marx ridicules 'the presupposition that the theory of value, developed for the explanation of bourgeois society, has validity for the "socialist state of Marx".'[10] Such arguments as these were almost axiomatic for all Soviet economists during the first decade and a half after the revolution.

After a decade of almost complete silence on the question, a bombshell was dropped in 1943. The theoretical organ of the Party, *Pod Znamenem Marksizma*, published a long, unsigned article entitled 'Some Questions of Teaching Political Economy', which made a complete break with the past.[11] The reader was informed that 'the instruction of political economy in our colleges has been renewed after a lapse of several years. Before this interruption, the teaching of political economy, as well as the existing textbooks and the curricula, suffered from serious defects.' 'With respect to the economic laws of socialism, many fundamental mistakes and faults often crept into the curricula and textbooks of political economy'. The main mistake 'of the former teaching', the article alleged, was 'in denying the operation of the law of value in socialist society'. All Soviet economists immediately toed the new line.

This *volte face* can be explained by a new readiness of the authorities to declare openly then much that in the past had been accepted in practice but publicly denied as characteristic of Russian life, such as Great Russian chauvinism, the glorification of Tsarist traditions, and many other things of a similar character.

It does seem, however, that the Soviet economists have become so involved in contradictions with the writings of Marx and Engels that the problem has had to be tackled over and over again. Even as late as February 1952, Stalin himself found it necessary to write:

> It is sometimes asked whether the law of value exists and operates in our country, under the socialist system.
> Yes, it does exist and does operate.[12]

Contrary to all marxian teaching on the subject, Stalin states: 'Is the law of value the basic economic law of capitalism? No.'[13] Marx states that where labour power is a commodity, the natural, inevitable result of its sale is the appearance of surplus value, of exploitation; Stalin finds it convenient to declare that while the law of value prevails in Russian economy, there is no sale of labour power and therefore no surplus value. He writes: 'Talk of labour power being a commodity, and of "hiring" of workers sounds rather absurd now, under our system: as though the working class which possesses means of production, hires itself and sells its labour power to itself.'[14] (The tacit, if untenable, assumption of Stalin's argument, of course, is that the state that owns the means of production and buys labour power is actually 'owned' and controlled by the workers and not by an omnipotent bureaucracy.) Furthermore, he writes: 'I think that we must ... discard certain other concepts taken from Marx's *Capital* – where Marx was concerned with an analysis of capitalism–and artificially pasted on to our socialist relations. I am referring to such concepts, among others, as "necessary" and "surplus" labour, "necessary" and "surplus" product, "necessary" and "surplus" time.'[15]

It is, of course, of the utmost importance to discover the true relationship between the marxian law of value and Russian economy, while remembering that Marx saw a close connection between this law and all the contradictions of capitalism.

The marxian law of value

Marx's theory of value may be explained briefly as follows.

Under capitalism, and only under capitalism, 'all, or even a majority of the products, take the form of commodities.'[16] For products to become commodities a division of labour must exist within society. But this alone is not enough. There was a division of labour within primitive tribes, but commodities were not produced. Nor were they in the system of society based on the ancient Roman latifundia with their slave labour and self-sufficiency. Within any one capitalist factory, too, there is a division of labour, without the fruit of each worker's labour becoming a commodity. Only between primitive tribes, between latifundia or between one capitalist factory and another, are products exchanged, and thus take the form of commodities. Marx writes: 'Only such products can become commodities with regard to each other, as result from different kinds of labour, each kind being carried on independently and for the account of private individuals,'[17] or 'groups of individuals'.[18]

Value is defined as the characteristic common to all commodities on the basis of which they are exchanged. Only as commodities do products have exchange-value; exchange-value being an expression of the social relations between producers of commodities, that is, of the *social* character of the labour of every producer. It is, in fact, the *only* expression of the social character of labour in a society of independent producers. Marx writes: 'Since the producers do not come into social contact with each other until they exchange their products, the specific social character of each producer's labour does not show itself except in the act of exchange. In other words, the labour of the individual asserts itself as a part of the labour of society, only by means of the relations which the act of exchange establishes directly between the products, and indirectly, through them, between the producers.'[19]

When he writes that a commodity is value, Marx is asserting that it is materialised abstract labour, that it is the result of a certain portion of the total productive labour of society. 'Magnitude of value expresses a relation of social production, it expresses the connection that necessarily exists between a certain article and the portion of the total labour-time of society required to produce it.'[20]

Why is exchange value the only expression of this connection, and why cannot this relation be expressed *directly*, instead of through the medium of things? The answer is that the only social connection between independent producers that there can be is through things, through the exchange of commodities.

In a society of independent producers the law of value determines:

a. the exchange relation between different commodities,

b. the total quantity of commodities of one kind which will be produced compared with commodities of another kind, and therefore,

c. the division of the total labour time of society among different enterprises.

Hence it determines the exchange relation between labour power as a commodity and other commodities, and so the division of the working day into time spent on 'necessary labour' (in which the worker reproduces the value of his labour power) and 'surplus labour' (in which he produces surplus value for the capitalist). The law of value also controls the proportion of social labour devoted to the production of producer and consumer goods, that is, the relation between accumulation and consumption (a corollary of a. above).

Marx contrasted the division of labour in capitalist society as a whole (which is expressed in the appearance of values) and the division of labour within a single factory (which is not):

Division of labour in a society is brought about by the purchase and sale of the products of different branches of industry, while the connection between the detail operations in a workshop, are due to the sale of the labour-power of several workmen to one capitalist, who supplies it as combined labour-power. The division of labour in the workshop implies concentration of the means of production in the hands of one capitalist; the division of labour in society implies their dispersion among many independent producers of commodities. While within the workshop the iron law of proportionality subjects definite numbers of workmen to definite functions, in the society outside the workshop, chance and caprice have full play in distributing the producers and their means of production among the various branches of industry. The different spheres of production, it is true, constantly tend to an equilibrium: for, on the one hand, while each producer of a commodity is bound to produce a use-value, to satisfy a particular social want, and while the extent of these wants differ quantitatively, still there exists an inner relation which settles their proportions into a regular system, and that system one of spontaneous growth; and, on the other hand, the law of the value of commodities ultimately determines how much of its disposable working-time society can expend on each particular class of commodities. But this constant tendency to equilibrium, of the various spheres of production, is exercised, only in the shape of a reaction against the constant upsetting of this equilibrium. The *a priori* system on which the division of labour, within the workshop, is regularly carried out, becomes in the division of labour within the society, an *a posteriori*, nature-imposed necessity, controlling the lawless caprice of the producers, and perceptible in the barometrical fluctuations of the market prices. Division of labour within the workshop implies the undisputed authority of the capitalist over men, that are but parts of a mechanism that belongs to him. The division of labour within the society brings into contact independent commodity-producers, who acknowledge no other authority but that of competition, of the coercion exerted by the pressure of their mutual interests.[11]

Thus in spite of the lack of central planning within a society of commodity-producers, the law of value creates order out of disorder, by the continuous change in demand and supply produced by competition. A certain equilibrium is established in the production of different goods, in the division of the total labour time of society between the different branches of the economy and so on. Within the individual factory, on the other hand, it is not impersonal anarchy, but the conscious will of the capitalist which determines the division of labour and the quantity of different goods to be produced.

It is obvious that in all the different forms of society, from the primitive communism of the ancient past to the future socialist society, there must be a certain division of the labour time of society among the different branches of the economy in order to produce suitable quantities of the goods which are needed. But the way in which this division is carried out has varied with every form of society. 'Every child knows,' wrote Marx,

> that a country which ceased to work, I will not say for a year, but for a few weeks, would die. Every child knows too that the mass of products corresponding to the different needs require different and quantitatively determined masses of the total labour of society. That this necessity of distributing social labour in definite proportions cannot be done away with by the *particular form* of social production, but can only change the *form it assumes*, is self-evident. No natural laws can be done away with. What can change, in changing historical circumstances, is the *form* in which these laws operate. And the form in which this proportional division of labour operates, in a state of society where the inter-connection of social labour is manifested in the *private exchange* of the individual products of labour, is precisely the *exchange value* of these products.[12]

A necessary condition for exchange value to be the mani-festation of the division of the total labour time of society between the production of different goods, is that the activity of people in the process of production should be 'purely atomic', there must be free competition between independent producers and between the owners of different commodities, including the sellers of labour power. The relation between the members of society in the course of production must not be determined by conscious action.

The applicability of the law of value to capitalist monopoly

In *Capital*, Marx took as the norm of capitalism a system of absolutely free competition. The only marxian economist who discussed in detail the law of value in relation to monopoly capitalism was Rudolf Hilferding in his book, *Das Finanz-kapital* (Vienna, 1910). He states that it is impossible to deduce from Marx's theory of value any general law by which to explain the quantitative *effect* of monopoly on the exchange relations between different commodities.

He writes:

What is undetermined and immeasurable under the rule of monopolies is demand. How this reacts on the raising of prices cannot be ascertained. Monopoly prices can be determined empirically, but their level cannot be determined theoretically ... Classical economy [in this Hilferding includes Marx] conceives prices as the form of appearance of anarchical social production, their level as dependent on the social productivity of labour. The objective price law is realised only through competition. When the monopolist associations abolish competition, they remove with this the only means by which an objective price law can be realised. Price ceases to be an amount determined objectively, and becomes a problem of calculation for those who determine it with will and consciousness; instead of a result it becomes an assumption, instead of being objective, subjective, instead of being inevitable and independent of the will and consciousness of the actors it becomes arbitrary and accidental. The realisation of the Marxian theory of concentration – the monopolistic merger – seems to lead to the invalidation of the Marxian theory of value.[11]

It is equally impossible to determine what quantities of different commodities will be produced, and how the total labour time of society will be divided between different branches of the economy. But it is possible to estimate what the *tendency* of the above factors will be under monopoly conditions in comparison with what they would have been under conditions of free competition. Under conditions of equilibrium, the exchange value of commodities produced by monopolies will rise in relation to others, fewer of them will be produced compared with non-monopoly commodities, hence the proportion of the total labour time of society absorbed by monopolised industry will be smaller. It can be asserted that under conditions of monopoly the exchange relations between commodities, the quantities produced and the division of the total labour time of society are modifications of the same factors as they would appear under free competition. The law of value is partially negated, but appears in modified form in essence to continue to exist. Competition, even though it is not absolutely free, exists, and, therefore, Marx's thesis is still correct, viz., that 'the behaviour of men in the social process of production is purely atomic. Hence their relations to each other in production assume a material character independent of their control and conscious individual actions.'[24]

Because of the competition between different monopolies either in the same branch or in different branches of the economy, the relations of exchange between commodities are related to, even if not exactly equivalent to, the labour time spent on their production or their derived cost of production ratios. Although the division of labour within society as a whole is not absolutely independent of the conscious actions of individuals or groups (such as monopolies) this division can be varied only within relatively narrow limits from what it would have been under completely free competition. In spite of 'planning' by monopolies, the division continues to be arbitrary and quite different from the division of labour *within* a factory, 'not only in degree, but also in kind.' Monopoly capitalism means a partial negation of the marxian law of value but on the basis of the law of value itself. But '*determinatio est negatio*'. The *partial* negation of the law of value *borders* on its total negation.

State monopoly capitalism and the law of value

How does the law of value operate when the state intervenes in the economic system by regulating the price of commodities, buying a substantial part of the products of the national economy, allocating raw materials, and regulating capital investment?

According to Lenin,

> When capitalists work for the defence, i.e., for the government treasury, it is obviously no more 'pure' capitalism, but a special form of national economy. Pure capitalism means commodity production. Commodity production means work for an *unknown* and free market. But the capitalist 'working' for the defence does not 'work' for the market at all. He fills the order of the government, and in most cases for money that had been advanced to him by the treasury.[14]

Does this mean that the supply of products to the state by capitalist enterprises is outside of the law of value? In Nazi Germany where the state bought more than half the total national product, concentrated in its hands the allocation of raw materials, regulated the flow of capital into the different branches of the economy, fixed the prices of commodities, and regimented the labour market, it was not left to the blind, automatic activity of the market to regulate the exchange relations of different commodities, the relative quantities of different goods produced and the division of the total labour time of society among the different industries. It is true that the Nazi state did not take *all* the decisions regarding production, but it did take the more decisive ones. In the Nazi economy the state fixed the quantity of consumer goods produced; there was no freedom in selling labour power, and the division of the total labour time of society among the different branches of industry was determined not by the automatism of the market, but by the state's allocation of orders and raw materials and by its control over capital investment. A very narrow field remained for the *autonomous* activities of different entrepreneurs within Germany.

As Hilferding wrote: 'In Germany ... the State, striving to maintain and strengthen its power, determines the character of production and accumulation. Prices lose their regulating function and become merely means of distribution. The economy, and with it the exponents of economic activity, are more or less subjected to the State, becoming its subordinates.'*

The term 'state capitalism' can denote both a capitalist war economy and the stage in which the capitalist state becomes the repository of all the means of production. Bukharin, for example, used it to denote both. Although, as will be seen, there is no basic *qualitative* difference between the two as regards their effect on (a) the exchange relation between commodities, (b) the relative quantities produced, and (c) the distribution of the total labour time of society, we think that it will be preferable to distinguish between the two in order to avoid confusion. The term 'state capitalism' will be used only to denote the stage in which the capitalist state becomes the repository of the means of production, while a capitalist war economy will be termed 'state monopoly capitalism'.

---

* R. Hilferding 'State Capitalism or Totalitarian Economy', *Left* September 1947. Written in 1940.

State monopoly capitalism is, in the last analysis, at the mercy of blind economic forces, and is not governed by the conscious will and decisions of any man or men. For example, government orders are allocated according to the relative strengths (expressed in production capacity) of the different companies tendering for them. Hence each company has to try and achieve a certain rate of capital accumulation. They are driven to raise profits at the expense of wages. They create an increased demand for means of production relative to the demand for means of consumption, and so on. In Germany, under Nazi rule, the division of the total national product between the different social classes, and the distribution of the total labour time between the production of consumer and capital goods, was not determined by an arbitrary decision of the government, but by the pressure of competition. The same resulted from the competitive pressure – economic and military alike – of the Powers against which Germany fought.

Notwithstanding, therefore, the distortions of competition and of the law of value under state monopoly capitalism, this law is, in the last analysis, all-decisive.

The marxian law of value and the Russian economy, viewed in isolation from world capitalism

At first sight the relationship between the different enterprises in Russia appears to be the same as that between different enterprises in the traditional capitalist countries. But this is only formally so. In a society of private producers the essential difference between the division of labour within a workshop and the division of labour within society as a whole, is that in the former the ownership of the means of production is concentrated in the hands of one man or one body of men, while in capitalist society as a whole there is no centre of decisions, but only the 'blindly working average', which determines how many workers shall be employed in different enterprises, what commodities shall be produced, and so on. No such distinction exists in Russia. Both individual enterprises and the economy as a whole are subordinated to the planned regulation of production. The difference between the division of labour within, say, a tractor factory and the division of labour between it and the steel plant which supplies it, is a difference in degree only. The division of labour within Russian society is in essence a species of the division of labour within a single workshop.

Formally, products are distributed among the different branches of the economy through the medium of exchange. But as the ownership of all the enterprises is vested in one body, the state, there is no real exchange of commodities. 'Only such products can become commodities with regard to each other, as result from different kinds of labour, each kind being carried on independently and for the account of private individuals'[26] or 'groups of individuals'.[27]

In a society of private producers, connected with one another only through exchange, the medium regulating the division of labour in society as a whole is the monetary expression of exchange value – price. In Russia there is a direct connection between the enterprises through the medium of the state which controls production in nearly all of them and so price ceases to have this unique significance of being the expression of the social character of labour, or regulator of production.

If the demand for shoes exceeds the supply in a traditionally capitalist country, the price of shoes will automatically rise relatively to the price of other commodities; profits in the shoe industry will increase, capital and labour will pour into it and more of the total labour time of society will be spent in shoe production. The law of value tends to equalise supply and demand, a situation in which price is equal to value, or more correctly, is equal to price of production.*

If in Russia the demand for shoes exceeded the supply, although there would be a rise in the price of shoes either officially or on the black market, there would be no increase in the production of shoes, nor, therefore, in the labour time devoted to their production.

To take another example. In the traditional capitalist countries, the ratio between the production of producer and consumer goods is determined by the law of value. If the supply of shoes is below demand and the supply of machinery is above, the price of shoes will rise and the price of machinery will decline; capital and labour are transferred from one branch of the economy to the other until the correct balance is restored. But in Russia the state owns *both* sections of industry, and, therefore, a high rate of profit in the production of consumer goods will not attract capital and labour into that section and out of the other, and *vice versa*, because the ratios existing between them are not derived from the uncontrolled mechanism of the Russian internal market.

The relationship between the production of the two departments (the production of producer goods, and of consumer goods) is directly dependent on the relationship between accumulation and consumption. While in the traditionally capitalist countries competition between different factory owners causes them to accumulate and increase the organic composition of capital, in Russia this factor does not exist as all the factories are owned by one authority. Here accumulation and technical improvement are not undertaken as measures of defence against an attack in the competitive war with other enterprises.

We have seen that price is not the medium through which

---

* The relation between the value and price of production is a very complicated one, and cannot be dealt with here. (See *Capital*, Vol. III, Part II.)

Russian production and the division of labour in Russian society as a whole are regulated. It is the government which regulates. Price is only one of the weapons the state uses in this activity. It is not the motor, but the transmission belt.

This does not mean that the price system in Russia is arbitrary, depending purely on the whim of the bureaucracy. The basis of price here, too, is the cost of production. (The large-scale use of subsidies on the one hand, and the turnover tax on the other, do not contradict this.) Nevertheless there is a fundamental difference between this price system and the type operating in traditional capitalism. The latter expresses the autonomous activity of the economy (which is freest under free competition, less so under monopoly); the former is a sign that the economy is not self-propelled at all. The difference between these two kinds of price will probably be clearer if an analogy is made with a less complex society, for instance, that of the Pharaohs in ancient Egypt.

Pharaoh had to calculate how to divide the total labour time – which is the real cost of production in any society – of his slaves among the needs of his society. His method of doing so was direct. A certain number of slaves was put to the production of food, a certain number to the production of luxury goods, others to the construction of the irrigation system, yet others to the building of the pyramids, and so on. As the process of production was relatively simple, there was no necessity for any checks beyond seeing that the number of slaves was distributed according to plan. In Russia, too, the state directly makes an almost* complete plan of the division

---

* 'Almost', because there are some border cases in which the control of the state is not complete. The labour time of the kolkhoz member on his private plot is an example of this. Likewise the labour of the artisan. But even if these are not consciously planned by the state, they are not quite free of control. Through the levers of prices, taxes, and especially the state's planning of the *main* field of production, these peripheral activities are also drawn into channels desired by the state.

of the total labour time, but as the process of production is much more complicated than it was a few thousand years ago, it is not sufficient simply to check the number of workers engaged in the different branches, for the economy to run according to the plan. Certain ratios must be fixed between the employment of machinery and workers, the use of machinery of one sort or another, the quantity produced, the raw material and fuel used, and so on. For this task it is necessary to have a measure common to all costs and all products. Price serves as this common measure. The difference between the division of labour without a price system under the Pharoahs, and that with a price system under Stalin is a difference in degree, but not in essence. Similarly, whether Ford directs all his enterprises as one administrative unit, or breaks them up into smaller units in order to make it easier to calculate and direct, the difference is only in degree, so long as the same will directs production.

There is one thing in Russia that appears on the surface to fulfil the requirements of a commodity: labour power. If it is a commodity, then the consumer goods that the workers receive in exchange for their labour power are also commodities, being produced for exchange. We should then have, if not a highly developed circulation of commodities, a huge truck or barter system comprising the total consumption of the workers. But Marx argues that 'The circulation of commodities differs from the direct exchange of products (barter), not only in form, but in substance.'[28] He goes on to point out that with the circulation of commodities, 'exchange ... breaks through all local and personal bounds inseparable from direct barter, and develops the circulation of the products of social labour; ... it develops a whole network of social relations spontaneous in their growth and entirely beyond the control of the actors.'[29]

In order to see whether labour power in Russia is really a

commodity, as it is under traditional capitalism, it is necessary to see what specific conditions are necessary for it to be so. Marx states two conditions for this: first, that the labourer *must* sell his labour power as he has no other means of subsistence, being 'free' of the means of production; secondly, that the labourer *can* sell his labour power as he is the sole owner of it, that is, he is free to do so. The freedom of the worker on the one hand, his bondage on the other, are shown by the 'periodic sale of himself, by his change of masters, and by the oscillations in the market price of labour power.'[30] Marx therefore says that in order for labour power to become a commodity it is necessary

> that the owner of the labour-power should sell it only for a definite period, for if he were to sell it rump and stump, once for all, he would be selling himself, converting himself from a free man into a slave, from an owner of a commodity into a commodity. He must constantly look upon his labour-power as his own property, his own commodity, and this he can only do by placing it at the disposal of the buyer temporarily, for a definite period of time. By this means alone he can avoid renouncing his rights of ownership over it.[31]

If there is only one employer, a 'change of masters' is impossible, and the 'periodic sale of himself' becomes a mere formality. The contract also becomes only a formality when there are many sellers and only one buyer. (That even this formal side of the contract is not observed in Russia is clear from the system of fines and punishments, the 'corrective labour', and so on.)

There is no doubt that 'oscillations in the market price of labour power' take place in Russia, perhaps more so than in other countries. But here, too, the essence contradicts the form. The point needs some elaboration. In the traditional capitalist economy, where there is competition between sellers of labour power, between buyers of labour power, and between sellers and buyers, the price of labour power is determined by the resulting anarchy. If the rate of accumulation is high, there is extensive employment, which, under normal conditions, raises the nominal wages. This increases the demand for consumer goods, the production of which duly increases, raising the real wages. (Under normal conditions of free competition this is a true picture of development; monopolies distort it somewhat.) This rise of real wages adversely influences the rate of profit, which, in turn, slows the rate of accumulation, and so on. In contrast to this, in Russia the total amount of real wages and salaries is fixed in advance by the quantity of consumers' goods planned. It may – and usually does – happen, that because of defects in the working out and realisation of the plan, the quantity of money distributed as wages and salaries is larger than the total price of the consumers' goods produced. If the difference is not taken by the state, it will cause a rise in prices (either on the official market or the black market) but not a rise in real wages. The only way it could cause a rise in real wages would be by causing the state to increase the production of that branch which experiences a rise in prices. The Russian state, however, does not do this. (There is a point below which real wages cannot fall for any length of time. This is the physical minimum, which applies to Russia just as much as to any other society, whether based on slave labour, serf labour, or wage labour. The fact that real wages are not distributed equally among Russian workers is, apropos the problem under discussion, of secondary importance to the fact that the total real wages are directly fixed by the state.)

Hence if one examines the relations within the Russian economy, abstracting them from their relations with the world economy, one is bound to conclude that the source of the law of value, as the motor and regulator of production, is not to be found in it. In essence, the laws prevailing in the relations between the enterprises and between the labourers and the employer-state would be *no different* if Russia were one big factory managed directly from one centre, and if all the labourers received the goods they consumed directly, *in kind*.

The marxian law of value and the Russian economy viewed in its relations with world capitalism

The Stalinist state is in the same position *vis-à-vis* the total labour time of Russian society as a factory owner *vis-à-vis* the labour of his employees. In other words, the division of labour is planned. But what is it that determines the actual division of the total labour time of Russian society? If Russia had not to compete with other countries, this division would be absolutely arbitrary. But as it is, Stalinist decisions are based on factors outside of control, namely the world economy, world competition. From this point of view the Russian state is in a similar position to the owner of a single capitalist enterprise competing with other enterprises.

The rate of exploitation, that is, the ratio between surplus value and wages (s/v) does not depend on the arbitrary will of the Stalinist government, but is dictated by world capitalism. The same applies to improvements in technique, or, to use what is practically an equivalent phrase in marxian terminology, the relation between constant and variable capital, that is, between machinery, building, materials, etc., on the one hand, and wages on the other (c/v). The same therefore applies to the division of the total labour time of Russian society between production of the means of production and of means of consumption. Hence when Russia is viewed within the international economy the basic features of capitalism can be discerned: 'anarchy in the social division of labour and despotism in that of the workshop are mutual conditions the one of the other ...'

If Russia tried to flood the world market with her products, or if other countries flooded the Russian market with theirs, the Russian bureaucracy would be forced to cut the costs of production by reducing wages relatively to the productivity of labour or absolutely (increasing s/v), improving technique (increasing c/v), or increasing production of producer goods relative to consumer goods. The same tendencies would manifest themselves if world competition took the form of military pressure instead of normal, commercial competition.

Up to now, Russia's economy has been too backward for her to be able to flood foreign markets with her goods. Her own markets are protected against the possibility of being flooded with foreign goods by virtue of the state's monopoly of foreign trade which can only be destroyed by military power. Hence the commercial struggle has so far been of less importance* than the military. Because internaticnal

Import and export of USSR in current prices[11]

	(million roubles)		
	Exports	Imports	Turnover
1913	6,596.4	6,022.5	12,618.9
1924	1,476.1	1,138.8	2,614.9
1928	3,518.9	4,174.6	7,693.5
1930	4,539.3	4,637.5	9,176.8
1937	1,728.6	1,341.3	3,069.9

competition takes mainly a military form, the law of value expresses itself in its opposite, viz. a striving after use values. This point requires elaboration. In so far as value is the only expression of the social character of labour in a society of independent producers, a capitalist tries to strengthen himself against his competitors by increasing the total values

---

*Thus during the period of the Five-Year Plans, when industrial production multiplied many times, imports and exports both declined in a most phenomenal manner.

which he owns. As value is expressed in money, it makes no difference to him whether he invests, say a million pounds in shoe production and receives a profit of £100,000 or in the production of armaments and receives a profit of £100,000. As long as his product has some use value, he is not concerned with what particular use value it is. In the formula of the circulation of capital, Money—Commodity—Money (M^1—C—M^2), C appears only as a bridge between M^1 and M^2 (M^2, if everything runs smoothly for the capitalist, being larger than M^1).

If Russia traded extensively with countries outside her empire, she would try to produce commodities which would fetch a high price on the world market, and to buy the cheapest possible commodities from abroad. Thus she would be aiming, like a private capitalist, at increasing the sum of values at her disposal by producing some use value or other, regardless of what use it would be. (This factor has great bearing on Russia's trade with her satellites.)[33]

But as competition with other countries is mainly military, the state as a *consumer* is interested in certain specific use values, such as tanks, aeroplanes, and so on. Value is the expression of competition between independent producers; Russia's competition with the rest of the world is expressed by the elevation of use values into an end, serving the ultimate end of victory in the competition. Use values, while being an end, still remain a means.

A similar process takes place in the countries of traditional capitalism also, although in a less obvious way. It makes no difference to the individual armament manufacturer whether he invests his capital in the production of guns or butter, provided he makes a profit. But the state to which he belongs is extremely interested in the use value of his products. His relations with the state are those of seller and buyer, the former being interested only in value and the latter in use value. But in fact these relations of exchange are only formal. The state does not offer another commodity in exchange for armaments. It pays for them out of taxes and loans levied on the whole economy. In other words, the burden of armaments is spread more or less over the whole economy. (This becomes crystal clear when the state, instead of collecting taxes and raising loans in order to buy arms from private firms, produces them itself.) The slogan 'guns before butter' means that competition between the capitalist powers has reached the stage where the international division of labour is disrupted, and competition through buying and selling is replaced by direct military competition. Use values have become the aim of capitalist production.

Further evidence of this is the difference between technical advance in war and in peace. In a war economy there is virtually no limit to the market, nor any need to cut costs of production in the interests of commercial competition. The overwhelming need is to increase the quantity of goods available. Hence during the World War II technical improvements were introduced which had been opposed in peacetime by the monopolies and cartels.

The fact that the Russian economy is directed towards the production of certain use values does not make it a socialist economy, even though the latter would also be directed towards the production of (very different) use values. On the contrary, the two are complete opposites. The increasing rate of exploitation, and the increasing subordination of the workers to the means of production in Russia, accompanied as it is by a great production of guns but not butter, leads to an intensification, not a lessening of the oppression of the people.

The law of value is thus seen to be the arbiter of the Russian economic structure as soon as it is seen in the concrete historical situation of today – the anarchic world market.

Can there be world state capitalism?

If the production of the whole world were controlled by one authority, that is, if the Stalinist bureaucracy could unite the world under its rule and the masses were forced to accept such a régime, the resulting economy would be a system of exploitation not subject to the law of value and all its implications. Examining the problem – in hypothetical form at that date (1915), of course – Bukharin reached this very conclusion. In his book, *World Economy and Imperialism*, he explains that if the national state were to organise the national economy, commodity production would remain 'in the first place [in] the world market', and the economy would be, therefore, state capitalist. But if 'the organisation of the whole *world* economy as one gigantic state trust' took place (which, incidentally, Bukharin did not believe possible), 'we would have an entirely new, unique, economic form. This would be capitalism no more, for the production of *commodities* would have disappeared; still less would it be *socialism*, as the domination of one class over the other will have remained (and even grown stronger). Such an economic structure would, most of all, resemble a slave-master's economy, with the absence of the slave market.'[34]

(Because of national and social conflicts, it is very unlikely that such a world empire could ever in fact exist.)

Marx's theory of capitalist crisis

It is impossible within the framework of the present work to deal adequately with Marx's analysis of the capitalist crisis of overproduction. We shall have to limit ourselves to a short summary.

Unlike all pre-capitalist forms of production, capitalism is forced to accumulate more and more capital. But this process is hampered by two complementary, and yet contradictory, factors, both arising out of the system itself. One is the decline in the rate of profit, which means the shrinking of the sources of further accumulation. The other is the increase in production beyond the absorptive capacity of the market. If it were not for the first contradiction, the 'underconsumptionist' solution of the crisis – to raise the wages of the workers – would be a simple and excellent answer. If it were not for the second contradiction, fascism could, by continuously cutting wages, have staved off the crisis for a long period at least.

Dealing with the second horn of capitalism's dilemma, the low purchasing power of the masses, Marx wrote:

> The entire mass of commodities, the total product, which contains a portion which is to reproduce the constant and variable capital as well as a portion, representing surplus-value, must be sold. If this is not done, or only partly accomplished, or only at prices which are below the prices of production, the labourer has been none the less exploited, but his exploitation does not realise as much for the capitalist. It may yield no surplus-value at all for him, or only realise a portion of the produced surplus value, or it may even mean a partial or complete loss of his capital. The conditions of direct exploitation and those of the realisation of surplus-value are not identical. They are separated logically as well as by time and space. The first are only limited by the productive power of society, the last by the proportional relations of the various lines of production and by the consuming power of society. This last-named power is not determined either by the absolute productive power nor by the absolute consuming power, but by the consuming power based on antagonistic conditions of distribution, which reduces the consumption of the great mass of the population to a variable minimum within more or less narrow limits. The consuming power is furthermore restricted by the tendency to accumulate, the greed for an expansion of capital and a production of surplus-value on an enlarged scale.[11]

And he adds:

The stupendous productive power developing under the capitalist mode of production relatively to population, and the increase, though not in the same proportion, of capital values (not their material substance), which grew much more rapidly than the population, contradict the basis, which, compared to the expanding wealth, is ever narrowing and for which this immense productive power works, and the conditions, under which capital augments its value. This is the cause of crises.[36]

Elsewhere he expressed the same idea in these words:

The last cause of all real crises always remains the poverty and restricted consumption of the masses as compared to the tendency of capitalist production to develop the productive forces in such a way, that only the absolute power of consumption of the entire society would be their limit.[37]

In the *final* analysis, the cause of the capitalist crisis is that a greater and greater part of the income of society falls into the hands of the capitalist class, and a greater and greater part of this is directed not towards buying means of consumption, but, instead, means of production, that is, it is directed towards the accumulation of capital. But, as all means of production are *potentially* means of consumption – that is, after a certain lapse of time, the value of the means of production becomes incorporated in means of consumption – the relative increase in the part of the national income directed to accumulation compared with the part directed towards consumption, must lead to overproduction. And this is a cumulative process. The increase in accumulation is accompanied by rationalisation, resulting in an increased rate of exploitation. The greater the rate of exploitation, the greater is the fund from which accumulation is drawn, as compared with the wages of the workers and the revenue of the capitalist. Accumulation breeds accumulation.

If 'the poverty and restricted consumption of the masses' were the only cause of the capitalist crisis, the crisis would be permanent, because the wages of the workers, on the whole, *always* lag behind a rise in the productivity of labour. We should then not have known the one-time catastrophic equation of different elements, but a permanent slump.

But there is the other horn of the dilemma, the decline in the rate of profit. The process of capital accumulation is accompanied by a rise in the organic composition of capital, that is, there is a substitution of dead labour (embodied in machinery, etc.) for living labour. Since the latter produces surplus value and the former does not, there is a constant tendency for the rate of profit to decline. This decline in its turn makes competition between the capitalists keener, for each must try to increase his total profits at the expense of his rivals. Competition leads to rationalisation, and so to an ever greater rise in the organic composition of capital. From this vicious circle there is no escape.

This tendency is not by itself the cause of the cycle of revival, boom, crisis and depression. Marx explains that the decline of the rate of profit is a *very* slow process,[38] which is subject to many counteracting forces. Nevertheless it constitutes the background of the economic cycle. The *immediate* causes of the cycle are changes in the wage rate resulting from the changes in the demand for labour power which accompany the process of accumulation. On the decline of the rate of profit Marx wrote: 'It promotes over-production, speculation, crises, surplus-capital along with surplus-population.'[39] 'The barrier of the capitalist mode of production becomes apparent . . . In the fact that the development of the productive power of labour creates in the falling rate of profit a law which turns into an antagonism of this mode of production at a certain point and requires for its defeat periodical crises.'[40]

On the rise of the level of wages following on increased employment during a boom, he declared that if it were said 'that the working class receive too small a portion of their own product, and the evil would be remedied by giving them a larger share of it, or raising their wages, we should reply that crises are precisely always preceded by a period in which wages rise generally and the working class actually get a larger share of the annual product intended for consumption.'[41]

On the connection between the trade cycle, the rate of profit, the level of wages, and the extent of employment, when this last factor is of decisive importance as marking the end of the boom and the beginning of the crisis, Marx wrote:

> the whole form of the movement of modern industry depends, therefore, upon the constant transformation of a part of the labouring population into unemployed or half-employed hands ... As the heavenly bodies, once thrown into a certain definite motion, always repeat this, so is it with social production as soon as it is once thrown into this movement of alternate expansion and contraction. Effects, in their turn, become causes, and the varying accidents of the whole process, which always reproduces its own conditions, take on the form of periodicity.[41]

According to his analysis, the rate of profit determines the rate of accumulation, the rate of accumulation determines the extent of employment, the extent of employment determines the level of wages, the level of wages determines the rate of profit, and so on in a vicious circle. A high rate of profit means a quick accumulation, hence an increase in employment and a rise in wages. This process continues to a point where the rise in wage rates so adversely affects the rate of profit that accumulation either declines catastrophically or ceases altogether.

The cycle of the rate of profit and the cycle of accumulation and the cycle of employment, is the life-cycle of fixed capital (i.e. machinery, buildings etc.):

To the same extent that the volume of the value and the duration of the fixed capital develop with the evolution of the capitalist mode of production, does the life of industry and of industrial capital develop in each particular investment into one of many years, say of ten years on an average. If the development of fixed capital extends the length of this life on the one side, it is on the other side shortened by the continuous revolution of the instruments of production, which likewise increases incessantly with the development of capitalist production. This implies a change in the instruments of production and the necessity of continuous replacement on account of virtual wear and tear, long before they are worn out physically. One may assume that this life-cycle, in the essential branches of great industry, now averages ten years. However, it is not a question of any one definite number here. So much at least is evident that this cycle comprising a number of years, through which capital is compelled to pass by its fixed part, furnishes a material basis for the periodical commercial crises in which business goes through successive periods of lassitude, average activity, overspeeding and crisis. It is true that the periods in which capital is invested are different in time and place. But a crisis is always the starting point of a large amount of new investments. Therefore it also constitutes, from the point of view of society, more or less of a new material basis for the next cycle of turn-over."

This theory explains why, in spite of the antagonistic mode of distribution and the tendency for the rate of profit to decline, there is not a permanent crisis of overproduction, but a cyclical movement of the economy. During the period when fixed capital is being renewed and added to, the introduction of new means of production does not result directly in an added supply of finished goods. But after a time, maybe a few years, the value of the new means of production begins to be incorporated in new products, in the form of both means of production and means of consumption. This takes place without any, or with only a relatively small amount of capital being invested at that time. In other words, for a few years investments in the construction of new industries or the expansion of existing ones are very large compared with the increase in the output of finished goods. These are the years of boom, and they are followed by a period in which the output of finished goods expands considerably, almost simultaneously with a decline in the rate of accumulation. This is the crest of the boom and the harbinger of the coming crisis. Then comes the crisis: production declines catastrophically while investment stops or even gives place to disinvestment.

There is another factor which must be considered in this connection – the disproportion between different industries. This may be the direct result of the anarchic character of capitalist production. The capitalists of one industry may over-estimate the demand for its products and therefore over-expand its productive capacity. As there are many capitalists, it is only *after* the goods are produced that the capitalist becomes aware, through the market, that supply has exceeded demand. This leads to a fall in prices, decline of profits, restriction and a decline in the demand for labour power, raw materials and machinery produced by other factories, and so on. This restriction is not necessarily compensated for by the expansion of production in other industries. On the contrary the contraction of production in one industry can lead to similar results in other industries which are directly or indirectly dependent on it. If the industry which suffers first from over-production is an important one, a *general crisis* may result. 'That a crisis (and hence also overproduction) be general it is enough that it seize hold of the leading articles of commerce.'[44]

In this case the disproportion between different industries is the *cause* of the decline of the rate of profit and the decline of the consumption of the masses, and these three factors together bring about the crisis.

But disproportion between different industries may be the

result of the decline of the rate of profit or the underconsumption of the masses as well as, in its turn, their cause. If on the basis of a certain rate of profit there is a certain rate of accumulation, the rate of profit determines the demand for means of production and leads to a certain relationship between the demand for producer and consumer goods. A decline in the rate of profit, by causing a decline in the rate of accumulation, immediately changes the pattern of demand; and so upsets the balance of the demand for the two types of production. A similar relation exists between the underconsumption of the masses and the proportion or disproportion between the different industries. 'The "consuming power of society", and "the proportionality of the various branches of production" – these are absolutely not individual, independent, unconnected conditions. On the contrary, a certain state of consumption is one of the elements of proportionality.'[45]

One of the symptoms of disproportion between different industries is a change in the relation between the output of raw materials and the demand for them. Generally at the beginning of the revival the supply of raw materials exceeds the demand, and their prices are therefore low. As economic activity increases, these prices rise, thus increasing the cost of production, which adversely affects the rate of profit.[46] During a boom the prices of raw materials usually rise more than those of finished goods, and during a crisis fall much more steeply: the reason for this is that the supply of raw materials is far less elastic than that of finished goods.

Another indication of the same disproportion, which is a result rather than a cause of the economic cycle, but which has nevertheless and important reflex influence, is the rate of interest. The capitalist entrepreneurs do not receive the whole surplus value produced in their undertakings, but only what remains after the deduction of rent, taxes and interest.

At the beginning of a trade revival, there is generally an excess of credit over the demand for it. Hence the rate o interest is low, and this in turn encourages the revival. During a boom the rate of interest continues to be low, until shortly before its end, when it rises sharply, reaching its maximum with the onset of the crisis. After this it falls very sharply.[47] Thus, while the curve of the general rate of profit and the curve of the economic cycle as a whole roughly correspond, the rate of interest curve shows much greater zig-zags which cut across the curve of the economic cycle. The changes in the rate of interest spur the revival on at an ever wilder pace on the one hand, and on the other plunge the economic system into ever-deepening crises.

Credit has made it possible for capitalism to develop at an unprecedented tempo, but it also increases the instability of the system. It blinds the industrialists to the real condition of the market, so that they continue to expand production beyond the point at which they would have stopped if all payments were made in cash. This postpones the onset of the crisis, only to make it more serious.

One further factor contributing to the onset of a crisis is the existence of a chain of middlemen between the industrial capitalist and the consumers. Owing to their activity, production can, within certain limits, increase without a corresponding increase in the sale of products to consumers. The unsold products remain as stocks in the hands of merchants, making the crisis, when it comes, more severe.

This, in brief, is Marx's theory of the capitalist crisis.

State capitalism and the crisis - the posing of the problem

It is obvious that some of the causes of crises of over-production in traditional capitalism would not exist in a system of state capitalism. For instance, middlemen not only would not exist under state capitalism, but even in private enterprise can be eliminated by the industrialist selling his product directly to the consumer through his own trading network. Again, credit would cease to be a factor if all payments were made in cash. Also, under state capitalism, the rate of interest would not contribute to the fluctuations in the tempo of production. As the state would own all the capital, the use of credit would be no different from the use by each capitalist of his own capital. Yet again, the disproportion between different branches of the economy likewise would not act as the initial cause of the crisis. Although there might be miscalculations in investment, and the supply of a certain product might exceed the demand, the fact that the state would plan production and demand makes any serious disproportion impossible. Moreover, as the state would own all the industries, there would not be a cumulative process of decline in prices and a decline of the rate of profit spreading from one industry to another, but the effect of a partial over-production would be spread *directly* over the whole economy. When the next cycle of production began, the production of certain goods would be decreased and equilibrium restored.

These factors would, it is true, cease to have an effect only if the state capitalist economy were self-sufficient. If it were to produce for the world market, to receive credit from other countries, etc., the factors would then have a certain influence.

But what of the fundamental dilemma which faces traditional capitalism? How can a high rate of profit be achieved while surplus value is realised? How can capital be quickly accumulated without undermining the market which it requires? In a certain phase of the cycle – the boom – traditional capitalism temporarily solves the problem: a high rate of profit leads to quick accumulation, that is, a big increase in the production of means of production compared with production of means of consumption. Hence a big part of the surplus value can be realised in the industries manufacturing means of production, that is, in the system of production itself. (This alone is a sufficient explanation why the under-consumption of the masses does not cause a permanent crisis, and prevent any expansion of production under capitalism.) If capitalism could transform the boom from a temporary phase to a permanent condition, there would be no over-production. Can state capitalism do this? Can it ensure a high rate of profit, a high rate of accumulation, a high level of production, while yet preserving the antagonistic way of distribution, 'the poverty and restricted consumption of the masses'?

Bukharin on the crisis in state capitalism

The only marxian economist to consider the theoretical problem of the crisis of over-production within a state capitalist economy was Bukharin. In his discussion of Rosa Luxemburg's theory of accumulation, he poses, among other problems, the question of how reproduction on an enlarged scale would take place under state capitalism,* and discusses whether there would be a crisis of overproduction. He writes:

Is accumulation possible here? Naturally. The constant capital grows, since the consumption of the capitalists grows. New branches of production corresponding to new needs are always established. The consumption of the workers, although definite limits are placed upon it, grows. Despite this 'underconsumption' of the masses no crisis arises, *as the demand of the various branches of production for each other's products as well as the demand of the*

---

* Bukharin defines state capitalism in these words: 'the capitalist class united in one united trust, an organised economy, but one which is at the same time, from the standpoint of the *classes*, antagonistic.'[48]

consumers, capitalists as well as workers, is fixed in advance. (Instead of 'anarchy' of production — what is, from the standpoint of capital, a rational plan.) If a mistake is made in production goods, the surplus is added to inventory and a corresponding correction is made in the next production period. If a mistake is made in workers' consumption goods, the surplus can be divided among the workers or destroyed. Also in the case of a mistake in the production of luxury goods 'the way out' is clear. Thus there can be no kind of crisis of general overproduction. The consumption of the capitalists is the motive power for production and for the production plan. Consequently there is in this case not a *specially* rapid development of production (there is a small number of capitalists).'[48]

Bukharin's words 'in this case not a *specially* rapid development of production' may be misleading. Not only will production be 'not especially rapid', but it will be slowed down compared with the tremendous productive capacity of a 'free' capitalist economy: there will be virtual stagnation.

It is interesting to note that Marx connected stagnation or 'a dormant state' with a decrease in the number of capitalists to a mere handful in the whole world. 'The rate of profit', he wrote, 'that is, the relative increment of capital, is above all important for all new offshoots of capital seeking an independent location. And as soon as the formation of capital were to fall into the hands of a few established great capitals, which are compensated by the mass of profits for the loss through a fall in the rate of profits, the vital fire of production would be extinguished. It would fall into a dormant state.'[50]

Tugan-Baranovsky's 'solution'

Could there not be a capitalist mode of production with a high and continuously rising level of production together with the present antagonistic mode of distribution?

It would be possible to construct a model on the following

lines. Every rise in the productivity of labour would be accompanied by a corresponding rise in the production of means of production, while production of means of consumption would not outpace the rate of growth of the population and the consumption of the capitalist class. As techniques changed, workers and capital would be transferred from the production of means of consumption to the production of means of production: more people and capital would be engaged in the production of machinery in order to produce machinery in order to produce machinery, and so on, while the production of means of consumption would not increase in proportion to the rise in the productive capacity of society. Production would become more and more roundabout, and so the market for which capitalism would produce would be within itself. Provided the correct relationship were kept between the two sectors of industry, there would be no crisis of overproduction, however low the purchasing power of the masses.

This was the argument of Mikhail Tugan-Baranovsky, a Russian non-marxist economist. He wrote:

The schemes quoted above were to prove a principle which might meet with objections; unless the process be adequately understood, namely, the principle that capitalist production creates a market for itself. So long as it is possible to expand social production – if the productive forces are adequate for this – the proportionate division of social production must also bring about a corresponding expansion of the demand, as under such conditions each newly produced good represents a newly created purchasing power for the acquisition of other goods. From the comparison of simple reproduction of the social capital with its reproduction on an expanded scale, the most important conclusion to be deduced is that in a capitalist economy the demand for commodities is in a sense independent of the total volume of social consumption: it is possible that the aggregate volume of social consumption as a whole goes down while at the same time the total social demand for commodities grows, however absurd it may seem to 'common sense'. [41]

Only a disproportion in the rate of expansion of the two sectors of industry can cause a crisis. 'If ... the expansion of production is practically unlimited, then we must assume that the expansion of markets is equally unlimited, for *if social production is distributed proportionately, there is no limit to the expansion of the market other than the productive forces available to society.*'[52]

Technical progress is expressed by the fact that the importance of the means of labour, the machine, increases more and more as compared to living labour, to the worker himself. Means of production play an ever growing role in the process of production and in the commodity market. Compared to the machine, the worker recedes further into the background and so also the demand resulting from the consumption of the workers as compared with the demand resulting from productive consumption of means of production. The entire workings of the capitalist economy take on the character of a mechanism existing for its own sake, in which human consumption appears as a simple moment of the process of reproduction and the circulation of capitals.[53]

In another work, Tugan-Baranovsky reduced the idea to an absurdity:

If all workers except one disappear and are replaced by machines, then this one single worker will place the whole enormous mass of machinery in motion and with its assistance produce new machines – and the consumption goods of the capitalists. The working class will disappear, which will not in the least disturb the self-expansion process (*Verwertungsprozess*) of capital. The capitalists will receive no smaller mass of consumption goods, the entire product of one year will be realised and utilised by the production and consumption of the capitalists in the following year. Even if the capitalists desire to iimit their own consumption, no difficulty is presented; in this case the production of capitalists' consumption goods partially ceases, and an even larger part of the social product consists of means of production, which serve the purpose of further expanding production. For example, iron and coal are produced which serve always to expand the production of iron and coal. The expanded production of iron and coal of each succeeding year uses up the increased mass of products turned out in the preceding year, until the supply of necessary minerals is exhausted.[54]

Clearly, as Tugan-Baranovsky himself remarks, the main-point of his analysis is not 'the wholly arbitrary and unreal assumption that the replacement of manual labour by machinery leads to an absolute diminution in the number of workers ... but rather the thesis that, given a proportional distribution of social production, no decline in social consumption is capable of producing a superfluous product.'[55]

Tugan-Baranovsky's 'solution' is impossible of application under individual capitalism because of the dependence on one another of the two sectors of the economy, and because of the uncontrolled exchange between them.

Under capitalism there is production both of use values and of values. The purpose of the former is the satisfaction of human needs, independent of the particular form of the economy; but the purpose of the latter (the production of values) is 'accumulation' – in order, as Marx expressed it, 'to conquer the world of social wealth, to increase the mass of human beings exploited by him [the capitalist].'[56]

Although the capitalist may consider use value only as the bearer of value, and although he may consider consumption only as a means and not an end, the means is nevertheless vital, because without it the end could not be achieved. 'Consumption produces production by creating the necessity for new production ... No wants, no production. But consumption reproduces the want.'[57]

The dependence of accumulation on consumption means that the sector of the economy producing capital goods depends on the sector producing means of consumption. Under private capitalism this relationship is achieved without conscious planning. If the supply of capital goods exceeds the demand for them to a greater extent than the supply of consumer goods exceeds the demand for them, the price of the former decreases relatively to the price of the latter. Hence the rate of profit decreases in industries producing means of production and increases in industries producing means of consumption. This leads to a falling off of accumulation in the first and an increase in the rate of accumulation in the other sector of the economy. Capital will then be transferred from the first to the second until a balance is restored between the two.

This process requires free movement in the price of commodities, free movement of capital from one sector to the other, and a rise in wage rates consequent on the expanded employment in the first sector which originally causes an an increase in the demand for the products of the consumer goods industries.

These factors make the application of the Tugan-Baranovsky 'solution' impossible under individual capitalism. Nevertheless, from a capitalist standpoint it has a sound element in it. In actuality it is the extension of the phase of revival and boom in the economic cycle, a phase during which accumulation increases more than consumption, and the production of means of production increases more quickly than the production of means of consumption. For a number of years accumulation can far exceed consumption without disturbing the balance of the economy. This and the fact that the link between the cycles of the rate of profit, accumulation and employment is the rate at which fixed capital (machinery, buildings, etc.) wear out, suggest that if increased production of consumer goods could be prevented while production of capital goods steadily increased, the boom would last longer than is usual in the decennial cycle. This is possible under state capitalism, because the state owns all the capital of society, and can control its movement between one sector and another.

State capitalism eliminates another factor which under private capitalism causes the turn from boom to crisis, and thus makes the Tugan-Baranovsky 'solution' possible for a time. Under private capitalism, a high rate of profit leads to rapid accumulation, a high level of employment and high wages. This process reaches a point at which wages are so high that they eat into the rate of profit, which falls steeply, dragging down with it accumulation, employment and wages. The workers, being 'free' to bargain over the sale of their labour power, the 'relative surplus population is ... the pivot upon which the law of demand and supply of labour works. It confines the field of action of this law within the limits absolutely convenient to the activity of exploitation and to the domination of capital.'[58]

Under a totalitarian state capitalist regime, even if there is practically no surplus population, and full employment exists, wages can for a long time remain 'within the limits absolutely convenient to the activity of exploitation and to the domination of capital'.

The Tugan-Baranovsky 'solution' is therefore possible under state capitalism, if it is backward compared with world capitalism, if means of production are scarce and if, therefore, the paramount need of the economy is the production of machinery in order to produce more machinery, and so on. But when the production of machinery succeeds in bringing the economy up to the level of the rest of the world, will this state capitalist system be faced with overproduction? There can be only one reply to this question, the reply given by Bukharin, viz. that the economy will be practically stagnant.

At first glance Bukharin's description of the relation between state capitalism and the crisis of overproduction appears to be the exact opposite of Tugan-Baranovsky's 'solution'. Tugan-Baranovsky speaks of a capitalist system in which there is a very rapid rise of production and accumulation; Bukharin of a system in which production and accumulation are on a very small scale. The former describes accumulation increasing independently of consumption, the latter as accompanying and being dependent on consumption. Yet the two theories have this in common: both point to the fundamental contradiction in capitalism between accumulation and consumption. The former suggests that this contradiction can be resolved by freeing accumulation and production entirely from consumption; the latter by slowing down accumulation and production to the pace of consumption. The former says that increased production can take place with accumulation only benefiting from it; the latter argues that quick accumulation is impossible and that production must therefore slow down. The former reflects the boom, the latter the crisis in the capitalist cycle. Both 'solutions' leave the worker subordinated to capital.

The Tugan-Baranovsky 'solution' is possible under a system of state capitalism in a backward country. Bukharin's description applies to state capitalism which reaches saturation point in the means of production. The latter is a capitalism which, although apparently free from crisis is really in permanent crisis, for if production does not rise above demand, production is *restricted* to demand. Both are a product of the contradiction between the productive forces and the capitalist relations of production and distribution.

But besides these 'solutions', there is another means whereby state capitalism can eliminate the crisis, viz. a war economy.

Production and consumption of means of destruction

A unique feature of the consumption of the capitalists, according to Marx, is that it does not constitute part of the process of reproduction. The 'consumption' of means of production (depreciation of machinery, etc.) leads to the creation of new means of production or new means of consumption, the consumption of the workers results in the reproduction of labour power, but the products consumed by the capitalists do not contribute at all to the new production cycle. There is, however, one form of consumption which, although possessing this characteristic, is nevertheless a means to acquire new capital and new possibilities of accumulation, 'to conquer the world of social wealth, to increase the mass of human beings exploited'. This is war production.

Like the crisis of overproduction, the war economy, while being an integral part of capitalism, throws into relief the obstacles to the capitalist mode of production, which are present in the system itself. Furthermore, a capitalist war leads not only to a stoppage of accumulation and a destruction of capital on such a scale that accumulation becomes possible anew, but to such destruction that there is a tendency towards the complete negation of capitalism and a reversion to barbarism.

In spite of superficial resemblances, however, a war economy and a socialist economy are opposite poles. In a war economy, as in a socialist economy, the state takes control of the economy and plans production and distribution. In a war economy, as in a socialist economy, there is the maximum possible production. But if the relations of distribution are antagonistic, and if the enormous accumulation of the past impedes new accumulation, maximum production is possible only if a large proportion of the products is not exchanged, that is, is not produced as values, but as use values. In a socialist economy, the aim of production is the creation of use values; the main aim of a war economy, too, is the production of use values. But in a socialist society use values are those needed by the people, while in a war economy they are guns, military equipment, and stores – use values inimical to the interests of the people.

A war economy is inevitably accompanied not by a crisis of overproduction, but by a crisis of underproduction, because the demand for goods outstrips the productive capacity of the economy. Inflation, on a large or small scale, always accompanies a crisis of underproduction.

The part played by war preparations and war in Russian state capitalism is such that it has not yet had to face the Bukharin 'solution'. In so far as the economy is directed to the production not of means of destruction but of means of production in order to produce means of production, and so on, it follows the Tugan-Baranovsky 'solution'. In any case the production of means of consumption lags far behind the production both of war materials and capital goods.

Given the world situation today, it appears that the war-economy 'solution' is the only expedient of the Russian bureaucracy until such time as either socialism or barbarism will render a 'solution' to the contradictions inherent in capitalism – orthodox or state – superfluous.

Chapter 8: The imperialist expansion of Russia

The example of Japanese imperialism · The motives for the expansion of the Stalinist bureaucracy · The record of imperialist expansion – Russian ingestion of Eastern Europe · The idealisation of the Tsarist empire · The struggle for national freedom – 'Titoism'

Empires existed before the monopolistic stage of capitalism, and even before capitalism itself. The imperialism of every period, however, is different in its motives and results, and the use of the one word, imperialism, to describe the different phenomena is therefore liable to bring about more confusion than clarity. Lenin used the term for the highest stage of capitalism, for capitalism in decline, when the proletarian revolution is on the order of the day. But the empires of even this one period have very different characters. Zinoviev says in his article, 'What is Imperialism?':

> In doing this [defining what modern imperialism actually is] we must not forget that there are various types of imperialism. British imperialism differs from German imperialism, etc. There is a European imperialism, an Asiatic imperialism and an American imperialism; there is a white imperialism and a yellow imperialism. Japanese imperialism doesn't resemble the French type; Russian imperialism is of quite a unique type, because it is a backward (it is not even possible any longer to say an Asiatic) imperialism, developing on the basis of an extraordinary backwardness.[1]

If, as Lenin explains, the *typical feature* of imperialism is the search for fields for capital export, while for youthful capitalism the typical feature was the search for markets, it seems wrong to have called Tsarist Russia imperialist. But all the Marxists including Lenin and Trotsky, did call it imperialist. And they were correct. For in the context of world economy, and the relations prevailing between Tsarist Russia and the highly developed countries, which is the criterion for its definition, Tsarist Russia was imperialist in the Leninist sense.

Lenin's definition of imperialism gives the following five essential features:

1. The concentration of production and capital developed to such a stage that it creates monopolies which play a decisive role in economic life.
2. The merging of bank capital with industrial capital, and the creation, on the basis of 'finance capital', of a financial oligarchy.
3. The export of capital, which has become extremely important, and distinguished from the export of commodities.
4. The formation of international capitalist monopolies which share the world among themselves.
5. The territorial division of the whole world among the greatest capitalist powers is completed.[*]

State capitalism certainly bears the first feature, as it consists of one general state monopoly. As regards the second feature, the merging of bank and industrial capital reaches the highest stage when the state is the industrial and banking capitalist together. As regards the fourth feature, the increasing competition between the imperialist powers drives the state – especially emphasised in Germany and Japan – to cut across international capitalist monopolies. It is clear that the economic invasion of an international capitalist monopoly is nearly excluded in a state capitalist economy. (Some foreign concessions are, of course, conceivable.) The third and fifth features – the relation of Russian state capitalism to the export of capital, and to the territorial division of the world, need further elaboration.

The example of Japanese imperialism

Of all the countries in the world except Stalinist Russia, that which reached the highest centralisation of capital was Japan. It was estimated that the 'Big Four' zaibatsu (family monopoly organisations) controlled sixty per cent of the capital invested in all Japanese joint stock companies, and that Mitsui alone accounted for nearly 25 per cent of the total. In 1938 the six biggest zaibatsu together held 57 per cent of all funds deposited in banks, trust companies and insurance companies. (The corresponding figure for 1929 was 45 per cent.)

(This is an indication why it is not excluded theoretically, although in practice there is no ground to assume that it will happen, that all the national capital will be concentrated in the hands of one trust.)

Nevertheless, although the centralisation of capital in Japan is much higher than in any other capitalist country, excluding Stalinist Russia, the productive forces of Japan lag far behind these of the countries of the west. This combination of highly centralised capital and the great backwardness of the country as a whole, explain the specific character of Japanese imperialism, as distinct from other imperialisms, and its *great similarity* in many respects to Stalinist imperialism. An outline of the specific features of Japanese imperialism will therefore help us to clarify some of the aspects of Stalinist imperialism.

The industrial output of Japan increased very rapidly during the present century. In the years 1913 to 1928, the tempo of this advance was about three times that of Britain in the years 1860 to 1913, that is, every year, they produced on an average 6 per cent more than the year before. Between 1927 and 1936 the industrial output of Japan increased by approximately 100 per cent, and E.B.Schumpeter could justifiably write:

It is no longer possible to state, as one careful and well informed writer did in 1930, that Japan can never become a manufacturing nation of major importance because of the lack of fuel and iron, which are essential in peace as well as war. Japan has become a major manufacturing nation. The rise of the heavy industries has been the striking development of recent years. Before the depression it was the textile industries, food preparation, pottery, and paper manufacturing which predominated. In 1935 just under half, in 1937 about 55 per cent, and in 1938 about 61 per cent of the total value of industrial production was accounted for by metals, chemicals, machinery, and engineering products. This meant that Japan produced her own ships and many of her own airplanes, but imported automobiles and parts; she was no longer dependent on the outside world for a large part of her steel, fertilizer, arms, ammunition and machinery, although she still had to import a substantial part of the raw materials from which they were manufactured. Since 1937, Japan has made a great effort to develop the raw material resources of the Yen Bloc and of adjacent regions in the Pacific area.[*]

From 1920 to 1936 the output of pig-iron increased four times, that of steel eight times, and the kilowatt capacity of electric power stations five and a half times. The main increase in industrial output took place in the means of production: the value of the output of the chemical, metal and machine industries rose from about 2,000 million yen in 1926 to more than 9,000 million in 1937, i.e. four and a half times. The output of all the other industries increased from about 5,150 million yen to 7,420 million, i.e. an increase of 44 per cent. In the same years prices rose by 40 per cent, so that we may conclude that the output of means of production rose about three times, while the output of means of consumption remained unchanged.

During this rapid rise of industrial output in Japan, the result of its general backwardness on the one hand and its high concentration of capital on the other, 'superfluous' capital did not appear and the rate of profit remained high. Another important factor permitting this high rate of profit was the extremely low level of wages. 'Average corporate earnings in 1936 and 1937 were from 16 to 20 per cent of paid-up capital and dividends averaged 8 to 9 per cent.'[4]

In the light of this, it would be wrong to say that Japanese imperialism sought fields of capital investment because it was faced with a 'superfluity' of capital and a low rate of profit in Japan herself. That the rate of profit was high and that she did not suffer from an abundance of capital but from a lack of it, is, however, but the expression of her backwardness. This caused a very interesting dialectical development: her very backwardness drove her to export capital on an extremely large scale, and to conquer a tremendous empire. In the words of F. Sternberg:

> When Great Britain and France founded their empires they were both leading industrial countries. Their empires were never intended to strengthen their own industrial position. Japan was in a very different situation. Her aim was to achieve a rate of development which would reduce the industrial gap between her and the other capitalist countries, and to become at least as strong and if possible still stronger than they were.[5]

After the World War I, foreign investments of all the highly developed countries which suffered from an enormous 'superfluity' of capital, except the USA, did not increase,

Capital invested abroad

(000m francs of pre-1914 parity)

Year	By Gt. Britain	By France	By Germany	By USA	Together
1862	3.6				3.6
1872	15	10 (1869)			25
1882	22	15 (1880)	?		37
1893	42	20 (1890)	?		62
1902	62	27–37	12.5	2.6 (1900)	104–114
1914	75–100	60	44.0	9.9 (1912)	189–214
1930	94	31–40	4.9–6.1	81.0	211–220
1935	58			41.9	130–140*

* We have estimated the investments of France and Germany for 1935 to be 30–40 milliard francs. This is, if anything, an over-estimation.

but on the contrary, decreased. Even with the USA included, the foreign investments of these countries did not rise beyond the level of 1914, as the facing table shows:[6]

Thus, while in the years 1860–1914 the quantity of capital invested abroad by the advanced capitalist countries grew almost uninterruptedly, from 1914 onwards, when imperialism had reached maturity, the quantity of capital invested abroad never rose above the level of 1914, and even declined below it.

As against this, Japan undertook an immense export of capital, especially to Manchuria, her only important colony until the Sino-Japanese war.

Japanese investments in Manchuria[7]

(million yen)

1932	97.2	1937	348.3
1933	151.2	1938	439.5
1934	271.7	1939	1,103.7
1935	378.6	1940–43	2,340.0
1936	263.0		

The Manchurian Five-Year Plan (1937–41) planned an investment of 2,800 million yen, which was subsequently raised to 6,000 million yen. This figure was impossible of achievement owing to the lack of capital and the scarcity of skilled labour in Japan. Investments reached only about half the target in the period laid down by the plan. But even this caused a very big rise in production, as the following table shows:[8]

Output of some products of Manchuria

Year	Coal mill. tons	Iron ore mill. tons	Pig-iron thous. tons	Electricity mill. kwh
1932	7.1	0.7	368.2	593
1936	13.6	1.3	633.4	1,351
1940	21.0		1,061.2	3,250
1944	30.0	5.3 (1943)	1,174.9	

The steel industry, established in 1935, was producing more than a million tons per annum after a few years. Machinery factories which supplied the major part of the equipment of Manchurian industry were established. In 1939 a car industry, planned to employ 100,000 workers, was established. A large aeroplane factory was also built. The construction of ships was begun. The railway network of Manchuria increased by nearly three times between 1932 and 1943 – and outstripped the whole network of China proper.

Sternberg remarked:

> The given historical conditions in which Japanese imperialism developed caused it to encourage and force the development of industrialisation in its empire, whilst different historical conditions caused the European imperialists to prevent or retard industrial development in their empires.
>
> In the ten years between Japan's invasion of Manchuria and her entry into the Second World War (1931–41) she so accelerated the industrialisation of Manchuria that although Manchuria's population is only about 10 per cent of British India's, as much, if not more, industry was created there in one decade, as was created in India in a century of imperialist rule.[*]

The industrialisation of Manchuria was not left to the blind activity of the different Japanese companies, but was carried out according to a plan by mixed companies of the monopolies and the state. Such organisation was found necessary for rapid industrialisation.

The motives for the expansion of the Stalinist bureaucracy

The privileges of the Russian bureaucracy, as those of the bourgeoisie, are conditioned by the unceasing advance of accumulation. But, unlike the bourgeoisie of the west, Russian state capitalism in its 'Tugan-Baranovsky stage' suffers neither from a 'superfluity' of capital, i.e. from a restriction of the possibilities of accumulation which the antagonistic mode of distribution causes in traditional capitalist countries, nor from a rise of wages which would threaten the rate of profit. In these respects Russian state capitalism is more similar to Japanese imperialism before its defeat in the World War II than to the western imperialist countries. Seeing that nearly all the means of production in Russia belong to the state, the industrial development of her colonial regions, i.e. the areas of the nations oppressed by the Russian bureaucracy, is *directly* a part of the general industrial development of Russia herself. The Japanese state saw in Manchuria 'an extension of the homeland'. The Stalinist state looks upon the Ukraine, the Caucasus, Rumania, Bulgaria, etc. in the same way, and, because of her monopolistic economic position, her development of these regions is and will be more efficient than Japanese imperialism's development of Manchuria. In the same way as Japanese imperialism looked upon the development of Manchuria as a necessary step to bridge the distance between it and the advanced powers of the west, so the Stalinist bureaucracy is driven to an imperialist policy for the same reason.

The same relative backwardness drives Russia towards the establishment of industries in the countries of the oppressed nations, and as the obverse of the same, to loot capital wherever she can lay hold of it. Japanese imperialism carried out large-scale plunder in China. As regards Germany: 'In the conquered territories, German firms have taken over the assets of resident concerns by right of conquest, not through "business as usual".'[10]

Stalinist Russia looted the countries of Eastern Europe and Manchuria. She did so by transferring factories to Russia, and, as Nazi Germany did, by concluding barter agreements with her vassals which were ruinous to them.

The concentrated monopoly capitalism of Japan and Germany and the state capitalism of Russia thus reveal another feature characteristic of the period of the primitive accumulation of capital – that trade and plunder were indistinguishable. If Alfred Marshall could say of that time that 'silver and sugar seldom came to Europe without a stain of blood', today the looted property is much bloodier; and it is not silver or sugar that is plundered, but means of production.

An additional motive for the imperialist expansion of Russia is the lack of certain raw materials. For example, Middle East oil and that of Northern Iran in particular, plays a big role in the plans of the Stalinist bureaucracy. This is the result primarily of the tardy execution of the oil extraction plans in Russia. Thus, for instance, the Second Five-Year Plan set the increase in production from 23.3 million tons in 1932, to 47.5 million tons in 1937. In fact, it increased only to 30.5 million tons. In 1940 production did not reach more than 35 million tons, although the plan laid down a level of more than 50 million tons. With these miscalculations, the Fourth Five-Year Plan set a more moderate aim for 1950 – 35.4 million tons. On examining the general plan for increased production, it is clear that oil will be one of the most important bottlenecks in Russia. The Stalinist bureaucracy tried to overcome this bottleneck by taking over Rumania and Northern Iran. (She did not succeed in the latter.)

Another factor motivating the expansion of Russia is the need for new labour power. In highly developed countries the export of capital is a reaction to the rise of wages which cuts into the rate of profit; it is directed to areas where labour power is cheap, and thus increases the amount of labour exploited by the same quantity of capital. The same result was achieved in a different way when Nazi Germany brought millions of workers from the conquered countries, particularly of the East, into Germany. Cheaper labour power than that of the Russian worker, expecially of the slave labourer, is not to be found in Europe, however, so that the annexation of new areas to Russia cannot be motivated by the need to find cheaper labour power. But this does not mean that it is not motivated by the necessity to find an additional *quantity* of labour power. Even though the quantity of capital relative to the population in Russia is very small, she still suffers from a lack of labour power. This is to be explained by its wasteful use caused by the lack of capital, so that side by side with the lack of capital appears the lack of labour power: hence slave labour and the low productivity of labour in agriculture. Every factor that impedes the productivity of labour – the bureaucracy itself included – will increase the wastage of labour power. Thus in spite of the gigantic population of Russia, the government finds it necessary to take special measures to increase it, such as the prohibition of abortion, fines for bachelors, and prizes for families with many children. So a vicious circle is created: lack of capital causes a wastage of labour power which makes it difficult to accumulate sufficient quantities of capital, and so on. The addition to Russia of a hundred million people from the countries of Eastern Europe is therefore an important motive for the expansion of Russian imperialism, corresponding to the export of capital from the countries of advanced capitalism.

Another motive for the expansion of Stalinist Russia is strategical considerations.

The record of imperialist expansion - Russian ingestion of Eastern Europe

The traditional imperialist countries exploited their colonies in three ways: by buying the products of their colonies for low prices; by selling them the products of the 'mother' countries for high prices; and by establishing enterprises owned by the capitalists of the 'mother' country and employing 'natives'. Russian state capitalism uses the same three methods to exploit its colonies.

There are numerous statistics proving that Russia pays very low prices for the products she buys from her satellites. To give a few examples. The Russo-Polish Agreement, dated 16 August 1945, stipulated that from 1946 onwards, Poland was to deliver to Russia at a special price (said to be 2 dollars per ton) the following quantities of coal: 1946 – 8 million tons, from 1947 to 1950 – 13 million tons each year, and subsequently 12 million tons annually, as long as the occupation of Germany continued. This coal is not to be paid for by Russian products, but by reparations taken from Germany by Russia. As far as is known, Poland did not get anything on this account. Anyhow, 12–13 million tons of coal at 2 dollars a ton, when the price of coal on the world market is 12–15 dollars a ton, gives a net profit to Russia of 10–14 dollars a ton, or altogether 120–180 million dollars a year (a sum comparable with the maximum annual profits of British capitalists from their investments in India). *Borba*, the Yugoslav daily of 31 March 1949, writes that a ton of molybdenum, an essential ingredient of steel, that cost Yugoslavia 500,000 dinars to produce, was sold to USSR during the Stalin-Tito honeymoon period for 45,000 dinars. The former Bata plants of Czechoslovakia had to supply Russia with shoes (the leather for which was supplied by Russia) for 170 Czech crowns, although the actual cost price per pair was 300 crowns. A particularly flagrant case of capitalist exploitation was that of Bulgarian tobacco: bought by Russia for 0.5 dollars, it was resold by her in Western Europe for 1.5–2.0 dollars.[11]

What applies to Russia's trade relations with her European satellites, applies equally to her trade relations with China. Chinese pig bristles and tung oil, which constitute a large proportion of Chinese exports, are offered at present in the

Western European markets at prices below those in Shanghai and Tientsin, the main ports of export of these products. Russia is the exclusive agent selling Chinese products in the Western markets, and the fact that she can afford to sell them at prices below those prevailing in China itself – and there is no question that Russia makes a profit on the transaction – indicates clearly that she pays exceptionally low prices for them. It partially also explains why Peking is making such efforts to open direct trade relations with the West, thus eliminating the Russian intermediary.

So much for underpayment. As far as overcharging the satellites for Russian products is concerned, we shall cite the following blatant examples: Russia charges China much higher prices for its goods than are charged, for instance, in nearby Hong Kong by Western capitalist sellers. Thus, for instance, a Soviet Zis 4-ton truck in Tientsin was sold by Russia for a price equivalent to 50,000 Hong Kong dollars, while a comparable six-ton truck of Western make is sold in Hong Kong for 15,000 Hong Kong dollars. Czechoslovakian saccharine, imported via Russia, is sold in Tientsin for a price equivalent to 106.40 Hong Kong dollars per lb., while German saccharine of the same quality is sold in Hong Kong for 6.50 Hong Kong dollars.[12]

The position of Russian-owned enterprises in Eastern Europe shows up most blatantly the third means of capitalist exploitation carried out by Russia: exploitation of the 'natives' employed in enterprises owned by foreign capital.

In the Russian Occupation Zone of Germany, the Russian state took outright as its property about a third of all industry. This is owned by what is called 'Soviet Shareholding Companies' (SAGs). The importance of the SAGs is very great. Nearly all the large-scale enterprises are owned by them. Every SAG employed in 1950 on the average 2,400 workers, as against 139–146 in the LEBs (enterprises owned by the so-called German Democratic Republic) and about 10 in the private industries. The importance of the SAGs will be even clearer if we take into account that they control heavy industry entirely. In the SAGs German workers produce surplus value taken by the Russian bureaucracy.

In Rumania, Hungary and Bulgaria there are mixed companies, in which Russia owns 50 per cent and which are in reality completely under its control. Thus, for instance, such a company controls the richest oilfields in Rumania; others control steel, engineering, coal-mining, shipping, air communications, timber, chemical production, tractor production, the building material industries, the exploitation of natural gas deposits, banks, insurance companies, etc. – altogether making up far more than half the industries, transport, banking and insurance of Rumania. In Hungary and Bulgaria there are also mixed companies, but their importance is much smaller.

Taking up half the profits of the mixed companies, while all the workers are 'natives' – is not this a clear case of colonial exploitation?

The idealisation of the Tsarist Empire

The Stalinist bureaucracy cannot but give its approval to its forerunners in empire-building – Tsarist imperialism. For generations Russian socialists and democrats thought Tsarist Russia a 'prison of the peoples' and Tsarist imperialist oppression of the Poles, Finns, Lithuanians, Esthonians, Ukrainians, Georgians, Armenians, Uzbeks, Kazakhs, etc. a most reactionary force. Stalinist Russia teaches differently.

Thus a Russian journal stated: 'annexation by Russia represented the only path of socio-economic and cultural development and also the salvation of the national existence of the peoples of the Caucasus and Transcaucasus ... annexation by Russia was the only means of saving themselves, preserving their ancient cultures and developing economically and culturally.'[13]

Another journal wrote that from the sixteenth century onwards, the feudal monarchies of Turkey and Iran conducted a long and stubborn struggle to seize various territories in the Caucasus. Many Caucasian people, unable because of their dispersed character, to withstand foreign aggression, 'sought salvation and intercession from the Russian state, turning to it for assistance and patronage.'[14] In the middle of the sixteenth century the Circassian (Karbadian) princes appealed to Ivan IV to give them Russian citizenship and to protect them from the raids and plunderings of Turkey and the Turkish vassal, the Crimean Khan. The Transcaucasian peoples established ties with Russia towards the end of the fifteenth century, and those ties were strengthened in proportion as the military danger presented by Turkey and Iran increased. By their actions against Turkey and Iran, 'Russian troops often saved the peoples of the Caucasus from military danger.' How well put! The Tsarist troops which occupied the Caucasus saved it from military danger!

A Russian literary journal stated:

The annexation of Kazakhstan by Russia, which took place in the 18th century, was of profoundly progressive significance. This historic act was conditioned by economic and political causes, by the entire course of historical development of the Kazakh people tormented by incessant raids from the feudal states of the Moslem East. It created the conditions for the mighty impact of Russian economy and culture in Kazakhstan. The Kazakh people made their historic choice wisely and correctly. At that time, besides Russia, the Kazakhs could have fallen into the bondage of Central Asiatic Khanates backed by Britain. Not rejecting any means, British capital crept up on Kazakh lands and resources, calculating on rich gains.[16]

It said further:

258 · *State Capitalism in Russia*

the working people [of Kazakhstan] through their daily experience, comprehended the advantages of life in a mighty state, Russia.[16]

The Kazakh people chose to be annexed by Tsarist Russia! They preferred to be in 'a mighty state'! *Pravda* underlined the point: 'The Kazakh working people were vitally interested in the annexation of Kazakhstan to Russia.'[17]

Russian propaganda since Stalin's death pursues the same line. The following slant was given to the occupation of Latvia by Tsarist Russia:

> Many centuries have passed since the Latvians' ancestors settled on the shores of the Baltic Sea ... During all these centuries the Russians have been good neighbours of the Latvians. The conquest and enslavement of the Baltic by the German knights is a gloomy history filled with killings, plundering and violence by the bloodthirsty Western invaders. The freedom-loving Latvian and Esthonian tribes were not strong enough to defend their freedom and independence. But proximity and friendship with the Russians enabled the ancestors of the Latvians to defend their lands from enslavement by turning for help to Russian princes.[18]

The struggle for national freedom – 'Titoism'

The nations oppressed by Great Russian imperialism, or threatened directly by it, react with a struggle of ever-growing intensity for national independence, a struggle bearing the recently-coined name of 'Titoism'.

The most numerous non-Russian people in the USSR are the Ukrainians. Their national aspirations have constantly been suppressed by a series of purges. In 1930 the Ukrainian Academy of Sciences was dissolved and members of it arrested for 'national deviations'. In 1933, Skrypnik, the most prominent leader of the Ukrainian Communist Party and a member of its Central Committee and Political Bureau, committed suicide in order to avoid arrest. At the same time Kostubinsky, the Vice-President of the Council of People's Commissars of the Ukraine (the Ukrainian Government), Kovnar, the Commissar of Agriculture, and a few score of high officials were shot as nationalists. To prevent further deviations, Postyshev was sent to Ukraine from Moscow in 1933 to reorganise the party and the state administration. He was given dictatorial powers. At the 12th Congress of the Ukrainian Communist Party in 1933, he said:

> In Ukraine our leading Party members and Comrade Stalin himself are specially hated. The class enemy has been to a good school in this country and has learned how to struggle against Soviet rule. In Ukraine have settled the remnants of many counter-revolutionary parties and organisations. Kharkov has gradually become the centre of attraction for all sorts of national- istic and other counter-revolutionary organisations. They have all been drawn to this centre and they have spread their web all over the Ukraine, making use of our Party system for their own ends. You remember, Comrades, when twenty Secretaries of Party Regional Committees dared to declare that it was impossible to fulfil the Harvest Plan.[19]

Postyshev expelled more than a quarter of the members of the Ukrainian Communist Party. Three years later he him- self suffered a similar fate. He was expelled and arrested. In his place came Kosior, from Moscow. He also was arrested in due course. In 1937, Lyubchenko, Chairman of the Council of People's Commissars of Ukraine, committed suicide in order to avoid arrest. The Commissars Petrovsky and Eiche were liquidated. Lyubchenko's successor was arrested two months after his appointment for 'nationalist' tendencies; his successor was liquidated a few months later. In April 1937, there were thirteen members on the Ukrainian Political Bureau; by June 1938, not one of these was left.

Other republics have a similar history. Goloded, who for ten years was Chairman of the Council of People's Commissars in the Republic of White Russia, was arrested as a Trotskyist in 1937. Some months later his successor as chairman, Cherviakov, committed suicide to avoid arrest. He had been Chairman of the Central Executive Committee of White Russia (i.e. President of the Republic) for seventeen years.

In Tadjikistan, the Chairman of the Executive Committee was purged as a nationalist in 1934. His successor held the position for three years and then suffered a similar fate.

The following is a short list of some of the foremost people in the national republics who were liquidated as 'nationalists' in the big purges of the 'thirties:

Presidents	Republic
Petrovsky	Ukraine
Chervyakov	White Russia
Kung	Volga German
Luft	Volga German
Gyllig	Karelian
Arkupov	Karelian
Khodzhibaev	Tadjikistan
Shotemur	Tadjikistan
Maksum	Tadjikistan
Dolgat	Daghestan
Samursky	Daghestan
Lordkipanidze	Adjar

Prime Ministers	Republic
Lyubchenko	Ukraine
Bondarenko	Ukraine
Chubar	Ukraine
Goloded	White Russia
Welsch	Volga German
Rakhimbayev	Tadjikistan
Rakhinov	Tadjikistan
Mgalobishvili	Georgia
Khodjaev	Uzbekistan
Abdurakhmanov	Kirghizstan
Ovakabelashvili	Transcaucasia

These are just a few of the victims. Altogether in the big purge of 1937–38 the whole or the majority of thirty national governments were liquidated. The main accusation against them was their desire for secession from the USSR.

The strongest proof that Russia's national policy does not create harmonious and fraternal relations between the different people is the dissolution of a number of national republics.

A year before the war, when there was tension between Russia and Japan, on the Manchurian border, the *entire* Korean population on the Russian side of the border was transferred to Kazakstan and Uzbekistan.

On 28 August 1941, the entire population of the Volga German Republic was transferred East of the Urals. The German Republic was one of the oldest national republics of Russia. As early as 19 October 1918, the Workers' Commune of Volga Germans was constituted, and on 19 December 1923, it was reconstituted as the Autonomous Soviet Socialist Republic of Volga Germans. It was one of the first republics to achieve almost complete collectivisation. *International Press Correspondence* (the Comintern paper) of 18 April 1936, said:

> The German Soviet Republic on the Volga is a living proof of the cultural and national progress which follows on the victory of socialism and a living disproof of the lies and slanders spread by the fascist enemies of the proletariat.

Just two years before their expulsion, an article appeared in *Moscow News* called: 'Volga German Republic, a Vivid Illustration of Soviet National Policy in Practice.' Then, after the Volga Germans had for so many years been commended for their unanimous support of the regime, came the decree of the dissolution of their republic, with the following explanation:

> According to reliable information received by military authorities, there are thousands and tens of thousands of diversionists and spies among the German population of the Volga region who are prepared to cause explosions in these regions at a signal from Germany. No Germans [living in the Volga districts] ever reported to Soviet authorities the presence of such great numbers of

diversionists and spies. Therefore, the German population of the Volga regions are covering up enemies of the Soviet people and the Soviet power.

In the areas of the USSR formerly occupied by the Germans, a number of republics were dissolved. These dissolutions were not even mentioned in the press, and it was only when *Pravda*, on 17 October 1945, gave a list of the constituencies for the coming general elections, that it was discovered that a number of republics had disappeared, since when one cannot know: the autonomous Crimean Tartar, Kalmuk and Checheno-Ingush Soviet Republics and the autonomous Karachev region were abolished, and the non-Russian populations deported. The Kabardinian-Balkar autonomous Republic became the Kabardinian Republic after the expulsion of the Balkars.

In Ukraine, Khrushchev, head of the government, declared in August 1946, that half the leading personalities of the Ukrainian Party had been expelled during the previous eighteen months. It would be too much even for the Great Russian bureaucracy to expel 30 million Ukrainians and dissolve their 'republic'.

After the World War II the national struggle against Russian imperialism spread to the newly created Russian colonies of Eastern Europe. The most prominent instance was the successful revolt of Yugoslavia against the Kremlin. The other 'People's Democracies' in Europe also had 'Titoist', i.e. nationalist resistance movements against Russian rule, but mainly because of the pressure of Russian troops these movements did not succeed. Proof of the broad scope of these national resistance movements is the fact that most of the leaders of the Communist Parties of the 'People's Democracies' were accused of being 'Titoists' by the Kremlin. Of the six people who filled the post of General Secretary of the Party immediately after the establishment of the 'People's

Democracies', the following four were accused of Titoism: Tito, General Secretary of the Yugoslav Communist Party; Kostov, General Secretary of the Bulgarian Party (executed); Gomulka, General Secretary of the Polish Party (arrested), and Slansky, General Secretary of the Czechoslovakian Party (executed). Of the six Foreign Ministers, the following four were accused of the same crime: Kardelj of Yugoslavia, Anna Pauker of Rumania (arrested), Clementis of Czechoslovakia (executed), Rajk of Hungary (executed). The list could be lengthened considerably.[20]

The struggle for national independence against Russian imperialism is sure to continue as long as Russian imperialism does. It is one of the most important factors which could seal the fate of the Stalinist regime.

Chapter 9: The class struggle in Russia

It is wrong to speak of a Stalinist epoch · The initial direct influence of industrialisation and 'collectivisation' on the relation of forces between the proletariat and the bureaucracy · The pressure of the totalitarian police machine · The military victories of Russia · The bureaucracy creates its gravedigger · The declining efficiency of Stalinist propaganda · The social goals of anti-Stalinist opposition · In conclusion

It is wrong to speak of a Stalinist epoch

The rise of the bureaucracy to the status of a ruling class expresses the fact that the historical mission of the Stalinist bureaucracy, which is to establish capitalism in Russia, has already been exhausted on an international plane, but not yet exhausted on a national one. At the same time, the bureaucracy, by relying on planning, an element of the 'invading socialist society', which it applies to its capitalist mission of the accumulation of capital, runs through the traditional historical course which the bourgeoisie of the west took about two hundred years to cover, in a few decades. Relying on elements of the future society in order to fortify relations of the past, the bureaucracy quickly undermines these very relations and in so doing prepares a new, glorious edition of the proletarian revolution on a much stronger historical base than in 1917.

Already in its first years as a ruling class the bureaucracy has adopted the totalitarian characteristics of decaying, ageing capitalism; it already proves its nature as a historical anomaly with no future. The bureaucracy is compelled to carry on a vast propaganda campaign against bureaucrats, to pose as the defender of the workers against the bureaucracy: the bureaucracy has a guilty conscience, it is a usurper lacking historical legitimacy.

Capitalist state ownership raises the ire of the masses. From the beginning of the bureaucracy's formation as a class, therefore, the sword of Damocles has hung ominously above its head. Whereas the capitalist of the sixteenth to nineteenth centuries could visualise a glorious future with himself as the representative of the whole of humanity, the Stalinist bureaucracy, today fulfilling the historical function of this capitalist, cannot but feel that its roots are in a temporary and transient concatenation of national and international circumstances. Hence its totalitarianism.

The bureaucratic terror, striking at the bureaucrats themselves, reveals the anomalous position of this hybrid. In traditional capitalism, competition between the capitalists ensures that each will be as efficient as possible. In a socialist economy, social consciousness, care for the interests of society, harmonious relations between people, is the basis for efficiency. The Stalinist bureaucracy, however, is both a result and a cause of the lack of harmony in the relations between people, of class and personal antagonisms, of the unlimited egoism prevailing in Russia. Therefore the motive of a planned socialist economy – the control of producers in the interests of the producers themselves – does not exist in Russia and cannot ensure the efficiency of production; on the other hand the direct connection between the efficiency of the individual enterprise and the income of its directors, a connection that exists under individual capitalism, also does not exist. The one important means of ensuring efficiency left to the bureaucratic state is terror directed against the individual bureaucrats.

The terror of the bureaucracy against the bureaucrats has an additional function besides this. As Ciliga writes:

> This original method of calming the anger of the people [the terrorist purges] reminded me of Marco Polo's report of the Mongol Emperor who reigned in Pekin at that time. It was customary once every ten or fifteen years to deliver over to the crowd the minister most abhorred by it, which allowed the emperor quietly to oppress his people for the next ten or fifteen years. What I saw in Russia was to bring this Mongol Emperor repeatedly to my mind.[1]

As a much deeper abyss exists between the Stalinist bureaucracy and the masses than ever existed in history between rulers and ruled, it is of the utmost importance to the bureaucracy that scapegoats be found.

Although the bureaucracy was born with all the marks of a declining class, it would be too great a simplification to say that every advance of the productive forces, every addition to the working class, will directly and immediately undermine the position of the bureaucracy. No, reality is much more complicated than that.

The initial direct influence of industrialisation and 'collectivisation' on the relation of forces between the proletariat and the bureaucracy

The number of workers in Russia increased very rapidly during the First Five-Year Plan. In 1928 the number of people occupied in manufacturing industries and the extraction of minerals was three million, in 1932 it reached eight million, an increase of 160 per cent. The overwhelming majority of the working class were thus raw elements newly come from the villages, not yet educated and organised by the process of social production.

At the same time the quick industrial development, and the ensuing acute shortage of technicians, skilled workers, officials, etc., opened the gates of the bureaucracy to many veteran workers. And of course the more experienced and intelligent the worker, the greater his opportunity for rising in the hierarchy.

These two factors, the dilution of the working class by raw elements and the exodus of militant elements from it, were a grave impediment to the rise of an independent workers' movement some decades ago in the different historical circumstances of the USA.

In Russia the difficulties of the workers' movement during the Five-Year Plans are much greater than those experienced by the American labour movement. Besides the terrible pressure of the secret police, besides the weariness of the masses after many years of super-human effort, besides the ideological disorientation which appears both as a result and cause of the weakness of the Russian workers' movement at the time, there is another factor: the creation by the bureaucracy of a layer of elite among the oppressed. This is one of the most efficient weapons the oppressor can wield in its oppression of the masses.

When Napoleon said that even the heaviest cannons could not stand up against empty stomachs, he was not entirely correct. Empty stomachs under certain circumstances lead not to revolt but to submission. Such was the case in the first years of industrialisation by the Stalinist bureaucracy. As Victor Serge said:

A vast misery will spring from its [the bureaucracy's] policy, but in this misery the tiniest material benefits become precious. It will now suffice to offer a worker a plate of soup the least bit nourishing and a shelter the least bit habitable in the winter for him to attach himself to the privileged amid the general destitution ... In that way a stratum of subordinate bureaucrats will be formed in the enterprises, in the party cells, and in the villages where the collectivisation is to result in a new differentiation between leaders and led. Around the former will gravitate a clientele eager to serve. The misery will consolidate those who conjured it up.[*]

The pressure of the totalitarian police machine

One cannot overestimate the difficulties which the police machine makes for the independent organisation of the workers in Russia. The working class is atomised and any attempt at building up any independent organisation whatsoever or at giving expression to the desires of the masses is brutally suppressed. The workers are compelled to belong to organisations led and controlled by the state and teeming with its spies. The combination of propaganda and terror designed to ensure the bureaucracy's monopoly of propaganda puts no limit to the lies it spreads, to the rape of the soul of the masses, driving them to mass demonstrations and public meetings, compelling them to debase themselves and sing the praises of their oppressors. All these weapons of the bureaucracy make the molecular process of the organisation and education of the workers very difficult. There is every indication that even the experienced, cultured German proletariat would have taken many years, perhaps decades, to smash the oppressive Nazi machine by its own strength. Even in the hours of Nazi Germany's greatest military defeats no mass revolt of workers broke out on the home front.

(In connection with this, one must not overlook the important effect Ilya Ehrenburg's chauvinistic propaganda had in helping the Nazis to cement the cracks in the wall of German 'national unity'.)

The raw Russian proletariat, the overwhelming majority of whom came but a few years ago from the villages, of whom probably less than 10 per cent knew the conditions under Tsarism when trade unions were legal, when the different workers' parties had a legal press, will find the utmost difficulty in learning the ABC of organisation and socialist ideology under the rule of Stalin.

The military victories of Russia

A factor which strengthened the rule of the bureaucracy was its military victories. Many factors contributed to them. Firstly, the absolute suppression of the masses allows Stalin to devote a larger portion of the national income to war aims than is possible in the countries of the West. He could, for instance, achieve the 'miracle of the evacuation of Russian industry' by transferring millions of workers to the East, housing them in holes in the ground. Secondly, police oppression ensures quiet on the home front, another 'advantage' Russia has over the democratic capitalist countries. The same two factors caused the absolute supremacy of Germany over France and Britain, which was eventually outweighed only by the co-operation of the American industrial machine (producing four times as much as Germany) and the Russian. While the Russian military victories were to a large extent the result of the 'quiet' on the home front, of the depression and despair of the toiling masses, they become in turn an important factor in the stabilisation of the Stalinist regime. To make an analogy, one cannot underestimate Nazi Germany's victories in the Saar, Austria, Sudetenland, Czechoslovakia, Poland and France as a factor in influencing the psychology of the German masses.

The bureaucracy creates its gravedigger

The initial result of the industrialisation and 'collectivisation' in Russia was to strengthen the position of the bureaucracy. After a few years an opposite process began; now every step forward of the productive forces undermines the position of the bureaucracy.

In the First Five-Year Plan the number of workers employed in manufacture and mining rose from 3 million to 8 million, a rise of 160 per cent. In the Second Five-Year Plan it rose from 8 million to only 10.1 million, a rise of 25 per cent. The Third Five-Year Plan planned an increase to 11.9 million in 1942, a rise of 16.7 per cent. Thus despite the liquidation of many of the workers in the 'purges', the number of veteran workers with many years of participation in the process of production behind them is steadily growing.

At the same time the gates to the bureaucracy draw together as more and more obstacles are put in the way of higher education, and the recruitment of the best elements among the workers into the bureaucracy diminishes.

The crystallisation of the proletariat due to the dwindling stream of raw elements coming into it and the dwindling stream of experienced elements going out of it is a process of the greatest importance.

The historical task of the bureaucracy is to raise the productivity of labour. In doing this the bureaucracy enters into deep contradictions. In order to raise the productivity of labour above a certain point, the standard of living of the masses must rise, as workers who are undernourished, badly housed and uneducated, are not capable of modern production. The bureaucracy approaches the problem of the standard of living of the masses much in the same way as a peasant approaches the feeding of his horses: 'How much shall I give in order to get more work done?' But workers, besides having hands, have heads. The raising of the standard of living and culture of the masses, means raising their self-confidence, increasing their appetite, their impatience at the lack of democratic rights and personal security, and their impatience of the bureaucracy which preserves these burdens.

On the other hand, not to raise the standard of living of the masses means to perpetuate the present low productivity of labour which would be fatal for the bureaucracy in the present international situation, and would tend to drive the masses sooner or later to revolts of despair.

The bureaucracy increases the working class on the basis of the highest concentration history has known. And try as it may to bridge the abyss between concentrated wage labour and concentrated capital, try as it may to veil it under the slogan of 'socialist property', the bureaucracy is bringing into being a force which will sooner or later clash violently with it.

The fact that only a few years after the industrialisation and 'collectivisation' when the working class was yet young and relatively raw, Stalin was compelled to be entirely totalitarian and to make such mass frame-ups as have no precedence in history, indicates the quick tempo at which the class struggle in Russia develops.

The declining efficiency of Stalinist propaganda

The diminishing efficacy of Soviet propaganda and its infirmity when the hard facts of life give it the lie, are indicated by two phenomena not to be otherwise explained. One is a mass scale on which Soviet POWs voluntarily joined the Nazi army; the other is the large numbers of Russian 'non-returners'.

During the war half a million or more Soviet nationals served in the Nazi army – in the *Osttruppen* – under German command.[3] Of some fifty Soviet generals captured by the Germans, about ten collaborated with Hitler against Stalin.[4] No other national group of POWs showed a comparable readiness to join the Nazis.

After the war, many Soviet nationals did not return to their homeland. That these 'non-returners' are, on the whole, not the same people who joined the Nazi troops is clear from the fact that the latter were forcibly repatriated by the Soviet army, as well as by the United States, Britain and France. The number of non-returners is considerable, although for obvious reasons it cannot be gauged accurately. According to a Soviet official statement, the number of Soviet citizens who had not returned to the USSR after the war was 400,000 (as against five and a half millions who had).[5] No other nationals displayed such reluctance to go home, such preference for the hazards and hardships of the DP camps. This is a reflection on Soviet reality and a pointer to the limited capacity of Stalinist propaganda.

The social goals of anti-Stalinist opposition

Anti-Stalinist opposition forces in the USSR, however unorganised and inarticulate, strive consciously or semi-consciously, even unconsciously, towards a goal which, by and large, can be inferred from the economic, social and political set-up of bureaucratic state capitalism, the set-up which these forces aim to overthrow. From a state-owned and planned economy there can be no retracing of steps to an anarchic, private-ownership economy. And this not only, or even mainly, because there are no individuals to claim legal or historical right to ownership of the major part of the wealth. The replacement of large-scale state industry with private industry would be a technical-economic regression. And so for the mass of the people, the overthrow of Stalinist totalitarianism could have real meaning only if political democracy had transformed the general wealth into the real property of society, thus establishing a socialist democracy. This deduction of the probable programme of the anti-Stalinist opposition from the objective data of bureaucratic state capitalism is clearly supported by the actual programmes of two organised anti-Stalinist movements which appeared during the World War II – the Vlassov movement and the Ukrainian Resurgent Army (UPA).

General Malyshkin, former Soviet general and one of General Vlassov's chief assistants, said:

> We take the position ... that all those industries which during the period of Bolshevism were erected at the expense of the blood and sweat of the whole people, must become the property of the state, national property ... Should it appear preferable, and be in the interests of the people, however, the state will raise no objections to the participation of private initiative... Private initiative will be made possible not only in peasant holdings and industry ... We believe that private initiative must also participate in other facets of economic life, for instance, in trade, handicrafts, artisan work ... To all former participants of the White Movement, we can say definitely the following: anyone does not belong to us who believes in the restoration in Russia of nobles and large landowners, in the restoration of privileges based on origin, caste, or wealth, in the restoration of outlived governmental forms.[6]

Whether the Vlassov leaders were sincere or not is irrelevant. The mere fact that they took a stand for state ownership of large industry – and that in Nazi Germany – is proof that only such a stand could have appealed to the Soviet POWs whom they tried to recruit.

A similar position was held by the UPA. This group conducted guerilla warfare against both German and Russian armies and managed to maintain an underground resistance in Soviet Ukraine. In 1943, in its publications in Volhynia, it put as its foremost slogan: 'Only in an independent Ukrainian state can the true realisation of the great slogans of the October Revolution be attained.'[7] The UPA proposed the following as its programme for a new social order in the Ukrainian state:

(1) For state-nationalised and co-operative-social property in industry, finance and trade.

(2) For state-national property in land with agriculture to be conducted either collectively or individually, depending on the wishes of the population.

(3) A return to capitalism in any instance is a regression.

Another publication of the UPA stated:

The complete liquidation of the class struggle demands the destruction of the source of classes itself, i.e., in the capitalist countries – the institution of private property in the means of production; in the case of the Soviet Union, the political monopoly of the Stalinist Party, the dictatorial, totalitarian regime.[9]

And again:

The Soviet order ... is not a socialist order, since classes of exploited and exploiters exist in it. The workers of the USSR want neither capitalism nor Stalinist pseudo-socialism. They aspire to a truly classless society, to a true popular democracy, to a free life in free and independent states. Today Soviet society, more than any other, is pregnant with social revolution. In the USSR, the social revolution is strengthened by the national revolutions of the oppressed nationalities.[10]

In conclusion

In the countries of capitalist democracy, and to a large extent even in Tsarist Russia and the colonial countries, the class struggle of the proletariat initially takes the form of partial, 'peaceful' organised and 'planned' economic struggles. In Stalinist Russia, because of the brutal police oppression, such struggles are excluded. Here, as in the armies of the capitalist countries where the soldiers are continuously under the whip of martial law, the molecular process of crystallisation of mass opposition to the rulers does not receive clear direct external expression. Only when conditions have become unendurable *and* it becomes clear to the masses that a *decisive* victory is possible, are they able to join battle. It is even more difficult for the Russian masses to strike today than it was for the soldiers in Tsarist Russia. The Tsarist soldiers rebelled only *after* they saw that the mass of the people was in revolt. The workers' barricades gave the soldiers confidence in the people's strength and inspired them to revolt against their officers. In Russia today there is no group of people which is not under closer surveillance than ever the Tsarist army was. Only when the anger and resentment embedded in the hearts of the masses cumulates till it is ready to burst, will the masses break out in revolt. (A proletarian revolution in the west can obviously accelerate this process to an incalculable extent). The class struggle in Stalinist Russia *must inevitably* express itself in gigantic spontaneous outbursts of millions. Till then it will seem on the surface that the volcano is extinct. Till then the omnipotent sway of the secret police will make it impossible for a revolutionary party to penetrate the masses or organise any systematic action whatsoever. The spontaneous revolution, in smashing the iron heel of the Stalinist bureaucracy, will open the field for the free activity of all the parties, tendencies and groups in the working class. It will be the first chapter in the victorious proletarian revolution. The final chapter can be written only by the masses, self-mobilised, conscious of socialist aims and the methods of their achievement, and led by a revolutionary marxist party.

Postscript 1988

From Stalin to Gorbachev
by Chris Harman

The first edition of this book[1] appeared when Stalinism was at its strongest – after the Russian occupation of Eastern Europe and before the split between Tito and Stalin.

In March 1953 Stalin died and within months enormous cracks were visible in the edifice he had created. His former lieutenants were soon quarrelling bitterly. At first Malenkov seemed to inherit Stalin's power, closely supported by the notorious police chief Beria. Then Beria was suddenly executed and Khrushchev displaced Malenkov from the dominating position in the leadership.

The quarrels were accompanied by sudden and sharp changes in policy. The terror machine that had been so important in Stalin's time suddenly went into reverse. The most recently discovered conspiracy (the so-called 'doctors' plot') was denounced as a frame-up, and those who had allegedly instigated the arrests were themselves arrested. In the three years that followed, 90 per cent of those in the labour camps were freed.

The new Russian leadership publicly admitted that enormous 'mistakes' had been made. For the first three years it heaped the blame for these on Beria and a 'gang of anti-socialist spies' who had 'infiltrated' the state machine. But then in 1956 Khrushchev denounced Stalin himself (although in secret) at the 20th Congress of the CPSU, and in 1962 made part of the denunciation public by removing Stalin's body from the Lenin mausoleum in Moscow.

The arguments at the top of Stalin's empire were accompanied by a sudden unleashing of discontent below. The slave labourers in the camps in Russia did not simply wait for the regime to reprocess their cases: in July 1953 the inmates of the biggest and most notorious of the camps went on strike, despite the shooting of 120 strike leaders. In East Berlin building workers reacted to an increase in work norms by a strike which turned into a near-insurrection by the whole working population of East Germany. In June 1956 this example was repeated by the workers of Poznan in Poland, and in October 1956 by the workers of the whole of Hungary.

These rebellions were put down in the bloodiest fashion. But not before they had shaken the illusions many socialists still held about Russia – and had also challenged any view of the Eastern states as lifeless monoliths in which rebellion was inconceivable.

The belief that Russia was different from and intrinsically superior to the West continued, however, to be taken for granted by most of the left internationally. As late as 1960 the British Labour politician Richard Crossman (previously editor of the Cold War book, **The God That Failed**) argued[2] that the superiority of Russian 'planning' over Western capitalism would eventually force Western states in a socialist direction. Further to the left the leading intellectual of the Fourth International, Ernest Mandel, argued in 1956:

The Soviet Union maintains a more or less even rhythm of economic growth, plan after plan, decade after decade, without the progress of the past weighing on the possibilities of the future . . . all the laws of development of the capitalist economy which provoke a slow down in the speed of economic growth are eliminated . . .[3]

Such reasoning led Mandel to express a preference for the attempt to reform the system from above by Gomulka in Poland to the workers' rebellion in Hungary.[4] It led the biographer of Trotsky, Isaac Deutscher, even further – to support the crushing of the Hungarian revolution.

Such hopes in the reforming intentions of the rulers of the Eastern states were widespread in the years after 1956. Although they were dashed when Khrushchev was removed from power in 1964, they revived briefly during the Dubcek period in Czechoslovakia in the first half of 1968. They are now reviving again with Gorbachev's programme of *glasnost* (openness) and *perestroika* (restructuring).

The Khrushchev period

Tony Cliff had extended his work on Stalinism with studies on the Eastern European states[5] and China[6] written in 1950 and 1957. In the late 1950s and early 1960s he set out to deepen his analysis of Russia so as to explain the reforms of the Khrushchev period and to point to their inbuilt limitations.

In 1947 he had already pointed to the central contradiction in Russia, which guaranteed growing crisis and an eventual workers' rebellion. The bureaucracy's role was to industrialise Russia by raising the level of productivity of labour. It could do so up to a point by coercion and the most minimal of living standards. But beyond a certain point, Cliff wrote, 'in order to raise the productivity of labour the standard of living of the masses must rise, as workers who are undernourished, badly housed and uneducated are not capable of modern production.' He suggested that the failure to raise living standards might already be leading to a decline in the rate of productivity growth and to 'jerky developments of production'.[7]

But the paucity of reliable information on the Russian economy and the newness of this theory of Russia meant that Cliff's arguments here were necessarily undeveloped – as was his argument about the form taken by economic crisis in state capitalism (the latter part of chapter 7 of the present edition). By the late 1950s much more information was available, although it still took a massive labour to excavate it from the mass of official statistics, newspaper reports and leadership speeches.

This Cliff did, first in a series of articles[8] and a short pamphlet,[9] then in a 140-page update for the 1964 edition of the present work, which was published under the title of **Russia: A Marxist Analysis**.

The additional material related specifically to the Khrushchev period, and has not been included in subsequent editions because by the time they appeared it was very dated. Yet many of the points Cliff made in it are worth summarising.

Cliff's central argument was that Khrushchev had inherited from Stalin an economy more and more plagued by elements of crisis. He had pushed through reforms because, without them, there was the danger of revolution.

Stalin's method of approach to each new failure or difficulty was to increase pressure and terrorism. But this rigid method became not only more and more inhuman, but also more and more inefficient. Each new crack of the whip increased the stubborn, if mute, resistance of the people.

Rigid, Stalinist oppression became a brake on all modern agricultural and industrial progress.

The crisis in Russia has not been limited to the economic base, but has engulfed the cultural, ideological and political superstructures too. It has affected not only the internal situation in Russia, but also the relations between Russia and the East European satellites, and the international communist movement.

Cliff then carried through a detailed examination of each of these areas of crisis.

The crisis in agriculture

The legacy Stalin left in the countryside is an agriculture bogged down in a slough of stagnation that has lasted over a quarter of a century. Grain output in 1949-53 was only 12.8 per cent higher than in 1910-14, while at the same time the population increased by some 30 per cent. Productivity of labour in Soviet agriculture has not even reached a fifth of that in the United States . . .

This stagnation became a threat to the regime for a number of reasons. First, after the hidden unemployment in the countryside was largely eliminated, it became impossible to siphon off labour to industry on the former scale without raising labour productivity in agriculture. Secondly, it became impossible beyond a certain point to siphon off capital resources from agriculture to aid the growth of industry.

Stalin's method of 'primitive accumulation' from being an accelerator became a brake, which slowed down the entire economy.[10]

Khrushchev attempted to deal with this crisis in two ways – 'the carrot and the stick'. The carrot involved reforms which raised the prices paid to agricultural producers, increased state investment in agriculture, giving the collective farms greater freedom to plan their own production and relaxing controls on production through the peasants' private plots of land. But such reforms were 'fraught with difficulties':

There have been some 25 years of Stalinist disincentives . . . It is very probable that a moderate rise in capital resources for agriculture, in consumer goods for agriculturalists, in prices paid by the state for agricultural output may for a time – perhaps for an extended time – have a disincentive rather than an incentive effect on the peasants. With higher prices, the will to work may decrease. Only massive incentives supplied over a very long period can overcome the past and spur agriculturalists on to increased activity. Unfortunately, Khrushchev lacks both capital surpluses of any size and also time; and their acquisition is rendered impossible by the international situation which causes a fantastic waste on armaments and the bureaucratic management of the economy (of which the crisis in agriculture is one of the most important aspects).[11]

It was this which led Russian leaders to resort repeatedly to the stick of greater central control, even if this contradicted their attempts to supply greater incentives. So the move to give peasants greater freedom on their private plots was followed by a tightening squeeze on these plots; the move to collective farm autonomy was followed by a campaign to build up the highly centralised state farms. And as both the stick and the carrot failed to deliver the goods, the leadership would storm round the country pushing great campaigns which were supposed to allow Russian agriculture to catch up with America overnight, such as the Virgin lands and maize campaigns of the mid-1950s.

But there was no way out of the crisis. Grain output was supposed to rise by 40 per cent between 1956 and 1960; instead it rose a mere 2.7 per cent and then stagnated so much that in 1963 the Russians had to buy millions of tons of grain from abroad. Meat production in 1960 was little more than a third of the original target.

'Solving the agricultural crisis,' Cliff wrote of Khrushchev, 'is meant to be the main plank in his programme; failure to deliver the goods may be his undoing.'[12] A few months later Khrushchev was removed from power by the rest of the politbureau, who complained of 'hare-brained schemes' that never worked.

The crisis in industry

Industry, unlike agriculture, had expanded massively through the Stalin period – and continued to grow under Khrushchev. But the rate of growth declined. And productivity, which had grown more rapidly than in the West in the 1930s, was now stuck at a considerably lower level than in the Russian bureaucracy's major rival, the United States. As Cliff noted:

At the end of 1957 the number of industrial workers in the USSR was 12 per cent larger than in the USA . . . Nevertheless, even according to Soviet estimates, the product turned out annually by industry in the USSR in 1956 was half that in the USA.[13]

Because of the crisis in agriculture, the lower level of productivity in industry could no longer be compensated for by a massive growth in the number of industrial workers. So the Russian bureaucracy had to pay increasing attention to the proliferation of waste and low-quality output within the Russian economy.

Cliff spelt out several of the sources of waste: the compartmentalism that led enterprises to produce internally goods that could be produced more cheaply elsewhere;[14] the hoarding of supplies by managers and workers;[15] the tendency of managers to resist technological innovation;[16] the stress on quantity at the expense of quality;[17] the neglect of maintenance;[18] the proliferation of 'paper work and muddle';[19] the failure to establish the efficient and rational price mechanism which managers required if they were to measure the relative efficiency of different factories.[20] He concluded:

If by the term 'planned economy' we understand an economy in which all component elements are adjusted and regulated into a single rhythm, in which frictions are at a minimum and above all, in which foresight prevails in the making of economic decisions, then the Russian economy is anything but planned. Instead of a real plan, strict methods of government dictation are evolved for filling the gaps made in the economy by the decisions and activities of this very government. Therefore, instead of speaking about a Soviet planned economy, it would be much more exact to speak of a bureaucratically directed economy . . .[21]

There had been accounts of the inefficiencies of Russian industry before Cliff, and there have been many since. They have provided the empirical 'evidence' of all those – on the left as well as the right – who claim that the Russian system is qualitatively inferior to the Western one. What characterised Cliff's account was not the stress on waste and inefficiency, but rather the way he saw these as following from the state capitalist nature of the system.

The immediate cause of the various sorts of waste was the way in which the planners set targets for production higher than what could easily be achieved. In order to protect themselves from these pressures, managers hoarded materials and supplies of labour. And in order to protect themselves from suddenly increased pressures from managers, workers worked at much less than full tempo. Awareness that this was happening throughout the economy led planners, in turn, to impose deliberately high targets. As Cliff put it:

What are the basic causes for anarchy and wastage in the Russian economy?
High targets of production together with low supplies – like two arms of a nutcracker – press upon the managers to cheat, cover up production potentialities, inflate equipment and supply needs, play safe, and in general act conservatively.

This leads to wastage and hence to lack of supplies, and to increasing pressure from above on the manager, who once more has to cheat, and on and on in a vicious circle.

High targets and low supplies lead to increasing departmentalism. Again a vicious circle.

High targets and low supplies make necessary priority awareness on the part of managers. But this priority system and 'campaign' methods, lacking a clear quantitative gauge, lead to wastage and hence to an increasing need to refer to priority schedules. Again a vicious circle.

All these requirements necessitate a multiplicity of control systems, which are in themselves wasteful and in their lack of systematisation and harmony make for even more wastage. Hence the need for more control, for paper pyramids and a plethora of bureaucrats. Again a vicious circle.

What has been said about the vicious circle resulting from the conflict between over-ambitious planned targets and low supply basis applies, *mutatis mutandis*, to the effect of the poor price mechanism. Thus for instance, the poor price mechanism leads to departmentalism, priority campaigns and a plethora of controls. And these lead to increasing faultiness of the price mechanism. Again a vicious circle.[22]

Cliff's 'vicious circle' has been described on innumerable occasions since 1964 by East European economists.[23] Some of these have made the connection between the over-high targets (sometimes referred to as 'overinvestment'), shortages (sometimes referred to as the 'inflation barrier'), the hoarding of supplies, and compartmentalism in the economy. A few have even gone further than Cliff in one respect by depicting how these different factors fit together into a cycle of investment and production somewhat akin to the classic boom-slump pattern of Western capitalist development.[24] But they miss one all-important point made by Cliff. The vicious, apparently irrational, cycle of inefficiency and waste has what is, from the ruling bureaucracy's point of view, a rational starting point. 'Overinvestment' is itself a result of the insertion of the bureaucratically run economy into a competitive world system:

> The great impediment on the path of lowering output targets are the world competition for power and the tremendous military expenditure.[25]

The Russian system cannot be regarded, as many of those who emphasise its waste today regard it, simply as a great failure:

> One should, however, avoid the mistake of assuming that the mismanagement corroding Russia's national economy precludes very substantial, nay, stupendous, achievements. Actually, between the bureaucratic mismanagement and the great upward sweep of Russia's industry, there is a tight dialectical unity. Only the backwardness of the productive forces of the country, the great drive towards their rapid expansion (together with a whole series of factors connected with this) and, above all, the subordination of consumption to capital accumulation, can explain the rise of bureaucratic state capitalism.
> The efforts and sacrifices of the mass of the people have raised Russia, despite bureaucratic mismanagement and waste, to the position of a great industrial power.
> However, state capitalism is becoming an increasing impediment to the development of the most important productive force — the workers themselves — which only a harmonious socialist society can liberate.[26]

To what extent low productivity is a result of mismanagement and blunders at the top or of resistance of workers from below cannot be estimated. The two aspects naturally cannot be divorced. Capitalism in general and its bureaucratic state capitalist species in particular is concerned with cutting costs and raising efficiency rather than satisfying human needs. Its rationality is basically irrational, as it alienates the worker, turning him into a 'thing', a manipulated object, instead of a subject who moulds his life according to his own desires. That is why workers sabotage production.[27]

As in agriculture, so in industry Stalin's heirs tried to deal with this problem by the carrot, found they could not succeed like that and returned at least in part to the stick.

The dismantling of the giant labour camps after Stalin's death was followed by the annulment of laws which had made workers liable for legal penalties if they were absent or late for work. Cliff compares these changes with what happened in the course of the development of Western capitalism: in the first stages of the industrial revolution all sorts of compulsions (the vagrancy laws, the workhouse system) were used to compel people to accept factory discipline; but once the new capitalist system had taken root, these tended to retard labour productivity and gave way to purely 'economic' forms of compulsion.[28]

But there were tight limits on the size of the carrot that could be used to entice workers to higher productivity. In 1953-4 the first post-Stalin prime minister, Malenkov, promised an increased output of consumer goods at the expense of means of production. But the honeymoon period for light industry was short-lived. In the framework of international economic and military competition, the subordination of consumption to accumulation is unavoidable. As early as the autumn of 1954 an offensive led by Khrushchev, Bulganin (then Minister of Defence) and Shepilov was launched against the 'pampering' of the consumers, and sought a return to a greater emphasis on heavy industry. In January 1955 Khrushchev declared that:

The paramount task, to the solution of which the party devotes all its efforts, has been and remains the strengthening of the might of the Soviet state and, consequently, the accelerated development of heavy industry.

A fortnight later Malenkov was forced to resign as prime minister. The share of light industry and the food industry in state industrial investment, which had been between 16 and 17 per cent in the five-year plans of the 1930s and 12.3 per cent in the second half of the 1940s, fell even lower in the 1950s and early 1960s – to around 9 per cent.[29]

Without any solution to the agricultural crisis and without any big increase in investment in consumer goods industries, there was a limit to the possible rise in workers' living standards in the Khrushchev years. By 1963,

In absolute terms consumer goods output has improved. However, on the whole the results have not in many cases reached the targets of even the first five-year plan as regards output per head . . . In spite of all the changes, living standards in Russia are still far below those in Western Europe and only marginally above those in Russia in 1928 (prior to the plan era).[30]

So even though things were much better for workers by the end of the Khrushchev period than they had been under Stalin (after all, they had fallen to only about three-fifths of the 1928 level in the mid-1930s), the improvements were by no means sufficient to produce massive increases in labour productivity. Cliff concluded his chapter on the Russian worker:

A central worry for the Russian leaders today is how to develop the productivity of the worker. Never has the attitude of their worker meant more to society.

By the effort to convert the worker into a cog in a bureaucratic machine, they kill in him what they most need, productivity and creative ability. Rationalised and accentuated exploitation creates a terrible impediment to a rise in the productivity of labour.

The more skilled and integrated the working class the more will it not only resist alienation and exploitation, but also show an increasing contempt for its exploiters and oppressors. The workers have lost respect for the bureaucracy as technical administrators. No ruling class can continue for long to maintain itself in the face of popular contempt.[31]

Changes in the 'superstructure'

Cliff's diagnosis of the Khrushchev period did not restrict itself to the economy. He went on to show how changing economic needs were reflected in the social and political 'superstructure'.

The most notable feature of the post-Stalin period was the relaxation of terror. Most of the labour camps were closed down and the mass purges became a thing of the past. Important elements of the rule of law were restored, with the police losing the power to imprison and execute people without judicial verdicts.

For Cliff, the main reason for these changes was that they were the other side of the shift from 'primitive accumulation', based on a great deal of forced labour, to 'mature state capitalism' based on free labour. But they also fitted in with the individual desires of the members of the bureaucracy:

The ruling class in Russia, for its own sake, wants to relax. Its members want to live to enjoy their privileges. One of the paradoxes of Stalin's regime was that even the socially privileged bureaucrats were not at one with it. Too often the MVD (the old name for the KGB) laid their hands even on the exalted bureaucrats. It was estimated that in 1938-40 some 24 per cent of the technical specialists were imprisoned or executed. The bureaucracy sought now to normalise its rule.[32]

Yet just as there were limits to the 'carrot' in the economic sphere, there were limits to the reduction in the power of the police. The KGB continued to be a very important centre of power within the state. Numerous laws remained in effect to punish people for any serious questioning of the power of the ruling class or for organising strikes and demonstrations. 'Comrades' courts' were set up to deal with 'infringements of soviet legality and code of socialist behaviour'. By this was meant a range of activities which challenged the bureaucracy's monopoly of state property or the obligation of the rest of society to work for the bureaucracy – 'illegal use of state or public material equipment or transport . . . shirking socially useful work and living as a parasite . . . poaching . . . damage to crops or plantations by animals . . . petty profiteering . . . drunkenness . . . bad language . . .'[33]

For Cliff, further reduction in the arbitrariness of state power was ruled out because of the general scarcity of goods, the inability to deal with 'bureaucratic arbitrariness and administrative *fiat*' in the economy, and by 'the fact that the state is the repository of all means of the production, the centre of educational and cultural organisation' and so, the focus for 'all criticism, of whatever aspect of the system'.

Hence state capitalism by its very nature, unlike private capitalism, excludes the possibility of wide, even if only formal, political democracy. Where the state is the repository of the means of production, political democracy cannot be separated from economic democracy.[34]

Behind the limitations on political reform lay the fact that power continued to lie with a narrow bureaucratic class:

The monopoly of power is not less the prerogative of the CPSU under Khrushchev than it was under Stalin. Its social composition has not changed much either. And the concentration of the commanding heights of the party in the hands of the bureaucracy is even more the case than under Stalin . . . Ordinary workers and collective farmers probably do not comprise more than a fifth, certainly no more than a quarter of the party membership. The higher one rises in the party hierarchy, the more scarce are workers and collective farmers.[35]

The tensions between Khrushchev's attempts at pushing through reform and his inability to do so beyond a certain point found expression in the relations between the different nationalities inside the USSR.

Stalin's death occurred at the height of the Russification campaign . . . Stalin's heirs had to decide whether they should continue these policies or offer concessions to the national minorities.[36]

At first concessions seemed on the cards:

The self-assurance of the non-Russian peoples of the USSR following their economic and cultural advance must lead to increasing opposition to national oppression . . . Where the retreat from Stalin's overcentralisation in economic management was made . . . the harshness and extremism of Stalin's nationalities policy became intolerable . . .
Pointers to change began to appear shortly after Stalin's death.

Cliff gave a number of examples of party leaders in the different republics who had been demoted for too zealous an identification with Stalin's nationalities policy and of others who were acquitted of previous accusations of 'bourgeois nationalism'. Khrushchev, in his 20th party congress speech, went out of his way to denounce Stalin's deportation of whole nationalities, and soon afterwards a number of them (but not the Crimean Tartars and the Volga Germans) were rehabilitated.

But 'the main lines of the nationalities policy have not really changed radically . . . In the governments of the Asian republics newly appointed in 1959, of the 118 ministers no fewer than 38 were Europeans' – and these usually held key portfolios such as those of state security, planning, and chair or deputy chair of the council of ministers. The idealisation of the Tsarist annexations continued, and 'the Russian language continues to edge out the national languages, even in the schools of the national republics'.

Although non-Russians constitute about half the population of the USSR, the circulation of newspapers in non-Russian languages constituted in 1958 only 18 per cent of the total circulation.[37]

Those who resisted this trend might not be taken out and shot as in Stalin's time, but they would find their careers ruined. 'Anti-nationalist' campaigns continued to take place in the different national republics, and continued to lead to widespread sackings and demotions.

The Russian leadership faced a 'national' problem outside as well as inside the borders of the USSR. In Stalin's time Moscow had been the centre of an international Communist movement that held power in a third of the world and had the support of many of the most militant sections of workers elsewhere. This was doubly useful to Stalin. The foreign Communist Parties could be used as counters in diplomatic games with the Western powers. And their praise for Russia could be used as an ideological weapon in the battle to keep control of Russia's workers and peasants – what better proof could there be of the correctness of Stalin's methods than that workers throughout the rest of the world praised them?

But the ability of Russia to control the other Communist Parties depended on it being the only independent Communist power:

> For a long time . . . the international Communist movement . . . has suffered one set-back after another: in Germany from the defeat of the revolution in 1919 to the rise of Hitler; in China the defeat of the revolution in 1925-27; the defeat of the Republic in the Spanish Civil War; the debacle of the People's Front in France, etc. The only Communist Party maintaining power was in Russia.
> If man's weakness in the face of the forces of nature or society lead to his imbibing the opiate of religion with its promise of a better world to come, Stalinism certainly became the opiate of the international labour movement during the long period of suffering and impotence.[38]

Things changed after the Second World War. First in Yugoslavia and Albania and then, much more importantly, in China and later Cuba and Vietnam, Communist regimes came to power which were not dependent on the Russians. Cliff showed in a number of books and articles[39] that these were propelled by the same logic of state capitalist accumulation as Russia. But this very logic inevitably led them into bitter conflicts with Russia's rulers.

Tito broke with Stalin in 1948 because Stalin attempted, in the interests of Russian capital accumulation, to impose policies which were detrimental to building an independent national state capitalism in Yugoslavia. Twelve years later Khrushchev was faced with a much more important split – that with the rulers of the giant Chinese People's Republic.

Cliff traced the roots of this split to the differing economic needs of the two ruling classes. The Russians were concerned with attempting to catch up with the US in productivity – and that involved concentrating investment in their own already relatively advanced industries and using what resources were left to try to raise Russian living standards. The Chinese, by contrast, were desperate for the investment needed to build new industries from scratch, using the most primitive methods if necessary, and needed to keep living standards as low as possible. Divergent interests led to increasingly bitter rows over the allocation of resources; and out of the economic divisions grew ideological divisions. The Russian leadership, making the transition from primitive accumulation to mature state capitalism, required an ideology which boasted of the immediate benefits to living standards of its policies. It needed to turn its back sharply on the Stalinist ideology of never-ending sacrifice and relentless mobilisation. The Chinese, still at the primitive accumulation stage, required that ideology more than ever:

> For China to belong to the same bloc while getting less and less materially from her rich partner is bad enough in itself. But as a morale-buster, the effect on Mao's highly disciplined camp can be catastrophic in the long run.[46]

Cliff's conclusion was that the split between Russia and China was not just a passing phase, but permanent. This meant, 'whichever way the conflict between Moscow and Peking develops, one thing is certain – the international Communist monolith has crumbled.'[41]

Again, it is a conclusion which may not seem particularly profound today. But in the early 1960s it was very much a minority view. On both the right and the left in the West the general view was that eventually Russia and China would soon mend their quarrel. Isaac Deutscher gave expression to the view of most socialists when he said that what the two had in common was so great the division could not last for long.[42]

The Brezhnev years

Nikita Khrushchev was removed from power by the Russian politbureau in the autumn of 1964 and died in official obscurity. His successor, Leonid Brezhnev, ruled for 18 years, twice as long as Khrushchev, and died in office. Yet hardly was his body cold than the Russian press were stigmatising the Brezhnev years as a period of 'stagnation'.

Brezhnev had been able to take power in 1964 because Khrushchev's succession of reforms and counter-reforms had upset a sizeable layer of the bureaucracy without producing outstanding economic results. It was easy to bring together a coalition of different bureaucratic interests opposed to any more 'hare-brained schemes'. By manoeuvring between these, the new leader was able to gain increasing control for himself until, combining the offices of party secretary and state president, he was unchallengeable.

He had to pay a price for his success, however. He had to placate all those who had helped him to rise, and that meant leaving established bureaucrats in their place, regardless of how well they did their jobs. The Stalin period had been characterised by massive, bloody purges, the Khrushchev period by bloodless ones. The Brezhnev period lacked both. It was a long period of bureaucratic stability, in which only death removed many top bureaucrats from office. When Stalin died in 1953 the average age of politbureau members was 55 and of Central Committee secretaries 52; by the time of Brezhnev's death the average had risen to 70 and 67.

At first there were token efforts to continue with reform. Brezhnev's first prime minister, Kosygin, tried to introduce a new system by which the success of factory managers was measured in terms of profitability, not just quantitative output. In 1967 the success of the Shchekino chemical combine in raising output while reducing the workforce was highlighted as an example for other enterprises to follow. But the new reforms soon petered out. Tinkering with the system did not produce the expected benefits, and the opposition of entrenched bureaucratic interests prevented more than just tinkering.

For a dozen years, it seemed that the problems that had so haunted Khrushchev could simply be ignored. The growth rate of the USSR's economy might be falling, but it was still faster than most Western states. The sheer size of the USSR and the continued existence of considerable mineral resources enabled it to ignore the weakness of whole sectors of its economy. If investment in agriculture and consumer goods was retarded by the pressures of military competition, it was still possible to raise output – and living standards. The average grain harvest in the Khrushchev years was 124.4 million tonnes; it was 176.7 million tonnes in Brezhnev's first decade in office.[43] In 1965 only 24 per cent of Soviet families had a TV set, 59 per cent a radio, 11 per cent a fridge and 21 per cent a washing machine; by 1984 the figures had risen to 85 per cent, 96 per cent, 91 per cent and 70 per cent.[44]

While things improved in this way, it seemed that all the problems that had so obsessed Khrushchev could be ignored. But they began to re-emerge with a vengeance in the late 1970s. The rate of economic growth began to decline precipitately. The 1976-80 plan set the lowest growth targets since the 1920s – and was still not fulfilled. If the annual growth rate had averaged 5 per cent in Khrushchev's last five years and 5.2 per cent in Brezhnev's first five years, it was only 2.7 per cent in 1976-80 (according to US estimates;[45] official Russian figures are a little higher, but show the same trend).

The trend to stagnation hit particular industries very hard: electricity and oil output was growing by 1980 at only about two-thirds of the rate of five years earlier, and coal, steel and metal-cutting machine tools output actually fell a little.[46] Even worse, the relatively good harvest of 1978 was followed by poor harvests in 1979 and 1980 and a disastrous one in 1981.

The Russian leadership say today that:

The unfavourable tendencies that surfaced in economic development in the 1970s grew sharper in the early 1980s rather than relaxing. The slowdown of the growth rates continued during the first two years. The quality indicators of economic management deteriorated. In 1982 the increment rate of industry was 33.4 per cent below the average of the period of the past five-year plan.[47]

The reaction of the Brezhnev generation of ageing bureaucrats was to try to evade all the problems the economic downturn posed. They tried to continue in the old way and to use political influence to protect their own little empires. Again, as the leadership now tells:

Both in the centre and the localities many leaders continued to act by outdated methods and proved unprepared for work in the new conditions. Discipline and order deteriorated to an intolerable level. There was a fall in exactingness and responsibility. The vicious practice of downward revision of plans became widespread.[48]

In the Stalin and Khrushchev periods bureaucrats at all levels could have a certain sense of pride in their achievements. They might have lived in fear of Stalin and have resented

Khrushchev's chopping and changing of policies, but at least they saw the economy grow under their collective control, and with it their individual prestige. They could believe in 'the relentless advance of communism' – not in the sense of the advance to human liberation preached by Marx and Lenin, but of the growth of Russian state capitalist power.

Under Brezhnev pride gave way to cynicism and cynicism easily spilled over into blatant corruption. At the top Brezhnev's own family was implicated in this: his daughter was suspected of involvement in a scandal concerning stolen diamonds and his brother-in-law, the deputy head of the KGB, in covering up for her.[49] A little further down the bureaucratic hierarchy, the national leaderships of a number of republics seem to have built a base for themselves by covering up for semi-criminal elements: accusations to this effect were thrown at the Kazakhstan, Uzbekistan, Georgian and Armenian leaderships after Brezhnev's death.

The cynicism of the bureaucracy was clearly matched by continuing mass alienation at the base. Drunkenness rose to record level. The quality of output from the factories did not improve. Productivity in industry remained at 55 per cent of the US level[50] and was rising only slightly faster than wages.[51]

Gorbachev

Yuri Andropov took over the leadership on Brezhnev's death. As head of the KGB he might have been expected to be conservative in his approach. But in a totalitarian state it is often the secret police who are most in touch with the real mood of the mass of the people: they have a network of informers who will report on what their neighbours are really saying, while members of the regime's party report only what those above them want to hear. So Andropov was aware of the cynicism, the corruption and the depth of popular alienation. He had also been Russian ambassador in Hungary in 1956 and had learnt how rapidly such ingredients could ignite into popular insurgency – a lesson reinforced by the sudden rise of *Solidarnosc* in Poland in 1980. He set out on the path of reform, as Khrushchev had 30 years before, to reduce such dangers to bureaucratic rule.

Andropov lived only another 14 months, and the conservative, Brezhnevite forces were still strong enough on his death to ensure that one of themselves, the ageing Chernenko, took over. But Andropov had managed to shift the balance of power to some extent. When Chernenko in turn died after 13 months in office, Mikhail Gorbachev was appointed general secretary.

In the interim, economic stagnation had continued: output of a whole range of goods from steel to fertilisers was actually lower than a year before. The new leader could hardly avoid leapfrogging backward over the Brezhnev years to the talk of reform and change that had been buried with the ousting of Khrushchev.

Gorbachev coined the slogans *perestroika* (restructuring) and *glasnost* (openness). He spoke of the need for a 'peaceful revolution'. He encouraged reform-minded economists to highlight faults in the organisation of industry and agriculture. He spoke of the need to replace corrupt local leaders and inefficient managers.

And talk of economic reform spilled over into talk of political reform. There was a reconciliation with the best-known of dissidents, Sakharov, who was allowed back to Moscow from exile in Gorki. There was renewed criticism of Stalin and the rehabilitation of Bolshevik leaders who had been executed by him, especially Bukharin. There was toleration of independent informal discussion groups. There was a change in the electoral system to allow for more than one candidate in certain cases. There was talk of allowing the secret ballot in internal party elections. There was even a promise of the election of factory managers by the workforce.

All this led many people on the left to develop the same sort of faith in Gorbachev's reforming zeal that people like Deutscher had shown in Khrushchev 30 years earlier. But, like Khrushchev, Gorbachev has shied away from the radical reform implied in some of his words. His economic reform is, like Khrushchev's, a case of the stick as well as the carrot.

Gorbachev has pointed enthusiastically to the Stakhanovite movement of the 1930s and 1940s as an example to be copied.[52] He told a meeting in Khabarovsk: 'The main thing needed now, and I say this to you and ask you, is: Work, work, work!'[53] His first major action to deal with economic inefficiency was to try to stop workers drowning their sorrows; he issued a decree restricting the sale of alcohol and raising its price 30 per cent. Indeed, for many workers the stick far outweighs the carrot: where the reform has been applied at the enterprise level it has led to wage cuts – and to strikes, as with the tram stoppage at Chekhov[54] and what Izvestia referred to as a 'wild demonstration' at the Kama River truck plant.[55] Gorbachev himself has admitted that there have been several 'work stoppages' over quality control measures which have lowered workers' bonuses.[56]

The promises of glasnost have not turned into even the very limited democracy known in the advanced Western states. There was a choice of candidates in the 1987 elections – but in only 5 per cent of constituencies, and even here there was no open campaigning for different policies.

The rules for the elections of managers made it clear that workers will not have real control. The workers do not themselves determine who is on the short list of candidates that is voted on. The successful candidate has to be approved by the 'superior organ' in charge of the enterprise[57] and it is not just the workers, but all employees (including managers, supervisors and foremen) who vote. Finally, in the elections that have taken place so far workers have not been allowed to campaign for or against an individual candidate (as workers in the Latvian factory of RAF cars complained in 1987).[58] It is easy to see how, in such conditions, the only group allowed to campaign within the enterprise, the party cell, will effectively be able to determine who wins. And statistics show that only 16.7 per cent of those in key positions in local party cells are workers.[59]

Alongside the alleged election of managers, elected enterprise councils have been set up. But again, the rules for elections make it clear that this is not an example of real workers' democracy. The councils' 'primary sphere of authority' is the monitoring of worker performance and the promotion of enterprise productivity:

> . . . the council concentrates its main attention on the development of the initiative of the working people and on the contribution of each worker to the common cause, and implements measures to achieve high end results . . . and to earn the collective economically accountable revenue.[60]

The first election campaigns were based entirely on candidates' records of promoting efficiency and productivity and their adherence to 'norms of socialist legality and morality'.[61] These bodies are clearly much closer to quality circles than to real factory councils!

If there were any doubt on the matter, article 6 of the new law spells out that the party organisation 'directs the work of the organisation of collective self-management'.

The same combination of talk of reform and real control from above is shown over the nationalities question. Many of the oppressed ethnic groups that make up more than half the USSR's population have taken *glasnost* to mean they can speak out for the first time in 70 years about the discrimination they face. In 1987 there were demonstrations in the Baltic republics and by the Crimean Tartars. February 1988 saw a million-strong demonstration in the Armenian capital. Yet the actions of the Gorbachev government have involved centralised direction from Moscow rather than reliance upon local initiative. At the end of 1986 a Russian was imposed on the Asian republic of Kazakhastan as first secretary in place of an allegedly corrupt local leader – and many thousands of Kazakhs poured into Alma Ata and clashed with the police in protests. The regime turned a blind eye to the protests in the Baltic republics and by the Tartars. When Gorbachev met a delegation elected from the mass demonstration of Armenians, he told them they would have to wait some years for satisfaction of their grievances. As with Khrushchev 30 years ago, Gorbachev's promise of reform is contradicted by his drive to make Russian industry more efficient – and that means a central, rather than a local direction of resources.

Again like Khrushchev, Gorbachev's period of rule has been marked by sudden chopping and changing. In 1984-86, he talked of reform but concentrated mainly on changing personnel, so as to replace former Brezhnev supporters with his own men. Then in the first ten months of 1987 he began to urge rapid change in a series of speeches and in his book **Perestroika**. But in October of that year there was a sudden shift back to older methods.

In the forefront of the campaign for reform had been Boris Yeltsin, the recently appointed leader of the Moscow party organisation. He introduced the October plenum of the Central Committee with a speech which, apparently (we don't know the exact contents of his speech, since *glasnost* does not amount to openness about such proceedings), involved swingeing attacks on those obstructing *perestroika*.

There followed attacks on him by no fewer than 26 speakers from the floor and the meeting then unanimously passed a resolution 'qualifying his statement as politically wrong'. The foreign press were told of the arguments taking place, but not the people of the USSR. The first they heard officially came three weeks later when a special meeting of the Moscow City party voted to sack Yeltsin.

The tone of the meeting was set by Gorbachev himself, who claimed that Yeltsin had 'adopted high-sounding statements and promises from the very beginning which were largely nourished by his inordinate ambition and fondness for staying in the limelight.' The language was not that different from that used by Stalin against his opponents in the late 1920s and early 1930s (before he turned to calling them 'agents of imperialism'). And Yeltsin's own response showed how little room there is in the *glasnost*-inspired leadership for open debate. Instead of defending himself, Yeltsin responded with a confession that could also have come from the Stalin era:

> I must say that I cannot refute this criticism . . . I am very guilty before the Moscow City Party organisation, I am very guilty before the City Party Committee, before the Bureau and, of course, before Mikhail Gorbachev whose prestige is so high in our organisation, in our country and throughout the world.[62]

The Yeltsin affair was no isolated occurrence. It marked some sort of turning point in the drive for *glasnost*. This is shown by a shift in Gorbachev's own approach. Before the Yeltsin affair, in the summer of 1987, he wrote his book **Perestroika**, which demands radical reform. After the attacks on Yeltsin at the Central Committee he gave a speech marking the 70th anniversary of the October revolution. This was widely expected to urge a speed-up of *perestroika* and *glasnost*. But instead it laid as much stress upon the 'dangers' of 'going too fast' as on the dangers of resistance to *perestroika*.

Such sudden reverses of policy are not accidental. The stagnation of the Russian economy produces pressure for reform. But that pressure encounters massive obstacles from inside the bureaucracy itself. It is not only that millions of individual bureaucrats are committed to the old ways of organising things; it is also that the whole bureaucracy fears that bitter arguments with each other might open up a space for millions of people below them to take action on their own accord.

It was precisely such splits within the bureaucracy which laid the ground for the East German rising of 1953, the Poznan rising of June 1956, the Hungarian revolution of October-November 1956 and the Czechoslovak events of 1968.[63] On each occasion what began as arguments between different sections of the bureaucracy partially paralysed the machine of repression and allowed students, intellectuals and finally workers to mobilise.

There have already been the first signs of such moves as a by-product of the arguments over *glasnost*. There was the clash between demonstrators and the police in Alma Ata in 1936, the nationalist demonstrations in the Baltic states in 1987, the huge demonstration in Armenia in late February 1988. Outside the USSR itself, in its sphere of influence in Eastern Europe, there have been signs that things might get completely out of control, with strikes and demonstrations in Hungary, a near-uprising in the Rumanian town of Brasov, and continuing discontent in Poland and Czechoslovakia.

What is more, those who resist reform have one very powerful argument: it is by no means self-evident that economic reform will solve the problems of the economy. In two East European countries, Hungary and Yugoslavia, far-reaching reforms in the direction of what is sometimes called 'market socialism' have been carried through. For a time these reforms received enormous praise in the Western media. Yet today the Hungarian and Yugoslav economies are in no better shape than that of Russia. Both are suffering from industrial stagnation, high levels of inflation and big foreign debts. Both are attempting to impose wage cuts and unemployment on their workers, creating growing discontent which led, in the Yugoslav case, to a massive wave of strikes in 1987.

The point is that reforms cannot deal with the root cause of the USSR's economic failings. This lies, as Cliff argued 40 years ago, in the way the ruling bureaucracy subordinates the whole economy to military and economic competition with the West (and, today, with China). This compels a level of accumulation which cannot be sustained by resources. And it leads the mass of the population – the workers and collective farmers – to such a deep alienation from their own work activity as not to care about the quality of their output.

The faults which the economic reformers focus on – the waste, the shoddy character of a lot of goods, the lack of interest of shop-floor workers in their work, the giant projects which rust, unused – are all matched within the giant corporations of Western capitalism. The disaster of the nuclear power plant at Chernobyl was matched by Three Mile Island in the USA and, before that, by the Windscale accident in Britain in 1957. The waste in Russian industry is matched by the idle modern steel and chemical plants scattered through Western Europe and North America, victims of the market which so many of the reformers see as Russia's salvation.

Russia may suffer from shoddy output. But so do whole industries of the West – witness the experience of countries like Britain where the system-building boom of the 1960s and early 1970s produced hundreds of thousands of flats and houses that were virtually unfit for human habitation less than 15 years later. If Russian bureaucrats try to dump low quality goods on an unsuspecting public, so did Western salesmen who pushed the drugs thalidomide and opren, who urged women to use the Dalken shield and who lured people onto the cross-Channel ferry *Herald of Free Enterprise*. Far from the market punishing the giant firms involved, it has often enabled them to reap massive profits.

Even firms that are inefficient in narrow cash terms are rarely driven into outright bankruptcy under conditions of modern Western capitalism: the state moves in to bail them out, as it did with Chrysler in the US, AEG in West Germany, Massey Ferguson in Canada and Britain. The units of modern capitalism are so large that the devastation threatened by leaving everything to the play of free market forces is too great even for the most market-oriented of governments, such as Thatcher's in Britain and Reagan's in the US. As a result measurements of in-firm inefficiency (baptised by one economist 'x-inefficiency') suggest that many firms could be working at double their present productivity.[64]

The Russian economy is half the size of its main competitor, the United States. It cannot afford to operate with smaller units of production than its rival. So the concentration of production is proportionately higher, and the impact of particular cases of inefficiency and waste proportionately bigger. And Russia's rulers certainly cannot deal with these simply by using the market to drive major units out of business, since the devastation caused would be so much greater than in the US.

The Russian leadership today is therefore caught in a terrible dilemma. It dares not leave things as they are any longer. Economic stagnation, it fears, could suddenly lead to the same sort of popular insurgency that gave birth to *Solidarnosc* in Poland in 1980. Yet it is afraid to push reform through consistently and does not even know if reform will work. It swings from one policy to another and back again, to the accompaniment of bitter rows inside the bureaucracy itself. These can make it increasingly difficult for the bureaucracy to impose its will on the rest of the population. Such were the ingredients which opened the way for the events of East Germany in 1953, Hungary in 1956 and Czechoslovakia in 1968.

Marx wrote in 1859 that 'from forms of development of productive forces', existing 'relations of production . . . turn into fetters. Then begins an epoch of social revolution.' The relations of production established by Stalinist bureaucracy have quite clearly become such fetters. Russia could well be on its way to a new 'epoch of social revolution'.

Marx warned that it is impossible to 'determine with the precision of natural science' the 'legal, political, religious, aesthetic or philosophical – in short, ideological, forms in which men become conscious of the conflict and fight it out'. We certainly cannot foresee either the speed at which the new period will develop in Russia or the political and ideological formations which will be thrown up. What we can say, with certainty, however, is that the bureaucracy faces a period of very grave crisis. This crisis has already seen the biggest nationalist demonstrations since the 1920s and a proliferation of reformist arguments. Working-class struggles are likely to follow. But if workers are to impose their solution to the crisis they will need to have a clear understanding of where the system comes from and what its dynamics are – an understanding that can only come from a theory of state capitalism like that developed by Tony Cliff forty years ago.

Appendix: An examination of Trotsky's definition of Russia as a degenerated workers' state

Can a state not under workers' control be a workers' state? · Russia's definition as a workers' state and the marxist theory of the state · The form of property considered independently of the relations of production - a metaphysical abstraction · Arab feudalism - an example of class society based on state property · The Russian bureaucracy - a gendarme who appears in the process of distribution? · Social revolution or political revolution? · Trotsky's last book · The internal forces are not able to restore individual capitalism in Russia : what conclusion as regards its class character? · The 'new democracies' and the definition of Russia as a workers' state · Are Russia's war victories proof that she is a workers' state? · What prevented Trotsky from renouncing the theory that Russia is a workers' state?

Trotsky's analysis of the Stalinist regime has its point of departure in Bolshevism, counterposes marxism and Stalinism, the October socialist revolution and the bureaucratic counter-revolution. Being a disciple of Trotsky and believing with him that what is vital in assessing Stalinism is to approach it from the standpoint of its relation to Marxism-Leninism, the present writer thinks it is necessary to devote the greatest attention to a critical assessment of Trotsky's analysis of the Stalinist regime.

Can a state not under workers' control be a workers' state?

In Trotsky's works we find two different and quite contradictory definitions of a workers' state. According to one, the criterion of workers' state is whether the proletariat has direct or indirect control, no matter how restricted, over the state power: that is, whether the proletariat can get rid of the bureaucracy by reform alone, without the need for revolution. In 1931 he wrote:

> The recognition of the present Soviet State as a workers' state not only signifies that the bourgeoisie can conquer power in no other way than by armed uprising but also that the proletariat of the USSR has not forfeited the possibility of submitting the bureaucracy to it, or reviving the Party again and of mending the regime of the dictatorship – without a new revolution, with the methods and on the road of reform.[1]

In a letter to Borodai, a member of the Opposition group called Democratic Centralists, he expresses this idea even more clearly. The letter is undated, but all indications show that it was written at the end of 1928. He writes:

> 'Is the degeneration of the apparatus and of the Soviet power a fact? That is the second question,' you write.
> There is no doubt that the degeneration of the Soviet apparatus is considerably more advanced than the same process in the Party apparatus. Nevertheless, it is the Party that decides. At present, this means: the Party apparatus. The question thus comes down to the same thing: is the proletarian kernel of the Party, assisted by the working class, capable of triumphing over the autocracy of the Party apparatus which is fusing with the state apparatus? Whoever replies in advance that it is *incapable*, thereby speaks not only of the necessity of a new party on a new foundation, but also of the necessity of a second and new proletarian revolution.[1]

Later in the same letter he says:

If the Party is a corpse, a new party must be built on a new spot, and the working class must be told about it openly. If Thermidor is completed, and if the dictatorship of the proletariat is liquidated, the banner of the second proletarian revolution must be unfurled. That is how we would act if the road of reform, for which we stand, proved hopeless.'

Trotsky's second definition has a fundamentally different criterion. No matter how independent the state machine be from the masses, and even if the only way of getting rid of the bureaucracy be by revolution, so long as the means of production are statified the state remains a workers' state with the proletariat the ruling class. Thus, in 'The Revolution Betrayed', Trotsky writes:

The nationalisation of the land, the means of industrial production, transport, and exchange, together with the monopoly of foreign trade, constitutes the basis of the Soviet social structure. Through these relations, established by the proletarian revolution, the nature of the Soviet Union as a proletarian state is for us basically defined.'

Three conclusions are to be drawn from this:

a. Trotsky's second definition of the workers' state negates the first.

b. If the second definition is correct, the Communist manifesto was incorrect in saying: 'The proletariat will use its political supremacy to wrest, by degrees, all capital from the bourgeoisie, to centralise all instruments of production in the hands of the state . . .'; and it was incorrect in saying: 'the first step in the revolution by the working class is to raise the proletariat to the position of the ruling class.' Furthermore, in this case, neither the Paris Commune nor the Bolshevik dictatorship were workers' states as the former did not statify the means of production at all, and the latter did not do so for some time.

c. If the state is the repository of the means of production and the workers do not control it, they do not own the means of production, i.e. they are not the ruling class. The first definition admits this. The second avoids it, but does not disprove it.

Russia's definition as a workers' state and the marxist theory of the state

The assumption that Russia is a degenerated workers' state must lead to conclusions in direct contradiction to the marxist concept of the state. An analysis of the role of what Trotsky called political revolution and social counter-revolution will prove this.

In 'The Revolution Betrayed' Trotsky writes:

In order better to understand the character of the present Soviet Union, let us make two different hypotheses about its future. Let us assume first that the Soviet bureaucracy is over-thrown by a revolutionary party having all the attributes of the old Bolshevism, enriched moreover by the world experience of the recent period. Such a party would begin with the restoration of democracy in the trade unions and the Soviets. It would be able to and would have to, restore freedom of Soviet parties. Together with the masses, and at their head, it would carry out a ruthless purgation of the State apparatus. It would abolish ranks and decorations, all kinds of privileges, and would limit inequality in the payment of labour to the life necessities of the economy and the State apparatus. It would give the youth the free opportunity to think independently, learn, criticise and grow. It would introduce profound changes in the distribution of the national income in correspondence with the interests and will of the worker and peasant masses. But so far as concerns property relations, the new power would not have to resort to revolutionary measures. It would retain and further develop the experiment of planned economy. After the political revolution – that is, the deposing of the bureaucracy – the proletariat would have to introduce in the economy a series of very important reforms, but not another social revolution . . .

If – to adopt a second hypothesis – a bourgeois party were to overthrow the ruling Soviet caste, it would find no small number of ready servants among the present bureaucrats, administrators, technicians, directors party secretaries, and privileged upper circles in general. A purgation of the state apparatus would, of course, be necessary in this case too. But a bourgeois restoration would probably have to clean out fewer people than a revolutionary party. The chief task of the new power would be to restore private property in the means of production ... Notwithstanding that the Soviet bureaucracy has gone far towards preparing a bourgeois restoration, the new regime would have to introduce in the matter of forms of property and methods of industry, not a reform, but a social revolution.[1]

Let us examine this. During bourgeois *political* revolutions, for instance the French revolutions of 1830 and 1848, the form of government changed to a greater or lesser degree, but *the type of state remained the same* – 'special bodies of armed men, prisons, etc.' independent of the people and serving the capitalist class.

Hitler's victory in Germany certainly brought with it a large-scale purge of the state apparatus, but the state machine as a whole was not smashed, remaining fundamentally the same. There is a much closer connection between content and form in a workers' state than in any other state. Even, therefore, if we assume that political revolutions can take place in a workers' state, one thing is clear: the same workers' state machine must continue to exist as such after, as before, the political proletarian revolution. If Russia is a workers' state, even though the revolutionary workers' party may carry out a large scale 'purge' of the state apparatus when it comes to power, it must be able to use and will use the existing state machine: on the other hand, if the bourgeoisie comes to power, it will not be able to use the existing state machine but it will be compelled to smash it and build another on its ruins.

Are those the conditions obtaining in Russia? To pose the

question correctly goes half-way to answering it. It is surely evident that the revolutionary party will not use the MVD nor the bureaucracy nor the standing army. The revolutionary party will have to smash the existing state and replace it by Soviets, people's militia, etc.

As against this, if the bourgeoisie comes to power, it can certainly use the MVD, the regular army, etc. Trotsky avoids the application of the marxist theory of the state to the political revolution and social counter-revolution in Russia partly by saying that the revolutionary party 'would begin with the restoration of democracy in the trade unions and the Soviets'. But actually there are neither trade unions nor Soviets in Russia in which democracy can be restored. The question is not one of reforming the state machine, but of smashing it and building a new state.

Whether we assume that the proletariat must smash the existing state machine on coming to power while the bourgeoisie can use it, or whether we assume that neither the proletariat nor the bourgeoisie can use the existing state apparatus (the 'purgation of the State apparatus' necessarily involving such a deep change as would transform it qualitatively) – on both assumptions we must come to the conclusion that Russia is *not* a workers' state. To assume that the proletariat and the bourgeoisie can use the same state machine as the instrument of their supremacy is tantamount to a repudiation of the revolutionary concept of the state expressed by Marx, Engels, Lenin and Trotsky.

The form of property considered independently of the relations of production - a metaphysical abstraction

Every marxist recognizes that the concept of private property in itself, independent of the relations of production, is a supra-historical abstraction. Human history knows the private property of the slave system, the feudal system, the capitalist system, all of which are fundamentally different from one another. Marx ridiculed Proudhon's attempt to define private property independently of the relations of production. What transforms the means of production into capital is the sum total of the relations of production. As Marx said:

> In each historical epoch, property has developed differently and under a set of entirely different social relations. Thus to define bourgeois property is nothing less than to give an exposition of all the social relations of bourgeois production. To try to give a definition of property as of an independent relation, a category apart – an abstract eternal idea – can be nothing but an illusion of metaphysics or jurisprudence.[*]

All the categories which express relations between people in the capitalist process of production – value, price, wages, etc. – constitute an integral part of bourgeois private property. It is the laws of movement of the capitalist system which define the historical social character of capitalist private property, and which differentiate it from other sorts of private property. Proudhon, who abstracted the form of property from the relations of production 'entangled the whole of these economic relations [the capitalist relations of production] in the general juristic conception of "property".'

Therefore, 'Proudhon could not get beyond the answer which *Brissot*, in a similar work, had already, before 1789, given in the same words: "Property is theft." '[?]

That one private property can have a different historical character to another, can be the stronghold of a different class than the other, was made quite clear by Marx. That the same can apply to statified property also, is not so evident. The main reason for this is that the known history of humanity has in the main been the history of the class struggle on the basis of private property. Cases of class differentiation on the basis of other than private property are not very numerous and on the whole not very well known. Nevertheless they have existed.

As the first example let us take a chapter from the history of Europe: the Catholic Church in the Middle Ages.

The Church had tremendous tracts of land on which hundreds of thousands of peasants laboured. The relations between the Church and the peasants were the same feudal relations as existed between the feudal manor owner and his peasants. The Church as such was feudal. At the same time none of the bishops, cardinals, etc. had individual rights over feudal property. It is the relations of production which define the class character of the Church property, which was feudal, notwithstanding the fact that it was not private.

It might be said that the Catholic Church was only an appendage to the feudal system as a whole – hence its feudal character – but this argument is irrelevant, as we do not wish to explain why the Catholic Church rose, concentrating in its hands tremendous tracts of land and entering into feudal relations with the peasants tilling it. We only wish to show that one and the same relations of production can be expressed in different forms of property, the one private, the other institutional.

From the history of the east we may draw numerous examples of systems of economy with deep class differentiations, based not on private property but on state property. Such systems existed in Pharaonic Egypt, Moslem Egypt, Iraq, Persia and India. That the state owned land was, it seems, mainly due to the fact that agriculture depended entirely on the irrigation system in these countries, which in turn was dependent on the activity of the state. The following example is sufficiently instructive to warrant the digression.

Arab feudalism - an example of class society based on state property

Let us examine the main characteristics of Arab feudalism under the Mamelukes. Here the subjugation of the peasants to the strong feudal state was much harsher than in medieval Europe, but the individual member of the ruling class had no individual property rights whatsoever. The Sultan was the only landowner and he used to divide the right to collect the rent in the various regions among the different nobles (called Multazims). While in Europe every feudal lord was the owner of a certain domain which was handed down from father to son, in the Arab East the feudal lord had no permanent domain of his own, but was a member of a class which collectively controlled the land and had the right to appropriate rent. In Syria and Palestine the area from which these feudal lords collected rent was changed from year to year. In Egypt they received the right to collect the rent in a certain area for their whole lives, and their heirs had a prior right in the appointment of the deceased's successor. While in Europe the feudal lord was relatively an independent power as against the king, who was no more than the first feudal lord, in the Arab East only the feudal collective was a factor of any consequence; as individuals the Arab nobles were weak, because they were dependent on the state for their positions. The weakness of the feudal lord as against the state was clearly indicated by the way in which the fiefs were allocated: the Sultan distributed them by lot among the emirs and knights, each getting a portion of land differing in size and quality according to his rank. The Arab nobles were thus divided into different groups with different incomes, the distinction between them being very great (for instance, the 'emirs of the hundred' got 80,000 to 200,000 dinar jayshi a year, 'emir-al-tabl' 23,000 to 30,000, 'emirs of the ten'

9,000 and below, 'emirs of the five' 3,000 and so on). The form of appropriation was much more like that of a state official than that of a European feudal lord. As a result of this dependence of the nobles on the state, an unusual phenomenon recurred in the Arab East. From time to time whole feudal strata were 'purged' and annihilated, others arising in their places. The Arab lords were replaced by the Sultan's freed slaves – the Mamelukes – who were not of Arab origin and did not speak Arabic but Turkish. In the thirteenth and fourteenth centuries they mostly originated from the Mongolian state, the Golden Horde, whose centre was on the banks of the Lower Volga; in the fifteenth and sixteenth centuries they were mainly Caucasian. With the Tsar's increasing resistance to conscription in the Caucasus for the Sultan, the Balkan element (Albanians, Bosnians, etc.) predominated.

The ownership of the land by the state not only prevented the rise of feudalism based on private property, but also of any social group with individualistic tendencies, whatsoever. The town was a military camp; the majority of the artisans were not independent. Even when guilds (Hirfeh) did develop, they did not attain any importance at all in the towns and did not become an independent force of any importance. The government subordinated them to itself by appointing many of the heads of the guilds, making them its officials, and turning the guilds into government organisations.

The fact that the main means of production – the land – belonged not to individuals, but to the state, and that the Arab nobles and the Mamelukes lacked juridical footholds and therefore did not have the right to inherit, did not improve the position of the peasant masses. Nor did the plebeian origin of the Mamelukes effect any change. The concentration of the ruling class of the Arab East in the towns, afforded them great military power over the peasants and, furthermore, increased their appetites. In this, too, they differed from the European feudal lords in the Middle Ages. The produce which the European serfs gave to their feudal lords as rent, was generally not sent out to be sold; the serfs therefore did not need to give their feudal lord more than he and his household needed for the daily use. 'The walls of his (the feudal lord's) stomach set the limits to his exploitation of the peasants.' (Marx). The Arab feudals had different tastes, and their point of view might best be summed up in the words used by Khalif Suliman to his emissary about the peasants: 'Milk till the udder be dry, and let blood to the last drop.'

The mode of production, the form of exploitation, the relation of the toilers to the means of production in the Arab East, was the same as in medieval Europe. The source of income of the ruling class was also the same; the only difference was in the mode of appropriation, in the legal expression of the right to exploit.[8]

The Russian bureaucracy - a gendarme who appears in the process of distribution?

Trotsky writes that the Stalinist state's coercion of the masses is the result of

the fact that the present transitional structure is still full of social contradictions, which in the sphere of *consumption* — most close and sensitively felt by all — are extremely tense, and forever threaten to break over into the sphere of production.[9]

Therefore,

The basis of bureaucratic rule is the poverty of society in objects of consumption, with the resulting struggle of each against all. When there is enough goods in a store the purchasers can come whenever they want to. When there is little goods the purchasers are compelled to stand in line. When the lines are very long, it is necessary to appoint a policeman to keep order. Such is the starting-point of the power of the Soviet bureaucracy. It 'knows' who is to get something and who has to wait.[1]

Is it true that the bureaucracy appears as the 'gendarme' in the process of distribution only, or does it appear so in the process of reproduction as a whole, of which the former is but a subordinate part? This is of infinite theoretical and political importance.

Before attempting to answer this question, let us examine what Marx and Engels thought about the connection between the relations of production and distribution. Marx writes:

> To the single individual distribution naturally appears as a law established by the society determining his position in the sphere of production, within which he produces, and thus antedating production. At the outset the individual has no capital, no landed property. From his birth he is assigned to wage-labor by the social process of distribution. But this very condition of being assigned to wage labor is the result of the existence of capital and landed property as independent agents of production.
>
> From the point of view of society as a whole, distribution seems to antedate and to determine production in another way as well, as a pre-economic fact, so to say. A conquering people divides the land among the conquerors establishing thereby a certain division and form of landed property and determining the character of production; or, it turns the conquered people into slaves and thus makes slave labor the basis of production. Or, a nation, by revolution, breaks up large estates into small parcels of land and by this new distribution imparts to production a new character. Or, legislation perpetuates land ownership in large families or distributes labor as an hereditary privilege and thus fixes it in castes.
>
> In all of these cases, and they are all historic, it is not distribution that seems to be organised and determined by production, but on the contrary, production by distribution.
>
> In the most shallow conception of distribution, the latter appears as a distribution of products and to that extent as further removed from, and quasi-independent of production. But before distribution means distribution of products, it is first a distribution of the means of production, and second, what is practically

another wording of the same fact, it is a distribution of the members of society among the various kinds of production (the subjection of individuals to certain conditions of production). The distribution of products is manifestly a result of this distribution, which is bound up with the process of production and determines the very organisation of the latter.[11]

This extract from Marx, the essence of which is repeated time and time again throughout his works, is sufficient as a point of departure for the analysis of the place of the Stalinist bureaucracy in the economy.

Let us pose these questions in connection with the Russian bureaucracy:

Does the bureaucracy only administer the distribution of means of consumption among the people, or does it also administer the distribution of the people in the process of production? Does the bureaucracy exercise a monopoly over the control of distribution only, or over the control of the means of production as well? Does it ration means of consumption only or does it also distribute the total labour time of society between accumulation and consumption, between the production of means of production and that of means of consumption? Does not the bureaucracy reproduce the scarcity of means of consumption, and thus certain relations of distribution? Do the relations of production prevailing in Russia not determine the relations of distribution which comprise a part of them?

Social revolution or political revolution?

If one agrees with Trotsky that a revolution by the working class of Russia against the bureaucracy is not a social revolution, one enters into immediate contradictions with marxian sociology.

The Civil War in the United States was defined by Marx

as a social revolution. The liberation of slaves and their transformation into wage-earners, was a social revolution: one class in society disappeared and gave place to another. Why should the overthrow of Stalin's bureaucracy and the liberation of the millions of slaves in the labour camps not be a social revolution, but merely a political one? The agrarian revolution, transferring the feudal estates to peasant hands, transferring serfs into free peasants, was a social revolution. Why should not the cessation of state plunder, of 'obligatory deliveries', the transformation of the kolkhozes into the real property of the kolkhoz members, owned and controlled by them, not be a social revolution?

A political revolution assumes that with the change in government, only individuals, groups, or ruling layers change, but that the same class retains power. Accordingly, the bureaucrat and the worker, the NKVD guard and his prisoner, belong to the same class. How can this be, when their positions in the process of production are so antagonistic, when their attitudes to the means of production not only are not the same, but actually clash sharply?

If we accept that the workers and bureaucrats do belong to the same class, then we must conclude that in Russia there is a struggle inside one class, but no struggle between classes, that is, no class struggle. Does not this take the ground from under Trotsky's attack on Stalin's assertion that there is no class struggle in Russia?

Trotsky's last book

As the working class in Russia was the only one to hold power for any length of time, as its overthrow took an unpredictable form in the very complicated economic and political circumstances of Russia, it is no accident that even Trotsky with his brilliant analytical faculties had to re-evaluate his basic analysis of the Stalinist regime from time to time. A tremendous shift took place in Trotsky's position, if only in emphasis from the time the acceptance of the theory of the degenerated workers' state was a condition for membership of the Left Opposition till the time that Trotsky did not propose the exclusion of the anti-defencists from the International, although he did not accept their position. It was no accident that in his polemics with Shachtman at the end of 1939 and in 1940 he could say that even though he might be in a minority against Shachtman and Burnham, he would oppose a split and would continue to fight for his position in the united party.[12]

A clear step in the direction of a new evaluation of the bureaucracy as a ruling class finds expression in Trotsky's last book, *Stalin*. In explaining the social nature of the Stalinist bureaucracy's rise to power he said:

> The substance of the Thermidor was, is and could not fail to be social in character. It stood for the crystallisation of a new privileged stratum, the creation of a new sub-stratum for the economically dominant class. There were two pretenders to this rule: the petty bourgeoisie and the bureaucracy itself. They fought shoulder to shoulder [in the battle to break] the resistance of the proletarian vanguard. When that task was accomplished a savage struggle broke out between them. The bureaucracy became frightened of its isolation, its divorcement from the proletariat. Alone it could not crush the *kulak* nor the petty bourgeoisie that had grown and continued to grow on the basis of the NEP; it had to have the aid of the proletariat. Hence its concerted effort to present its struggle against the petty bourgeoisie for the surplus products and for power as the struggle of the proletariat against attempts at capitalist restoration.[13]

The bureaucracy, Trotsky says, while pretending to fight against capitalistic restoration, in reality used the proletariat only to crush the kulaks for 'the crystallisation of a new privileged stratum, the creation of a new substratum for the economically dominant class'. One of the pretenders to the role of the economically dominant class, he says, is the bureaucracy. Great significance must be attached to this formulation especially if we connect this analysis of the fight between the bureaucracy and the kulaks with Trotsky's definition of the class struggle. He says:

> The class struggle is nothing else than the struggle for surplus-produce. He who owns surplus-produce is master of the situation – owns wealth, owns the State, has the key to the Church, to the courts, to the sciences and to the arts.[14]

The fight between the bureaucracy and the kulaks was, according to Trotsky's last conclusion, the 'struggle ... for the surplus products'.

The internal forces are not able to restore individual capitalism in Russia: what conclusion as regards its class character?

When Trotsky spoke about the danger of social counter-revolution in Russia, he meant the restoration of capitalism, based on private property. Stalinist Bonapartism is represented as a balancing factor between two forces on the national arena – on the one hand the working class supporting statified property and planning, and, on the other, the bourgeois elements striving towards individual property. He writes:

> It [the bureaucracy] continues to preserve State property only to the extent that it fears the proletariat. This saving fear is nourished and supported by the illegal party of Bolshevik-Leninists, which is the most conscious expression of the socialist tendencies opposing that bourgeois reaction with which the Thermidorian bureaucracy is completely saturated. As a conscious political force the bureaucracy has betrayed the revolution. But a victorious revolution is fortunately not only a programme and a banner, not only political institutions, but also a system of social relations. To betray it is not enough. You have to overthrow it.[15]

This presentation exposes most clearly the juridical abstraction of the form of property, and it exposes most clearly, therefore, the internal contradictions of the analysis. The Russian proletariat was not strong enough to keep its control over the means of production, and was ousted by the bureaucracy, but it is strong enough to prevent the promulgation of this relation in law! The proletariat was not strong enough to check a most antagonistic distribution of the product, to prevent the bureaucracy from brutally depressing its standard of living and denying it the most elementary rights, to prevent the sentence of millions of its members to slave labour in Siberia; but it is strong enough to defend the form of property! As though there is any relation between people and property other than that based on the relations of production.

Moreover, if the fear of the proletariat is the only factor preventing the restoration of private capitalism in Russia; if, as Trotsky said, the bureaucracy are conscious restorationists, his statement that the Stalinist regime is as stable as a pyramid standing on its head, would have proved correct, and his prognosis of the fate of the statified economy during the war would have been realised. He summed up his position thus:

In the heated atmosphere of war one can expect sharp turns toward individualistic principles in agriculture and in handicraft industry, toward the attraction of foreign and 'allied' capital, breaks in the monopoly of foreign trade, the weakening of governmental control over trusts, the sharpening or competition between the trusts, their conflicts with workers, etc. In the political sphere these processes may mean the completion of Bonapartism with the corresponding change or a number of changes in property relations. In other words, in case of a protracted war accompanied by the *passivity of the world proletariat* the internal social contradictions in the USSR not only might lead but would have to lead to a *bourgeois-Bonapartist* counter-revolution.[16]

Before the experience of the World War II, it was an understandable if incorrect assumption that private capitalism could be restored in Russia without its occupation by an imperialist power. But the victory of the concentrated, statified Russian economy over the German war machine silenced all talk of such a possibility.

The fact that external forces could restore individual capitalism, or even that a devastating war, accompanied by the annihilation of most of the Russian population, could cast her back to a much lower level of historical development than private capitalism is not excluded, however.

When Trotsky defined Russia as a society in transition, he emphasised correctly that as such it must by its own immanent laws lead either to the victory of socialism, or to the restoration of private capitalism. If the latter is ruled out, one of three possibilities remain:

1. The internal forces in Russia lead in one direction only – towards communism. This point of view is held by the Stalinists and also by Bruno R.*

2. Russian society is neither capitalist nor socialist, and although the productive forces rise uninterruptedly it will not lead to communism; although the exploitation of the masses continues unabated, it will not lead to capitalism. This is the theory of the 'Managerial Revolution' and of Bureaucratic Collectivism in Shachtman's 1943 formulation.

3. Russian society is either a transitional society which has two possible paths before it – state capitalism or socialism – or it is already state capitalism.

Denying the possibility of the internal forces leading to private capitalism and at the same time repudiating Stalinism, Bureaucratic Collectivism (according to both Bruno R's and

---

* In his book *La Bureaucratisation du Monde*, Paris, 1939.

Shachtman's formulation) and Burnhamism, we are left with the third alternative only.

Under both state capitalism and a workers' state, the state is the repository of the means of production. The difference between the two systems cannot be in the form of property. Therefore the state ownership of the means of production which Trotsky uses as the basis for his definition of the class character of Russia must be dismissed as an unsound criterion.

The 'new democracies' and the definition of Russia as a workers' state

The appearance of the 'new democracies' provided a test of the definition of Russia as a workers' state.

If state property, planning and the monopoly of foreign trade define a country as a workers' state, then without doubt Russia, as well as the 'new democracies' are workers' states. This means that in the latter proletarian revolutions have taken place. These were led by the Stalinists on the basis of national unity, governmental coalitions with the bourgeoisie and chauvinism which led to the expulsion of millions of German toilers and their families. Such policies merely served to oil the wheels of the proletarian revolution.

What, then, is the future of international socialism; what is its historical justification? The Stalinist parties have all the advantages over the international socialists – a state apparatus, mass organisations, money, etc. etc. The only advantage they lack is the internationalist class ideology. But if it is possible to accomplish the proletarian revolution without this ideology, why should the workers move away from Stalinism?

If a social revolution took place in the Eastern European countries without a revolutionary proletarian leadership, we must conclude that in future social revolutions, as in past ones, the masses will do the fighting but not the leading.

To assume that the 'new democracies' are workers' states means to accept that in principle the proletarian revolution is, just as the bourgeois wars were, based on the deception of the people.

If the 'new democracies' are workers' states, Stalin has realised the proletarian revolution; moreover he has carried it out quite speedily. Forty-seven years passed by from the Paris Commune till the establishment of the first workers' state in a country of 140 million people. Less than forty years passed until a number of additional countries became workers' states. In the West, Poland, Yugoslavia, Hungary, Rumania, Bulgaria and Czechoslovakia added their 75 million people (and this does not include the Baltic states, Eastern Poland and Bessarabia, containing 20 million people, which were annexed to the USSR). In the East, China, with 600 million people, was added. If these countries are workers' states, then why marxism, why the Fourth International?

If the 'new democracies' are workers' states, what Marx and Engels said about the socialist revolution being 'history conscious of itself' is refuted. Refuted is Engels' statement:

> It is only from this point [the socialist revolution] that men, with full consciousness, will fashion their own history; it is only from this point that the social causes set in motion by men will have, predominantly and in constantly increasing measure, the effects willed by men. It is humanity's leap from the realm of necessity into the realm of freedom.[17]

Rosa Luxemburg, too, must have spoken nonsense in her summing up of what all the marxist teachers wrote about the place of proletarian consciousness in a revolution:

> In all the class struggles of the past, carried through in the interests of the minorities, and in which, to use the words of Marx, 'all development took place in opposition to the great masses of

328 · *State Capitalism in Russia*

the people', one of the essential conditions of action was the ignorance of these masses with regard to the real aims of the struggle, its material content, and its limits. This discrepancy was, in fact, the specific historical basis of the 'leading role' of the 'enlightened' bourgeoisie, which corresponded with the role of the masses as docile followers. But, as Marx wrote as early as 1845, 'as the historical action deepens the number of masses engaged in it must increase!' The class struggle of the proletariat is the 'deepest' of all historical actions up to our day, it embraces the whole of the lower layers of the people, and, from the moment that society became divided into classes, it is the *first* movement which is in accordance with the *real* interests of the masses. That is why the enlightenment of the masses with regard to their tasks and methods is an indispensable historical condition for socialist action, just as in former periods the ignorance of the masses was the condition for the action of the dominant classes.[18]

Are Russia's war victories proof that she is a workers' state?

Whereas Trotsky, following up his analysis that Russia is a degenerated workers' state, predicted that the bureaucracy would not stand up to a war, many Trotskyists today conclude from these very victories that Russia is a workers' state. This post factum argument, however, cannot stand up to criticism.

The argument can be broken into two parts: 1. The enthusiasm of the masses in the war proves that they have something to lose besides their chains, that they are the ruling class. 2. The industrial-military strength of Russia proves the historical superiority of the Russian regime over capitalism.

The first part of the argument, prevalent in the Fourth International press in 1941–43, had the bottom knocked out of it by the course of events. The German army, too, in the years when all hope of victory had already vanished, fought with all its strength to the very gates of Berlin. Had the German soldiers also something to lose besides their chains? Was the German working class also the ruling class?

As regards the second part of the argument, there is no doubt that large scale enterprise has tremendous advantages over small-scale. This, indeed, explains to a large extent the superiority of American production to British although both are based on the same social system. Russian industry, newer and technically more modern, is built on an even larger scale than American. Besides, the overlapping and lack of co-ordination prevalent in the countries of individual capitalism is avoided in Russia by state ownership of the means of production. And yet another advantage in a war, which many other countries cannot claim, is that her workers lack all democratic rights. In Russia, as in Nazi Germany, it is possible to produce guns instead of butter, to transfer millions of workers from the West to beyond the Urals, housing them in dug-outs in the ground, without fear of organised opposition. The authority of the state over the economy and over the workers – these are the strong points of Russia's industrial-military production. But these are the very factors which explain Nazi Germany's military superiority over bourgeois democratic France, which, as we know, collapsed before her advancing armies like a house of cards, and even Britain, this ex-'workshop of the world', was saved from invasion only by the English Channel, by American help from the West and by the Russian threat to Germany from the East.

Germany's military victories of the beginning of the war fooled some people into believing that Germany was not a capitalist country, but represented a new and superior system of society. Burnham was notable among these.

The belief that the Russian military victories in themselves prove that Russia represents a new system of society has no more foundation than the belief that Nazi Germany did so.

What prevented Trotsky from renouncing the theory that Russia is a workers' state?

One tends to see the future in the trappings of the past. For many years the socialists who fought exploitation fought against the owners of private property – the bourgeoisie. When Lenin, Trotsky and the rest of the Bolshevik leaders said that if the workers' state of Russia remained isolated it was doomed, they envisaged that doom in a definite form – the restoration of private property, while state property was seen as the fruit of the struggle of the working people. From here it was only one step to the conclusion that if state ownership existed in Russia, it was thanks to bureaucracy's 'fear of the working class', and conversely, if the bureaucracy strove to increase its privileges (including the right of inheritance) it strove to restore private ownership. *Past experience* was Trotsky's main impediment in grasping the fact that a triumph for reaction does not always mean a return to the original point of departure, but may lead to a decline, in a spiral form, in which are combined elements of the pre-revolutionary and of the revolutionary pasts, the latter subordinated to the former; the old capitalist class content will then emerge in a new, 'socialist' form, thus serving as further confirmation of the law of combined development – a law which Trotsky himself did so much to develop.

In summing up it may be said that while Trotsky contributed incomparably more than any other marxist to an understanding of the Stalinist regime, his analysis suffered from one serious limitation – a conservative attachment to formalism, which by its nature is contradictory to marxism that subordinates form to content.

Appendix 2:

The theory of bureaucratic collectivism: A critique

Introduction

For obvious reasons, discussion of the nature of Soviet society was central to the thinking of most socialists of the last generation.

The conception of Russia under Stalin and his heirs as socialism, or a deformed kind of socialism ('degenerated workers' state' in the language of dogmatic 'orthodox' Trotskyists), has met two kinds of critique by Marxists. The first, to which the present writer subscribes, defines the Stalinist regime as state capitalist. The second sees it as neither socialism of any sort – nor capitalism. This last school of thought coined a special term for the Stalinist regime – Bureaucratic Collectivism. The first writer to coin this term was the Italian Marxist, Bruno R, in his book **La Bureaucratisation du Monde** (Paris 1939). The same term was adopted and the idea developed (without acknowledgement of the work of Bruno R) by the American socialist, Max Shachtman.

The subject of the present article is an evaluation and criticism of this thesis.

It is difficult to make a critique of Bureaucratic Collectivism because the authors never actually published a developed account of the theory. It is true that Shachtman wrote hundreds of pages of criticism of the theory that Stalinist Russia was a socialist country or a workers' state of any sort (he dismissed the theory of state capitalism in a sentence or two). But he wrote scarcely a paragraph on the laws of motion of the 'Bureaucratic Collectivist' economy, and made no analysis at all of the *specific* character of the class struggle within it. The place of Bureaucratic Collectivist society in the chain of historical development is not clearly stated, and, in any case, Shachtman's account is often inconsistent.

A central thesis of the present article is that the theoretical poverty of the theory of Bureaucratic Collectivism is not accidental. We will try to show that the theory of Bureaucratic Collectivism is only *negative*; it is thus empty, abstract, and therefore arbitrary.

Criticism of the theory will suggest a number of characteristics that are common – implicitly at least – to other conceptions of Stalinism – from that of the apologists to that of George Orwell's **1984**. In criticising the theory, the strength or weakness of the alternative theory of Stalinist Russia – as state capitalist – will emerge.

The place of Bureaucratic Collectivism in history

At first glance what is more plausible than describing Stalinist Russia as neither a capitalist nor a workers' state? But this simplification is of little value, for it tells us little about the regime; feudalism too was neither capitalism nor socialism, similarly slave society, and any other regime that has not existed but is created by our imagination. Spinoza was right when he said that 'definition is negation', but not all negations are definitions. The statement that the Stalinist regime was neither capitalist nor socialist left the latter's historical identity undetermined. Hence Shachtman could say on one occasion that Bureaucratic Collectivism was more progressive than capitalism (however unprogressive it was, compared with socialism), and, a few years later, that it was more reactionary than capitalism.

Shachtman first called Russia a Bureaucratic Collectivist state in 1941. A resolution on the Russian question passed at the 1941 Convention of his organisation, the now-defunct Workers' Party, stated:

> From the standpoint of socialism, the bureaucratic collectivist state is a reactionary social order; in relation to the capitalist world, it is on an historically more progressive plane.

On the basis of this, a policy of 'conditional defensism' was adopted. The Resolution states:

> The revolutionary proletariat can consider a revolutionary (that is, a critical, entirely independent, class) defensist position with regard to the Stalinist regime only under conditions where the decisive issue in the war is the attempt by a hostile force to restore capitalism in Russia, where this issue is not subordinated to other, more dominant, issues. Thus, in case of a civil war in which one section of the bureaucracy seeks to restore capitalist private property, it is possible for the revolutionary vanguard to fight with the army of the Stalinist regime against the army of capitalist restoration. Thus, in case of a war by which world imperialism seeks to subdue the Soviet Union and acquire a new lease of life by reducing Russia to an imperialist colony, it is possible for the proletariat to take a revolutionary defensist position in Russia. Thus, in case of a civil war organised against the existing regime by an army basing itself on 'popular discontent' but actually on the capitalist and semi-capitalist elements still existing in the country, and aspiring to the restoration of capitalism, it is again possible that the proletariat would fight in the army of Stalin against the army of capitalist reaction. In all those or similar cases, the critical support of the proletariat is possible only if the proletariat is not yet prepared itself to overthrow the Stalinist regime.

In logic, when, a few months after this Convention, Hitler's Germany attacked Russia, Shachtman and his followers should have come to the defence of Russia, as it was 'on an historically more progressive plane'.

The argument Shachtman put now was that, even though Russia was more progressive than capitalist Germany, her war was nevertheless only a subordinate part of the total war, the basic character of which was a struggle between two capitalist imperialist camps. He wrote:

The character of the war, the conduct of the war and (for the present) the outcome of the war, are determined by the two couples of imperialist titans which dominate each camp respectively, the United States and Great Britain, and Germany and Japan. (Within each of the two, in turn, there is a senior and a junior partner!) *All* the other countries in the two great coalitions are reduced to vassalage to the giants which differs in each case only in degree. This vassalage is determined by the economic (industrial-technical), and therefore the financial, and therefore the political, and therefore the military, domination of the war by the two great 'power-couples'. Italy is less dependent upon the masters of its coalition than Hungary, and Hungary less than Slovakia. But these facts do not alter the state of the vassalage – they only determine its degree. Stalinist Russia is less dependent upon the masters of its coalition than China (it would lead us too far afield to show in what sense, however, it is even more dependent upon US-England than China), and China less than the Philippines. But again, these facts only determine the degree of their vassalage. Except, therefore, for inconsequential cranks and special pleaders in the bourgeois world, everyone in it understands the total nature of the war as a whole; the total nature of each coalition; the relative position and weight of each sector of the coalition; the mutual interdependence of all fronts.[1]

Thus, although Bureaucratic Collectivism is more progressive than capitalism, a defeatist position was adopted because of Russia's vassalage to Anglo-American imperialism. The **New International** of September 1941 emphasised the point:

Stalin has lost the last vestige of independence . . . Soviet diplomacy is already dictated in London.

We shall not dwell on the factual mistakes. These are less serious than the method by which Shachtman arrives at his conclusions. Marxism demands that from sociological definitions we draw political conclusions. When the course of the war contradicted his judgement of Russia as a vassal state, Shachtman should have rejected his previous defeatist position, for Bureaucratic Collectivism, he said, is more progressive than capitalism. Instead, he held to the political conclusion of defeatism and altered the sociological basis. Bureaucratic Collectivism now came to be called the new barbarism, the decline of civilisation, etc. Yet in no document did he give any new analysis of the Russian economy after the Resolution of the 1941 Convention.

The only two constant alements in the theory have been: first, the conclusion that in any concrete conditions, Stalinist Russia must not be defended (no matter that the concrete conditions change all the time); second, that the name of the Stalinist regime is Bureaucratic Collectivism.

With regard to the first element, serious Marxists, while seeking to hold consistently to the same principles, often change their tactics, as tactics must change with changing circumstances. Marxists should not decide on one tactic and hold to it when the justification for it is proved incorrect. This is eclecticism, impressionism. But exactly this approach was adopted by Shachtman. He draws the same conclusion from two opposite and mutually exclusive assumptions, the one that Bureaucratic Collectivism is more progressive than capitalism, the other that it is the image of barbarism, more reactionary. Defeatism is the tactic. Why? Once because Russia was not the main power, but only a vassal of Anglo-American imperialism, now because Russia is a major imperialist power which threatens to conquer the world.

As for the name, we might well repeat Marx's apt criticism of Proudhon, who used to invent lofty words, thinking in this way to advance science. Marx quoted the following: '*wo Begriffe felhen Da stellt zur rechten Zeit ein Wort sich ein.*' (Where there is a lack of ideas, an empty phrase will do.)

In Marx's and Engels' analysis of capitalism, the fundamentals – the place of capitalism in history, its internal contradictions, etc. – remained constant from their first approach to the problem until the end of their lives. Their later years brought only elaborations of and additions to the basic theme. The theory of Bureaucratic Collectivism in its short history has had a much less happy fate. Shachtman first considered Bureaucratic Collectivism more progressive than capitalism, and then as 'totalitarian barbarism'. Another proponent of the theory, Bruno R, *at one and the same time* considers it both a slave society and the threshold of a peaceful transition to communism.

Bruno R on Bureaucratic Collectivism

Bruno R differs from Shachtman in many fundamentals. His analysis of the genesis of Bureaucratic Collectivism, for instance, is basically different from Shachtman's. They agree on the genesis of the system in Russia. But when they step beyond its borders, they are at variance. While the Resolution of the Workers' Party Convention of 1941 maintained that 'bureaucratic collectivism is a nationally-limited phenomenon, appearing in history in the course of a single conjuncture of circumstances,' Bruno R saw it as a society which would replace capitalism on a world scale through the expropriation of the bourgeoisie by the Stalinist bureaucracy and the fascist bureaucracy. However, on the characterisation, description, and analysis of Bureaucratic Collectivism *as such* – as a social order – they are in entire agreement.

In his book **La Bureaucratisation du Monde** (Paris 1939), Bruno R writes:

In our opinion, the USSR represents a new type of society led by a new social class: that is our conclusion. Collectivised property actually belongs to this class which has introduced a new – and superior – system of production. Exploitation is transferred from the individual to the class.[2]

In our opinion, the Stalinist regime is an intermediary regime; it eliminates outdated capitalism, but does not rule out Socialism for the future. It is a new social form based on class property and class exploitation.[3]

In our opinion, in the USSR, the property owners are the bureaucrats, for it is they who hold force in their hands. It is they who direct the economy as was usual amongst the bourgeoisie; it is they who appropriate the profits to themselves, as was usual amongst all exploiting classes, and it is they who fix wages and the prices of goods: once again, it is the bureaucrats.[4]

What is the character of the ruled class? Does there exist a Russian proletariat, or, just as the bourgeoisie was substituted by a new exploiting class, is the proletariat substituted by a new exploited class? Bruno R answers thus:

Exploitation occurs exactly as in a society based on slavery: the subject of the State works for the one master who has bought him, he becomes a part of his master's capital, he represents the livestock which must be cared for and housed and whose reproduction is a matter of great importance for the master. The payment of a so-called wage, consisting partly of State services and goods, should not induce us into error and lead us to suppose the existence of a Socialist form of remuneration: for indeed, it only means the upkeep of a slave! The sole fundamental difference is that in ancient times the slaves did not have the honour of carrying arms, whilst the modern slaves are skilfully trained in the art of war . . . The Russian working class are no longer proletarians; they are merely slaves. It is a class of slaves in its economic substance and in its social manifestations. It kneels as the 'little Father' passes by and deifies him, it assumes all the characteristics of servility and allows itself to be tossed about from one end of the immense empire to the other. It digs canals, builds roads and railways, just as in ancient times this same class erected the Pyramids or the Coliseum.

A small part of this class have not yet lost themselves in complete agnosticism; retaining their faith, they meet in caves for purposes of discussion, as of old, the Christians praying in the catacombs. From time to time the Pretorians organise a raid and round everybody up. 'Monster' trials are staged, in the style of Nero, and the accused, instead of defending themselves, say *'mea culpa'*. The Russian workers differ completely from the proletarians in every respect, they have become State subjects and have acquired all the characteristics of slaves.

They no longer have anything in common with free workers except the sweat on their brow. The Marxists will truly need Diogenes' lamp if they intend to find any proletarians in the Soviet towns.[5]

Even though Bruno R describes Stalinist Russia as the renewal of slavery (with all the historical retrogression connected with it), he nevertheless says that this regime is more progressive than capitalism, and, further, that it leads directly, without leaps or struggles, to communist society. He says:

We believe that the new society will lead directly to Socialism, because of the enormous volume attained by production.

The leaders (so will now be called those whom we have contemptuously labelled bureaucrats and the new class will be called leading class), having satisfied their material, intellectual and moral needs, may of course find a pleasurable occupation in the constant material, intellectual and moral elevation of the working class.[6]

The totalitarian State should not impress the Marxists. For the time being, it is totalitarian rather in the political than in the economic sense. These factors will be reversed in the course of the forthcoming and normal social developments. The totalitarian State will more and more lose its political characteristics and retain only its administrative characteristics. At the end of this process we will have a classless society and Socialism.[7]

A new 'withering away' – of 'collective slavery', of 'totalitarian bureaucratic collectivism', in communism! And this development Bruno R proudly proclaims *the triumph of historical materialism*! (See particularly the chapter in his book under this name.)

Bruno R's Bureaucratic Collectivism leads directly, automatically, to communism. It is undoubtedly a materialist conception, but it is not dialectical; it is a mechanical, fatalist approach to history which denies the class struggle of the oppressed as the necessary motive force.

The Stalinist Regime – Barbarism?

Shachtman writes about the Stalinist regime:

It is the cruel realisation of the prediction made by all the great socialist scientists, from Marx and Engels onwards, that capitalism must collapse out of an inability to solve its own contradictions and that the alternatives facing mankind are not so much capitalism or socialism as they are: *socialism or barbarism*. Stalinism is that new barbarism.[8]

If the Stalinist regime denotes the decline of civilisation, the reactionary negation of capitalism, then, of course, it is more reactionary than the latter. Capitalism has to be defended from Stalinist barbarism.

But Shachtman ties himself in knots.

When Marx spoke of the 'common ruin of the contending classes' – as in Rome after slave society disintegrated – it was associated with a general decline of the productive forces. The Stalinist regime, with its dynamic development of the productive forces, certainly does not fit this description.

Barbarism in Marx's concept meant the death of the embryo of the future in the womb of the old society. The embryo of socialism in the body of capitalism is social, collective, large-scale production, and associated with it, the working class. The Stalinist regime not only did not weaken these elements, but spurred them on.

The Motive for Exploitation in Bureaucratic Collectivist Society

Shachtman explains the motive for exploitation in Bureaucratic Collectivist society thus: 'In the Stalinist State, production is carried on and extended for the satisfaction of the needs of the bureaucracy, for the increasing of its wealth, its privileges, its power.'

Now if the motive for exploitation under Bureaucratic Collectivism was simply the needs of the rulers, how does this relate to the general historical roots of exploitation in different social systems?

Engels explains why, in the past, society was divided into exploiters and exploited:

The division of society into an exploiting and an exploited class, a ruling and an oppressed class, was the necessary outcome of the low development of production hitherto. So long as the sum of social labour yielded a product which only slightly exceeded what was necessary for the bare existence of all; so long, therefore, *as all or almost all the time of the great majority of the members of society was absorbed in labour, so long was society necessarily divided into classes.* Alongside of this great majority exclusively absorbed in labour, there developed a class, freed from direct productive labour, which managed the general business of society: the direction of labour, affairs of state, justice, science, art and so forth.[9]

In an economy in which the motive for production is the production of use values for the rulers, there are certain limits to the extent of exploitation. Thus, for instance, in feudal society, village and town alike were subjugated to the feudal lords' need for consumption goods, and so long as the produce which the serfs gave to their lord was not widely marketed, 'the walls of his stomach set the limits to his exploitation of the peasant' (Marx). This does not explain the existence of exploitation under capitalism. The walls of the capitalist's stomach are undoubtedly much wider than those of the feudal lord of the Middle Ages, but, at the same time, the productive capacity of capitalism is incomparably greater than that of feudalism. We should therefore be quite mistaken if we explained the increase in the exploitation of the mass of workers as the result of the widening of the walls of the bourgeoisie's stomach.

The need for capital accumulation, dictated by the anarchic competition between capitals, is the motivation for exploitation under capitalism.

Actually, if the Bureaucratic Collectivist economy is geared to the 'needs of the bureaucracy' – is not subordinated to capital accumulation – there is no reason why the rate of exploitation should not decrease in time, and as the productive forces in the modern world are dynamic – this will lead, willy-nilly, to the 'withering away of exploitation'.

With the dynamism of highly developed productive forces, an economy based on gratifying the needs of the rulers can be arbitrarily described as leading to the millenium or to 1984. Bruno R's dream and George Orwell's nightmare – and anything in between – are possible under such a system. The Bureaucratic Collectivist theory is thus entirely capricious and arbitrary in defining the limitation and direction of exploitation under the regime it presumes to define.

Class Relations under Bureaucratic Collectivism

The essence of Shachtman's position is summed up in the statement that the rulers of Russia under Stalin were neither workers nor private owners of capital. What is decisive, according to the Marxist method, in defining the class nature of any society? As the history of all class society is the history of the class struggle, it is clear that what does determine the place of any regime in the chain of historical development are these factors which determine the character of the class struggle in it. Now, the character, the methods and the aims of the class struggle of the oppressed class are dependent on the nature of the oppressed class itself: the position it has in the process of production, the relation between its members in this process, and its relation to the owners of the means of production. These are *not* determined by the mode of appropriation or mode of recruitment of the *ruling* class. A few examples will explain this.

We know that in the Middle Ages the feudal lord had the right to bequeath his feudal rights to his heirs; on the other hand the bishop did not have this right, nor even that of raising a family. The feudal lord was the son of a feudal lord, a nobleman; the bishops were recruited from different classes and layers of society, often from the peasantry. (Engels pointed to the plebian origin of the upper hierarchy of the Church – and even of a number of Popes – as one of the causes for the stability of the Church in the Middle Ages.) Thus the mode of recruitment of the bishops was *different* from that of the private feudal lords. As regards the form of appropriation, the difference was equally great: the feudal lord, as an owner, was entitled to all the rent he could collect from his serfs, while the bishop was legally propertyless and, as such, entitled only to a 'salary'. But did these differences between the mode of appropriation and the mode of recruitment of the feudal lords and the upper hierarchy of the Church make any *basic* difference to the class struggle of the serfs on Church land, or on the lord's land? Of course not. The peasant with his primitive means of production, with the individualistic mode of production, had the same relation to other peasants, the same relation to the means of production (primarily the land), and the same relation to his exploiter – the upper clergy (or as Kautsky calls them in a book, highly recommended by Engels, the 'Papacy Class').

Similarly, in slave society there was besides the private ownership of slaves, collective state ownership, as in Sparta.[10]

From the standpoint of the exploiters the question of their mode of appropriation and recruitment is of prime importance. Thus, for instance, Kautsky, in **Thomas More and his Utopia**, says:

It looked as if the Church aspired to become the sole landed proprietor in Christendom. But the mightiest were to be curbed. The nobles were always hostile to the Church; when the latter acquired too much land, the king turned to the nobles for assistance in setting limits to the pretensions of the Church. Moreover, the Church was weakened by the invasion of Heathen tribes and the Mohammedans.[11]

The Church acquired, not without a struggle (in which one of the weapons it used was the forging of deeds of gift), about a third of all the land in Europe as a whole, in some countries the majority share of the land (e.g. Hungary, Bohemia). Perhaps, therefore, the nobles considered the differences between themselves and the upper clergy – in their origin, and mode of appropriation – of importance.

But from the standpoint of the class struggle of the serfs or the rising bourgeoisie against feudalism, these differences were of quite *secondary* importance. It would not be correct to say that they were of no importance, as the differences in the composition of the ruling class to some extent conditioned the struggle of the serfs or the rising bourgeoisie. Thus, for instance, the concentration of the means of production in the hands of the Church made the struggle of the serfs against the Church much more difficult than their struggle against individual landlords; the ideological justification of feudal ownership was different in form when blue blood and coats of arms were presented than when religious phrases were quoted in Latin. And the fact that while Church property was officially called '*patrimonium pauperum*' (the inheritance of the poor), private feudal property was not endowed with this exalted title, helps to show that these judicial differences were not unimportant. But from the standpoint of the historical process as a whole, i.e. from the standpoint of the class struggle, all the differences in the mode of appropriation and method of recruitment of the different groups are only secondary.

Shachtman and Bruno R (as well as 'orthodox' Trotskyists) forget Marx's statement of a century ago: that the form of property considered independently of the laws of motion of the economy, from the relations of production, is a metaphysical abstraction.

Thus the big differences between the mode of appropriation and recruitment of the Russian bureaucrats and that of the bourgeoisie, in itself, does not at all prove that Russia represents a non-capitalist society, a new class society of Bureaucratic Collectivism. To prove this, it is necessary to show that the *nature* of the ruled class – its condition of life and struggle – is fundamentally different in Russia from what exists, even for Shachtman, in capitalism. And this is exactly what Bruno R, and later Shachtman, tried to do.

The Nature of the Working Class in Russia

On the question of whether the workers in Russia are proletarians, the proponents of the theory of Bureaucratic Collectivism answer, and must answer, that they are not. They compare the Russian with the classical worker who was 'free' of the means of production and also free of any legal impediments to selling his labour power. It is true that there often were legal impediments to the movement of Russian workers from one enterprise to another. But is this a sufficient reason to say that the Russian worker was not a proletarian? If so, there is no doubt that the German worker under Hitler was also not a proletarian. Or, at the other extreme, workers in power are also not proletarians inasmuch as they are not 'free' as a collective from the means of production. No doubt an American worker is very different from an indentured girl in a Japanese factory who is under contract for a number of years and must live in the company's barracks for that time. But basically they are members of one and the same class. They were born together with the most dynamic form of production history has ever known, they are united by the process of social production, they are in actuality the antithesis of capital, and in potentiality socialism itself (because of the dynamics of a modern economy, no legal impediments in fact put an end *altogether* to the movement of workers from one enterprise to another under Stalin's regime).

Hilferding, Bruno R, and Dwight MacDonald were consistent and maintained that just as they did not consider a Russian worker to be a proletarian, so they did not consider a worker in Hitler's Germany to be a proletarian. The Shachtmanites tried to avoid this conclusion. In so doing they were led to falsify facts. For instance, they claim that the German workers under Hitler were freer to move than the Russian, that they were freer to bargain with their employers, and that slave labour was never as widespread in Germany as in Russia. Thus Irving Howe, one of Shachtman's followers at the time, wrote:

The Nazis did not use slave labor to the extent that Stalinist Russia has; under the Hitler regime, slave labor never became as indispensable a part of Germany's national economy as it has become for Russia under Stalin . . . industry under Hitler was still largely based on 'free labor' (in the Marxist sense; that is, free from ownership of the means of production and thereby forced to sell labor power, but also possessing the freedom to decide whether or not to sell this labor power). For all of the Hitlerite restrictions, there was considerable bargaining between the capitalist and proletarian, as well as between capitalists for workers during labor shortages.[12]

In reality the Russian worker, notwithstanding all restrictions, moves from one factory to another *much more* than the German worker, or, for that matter, than any other worker in the whole world. As early as September 1930, workers were prohibited from changing their place of work without special permission, and year after year brought new prohibitions. Despite this, the rate of turnover was tremendous. In 1928, as against 100 workers employed in industry 92.4 leavings were registered; in 1929, 115.2; 1930, 152.4; 1931, 136.8; 1932, 135.3; 1933, 122.4; 1934, 96.7; 1935, 86.1. In later years figures were not published, but it is clear that the large turnover continued, to which the frequent declamations in the press bear witness. Even the war did not put an end to it. The German administration was incomparably more efficient in combating the free movement of labour under Hitler. This, in addition to other factors (especially the relatively much greater dynamism of the Russian economy), made the labour turnover in Germany much lower than in Russia.

What about the slave camps in Stalin's Russia? Shachtman tried to suggest that slave labour was the basic factor of production in Russia. But this is absolutely wrong. The labour of prisoners is suitable only for manual work where modern technique is not used. It is therefore employed in the construction of factories, roads, etc. Despite its cheapness, it is necessarily only of secondary importance to the labour of workers, as 'unfree' labour is always relatively unproductive. If not for the fact that slave labour were an impediment to the rise of the productivity of labour, the decline of Roman society would not have taken place. Likewise, although in different circumstances, slavery would not have been abolished in the Unied States. In the face of special circumstances – the lack of means of production and the abundance of labour power – it is explicable that the Stalinist bureaucracy should introduce and use slave labour on a large scale. But it is clear that the main historical tendency is in an opposite direction. All the factories in Russia producing tanks and aeroplanes, machinery, etc., were run on wage labour. During the war Hitler's Germany found it expedient to use twelve million foreign workers, most of whom had been recruited as prisoners and forced labourers.

Marx maintained that the historical tendency towards the degradation of the *proletariat*, its increased oppression by capital, is fundamental to capitalism, whereas the substitution of the proletariat by a new, or rather, ancient, class of slaves is quite contrary to the general tendency of history. As we have said, only a lack of means of production and an abundance of labour power can explain the widespread use of prison labour in Stalin's Russia. Hence its almost complete disappearance since the death of Stalin, since Russia reached industrial maturity.

Shachtman's theory of Bureaucratic Collectivism must lead to its logical conclusion. If the Russian worker is not a proletarian, the German worker under Hitler was not a proletarian, and in Hitler's Germany there was not a wage labour system, but a system of 'collective slavery'. Accordingly, the ruling class in Hitler's Germany could not be called a capitalist class, as capitalists are exploiters of proletarians. Bruno R, Dwight MacDonald and Hilferding, at least, have the merit of consistency. They drew these conclusions and were therefore justified in calling Hitler's Germany Bureaucratic Collectivist (Bruno R and Dwight MacDonald) or a 'Totalitarian State Economy' (Hilferding).

If we accepted that workers employed by the Stalinist state are not proletarians, we should have to come to the absurd conclusion that in the Western Powers' zones of Berlin the workers are proletarians, but in the Russian zone those employed in the nationalised German enterprises are not proletarians, while those employed in the Russian zone by private industry are proletarians!

Again, we should have to come to the absurd conclusion that non-workers under Stalin have been gradually transformed after his death into proletarians.

Above all, if Shachtman is right and there is no proletariat in the Stalinist regime, Marxism as a method, as a guide for the proletariat as the subject of historical change, becomes superfluous, meaningless. To speak about Marxism in a society without a proletariat, is to make of Marxism a supra-historical theory.

Historical Limitations of Bureaucratic Collectivism

If one accepts the state capitalist nature of the Stalinist regime, one not only accept its laws of motion – the accumulation of capital as dictated by the pressure of world capitalism – but also the historical limitations of its role. Once capital is amassed and the working class is massive, the ground is undermined beneath the feet of the bureaucracy.

For a Marxist who thinks Russia is state capitalist, the historical mission of the bourgeoisie is the socialisation of labour and the concentration of the means of production. On a world scale this task had already been fulfilled. In Russia the revolution removed the impediments to the development of the productive forces, put an end to the remnants of feudalism, built up a monopoly of foreign trade which defends the development of the productive forces of the country from the devastating pressure of world capitalism, and also gave a tremendous lever to the development of the productive forces in the form of state ownership of the means of production. Under such conditions, all the impediments to the historical mission of capitalism – the socialisation of labour and the concentration of the means of production which are necessary prerequisites for the establishment of socialism, and which the bourgeoisie was not able to fulfil – are abolished. *Post-October Russia stood before the fulfilment of the historical mission of the bourgeoisie*, which Lenin summed up in two postulates: 'increase in the productive forces of social labour and the socialisation of labour.'

Once the Stalinist bureaucracy created a massive working class and massive concentrated capital, the objective prerequisites for the overthrow of the bureaucracy had been laid. The Stalinist bureaucracy thus created its own gravedigger (hence the post-Stalin convulsions in Russia and Eastern Europe).

The theory of Bureaucratic Collectivism is inherently incapable of saying anything about the historical role and limitations of the Stalinist bureaucracy. Hence socialism also appears simply as a Utopian dream, not a necessary solution to contradictions inherent in the Stalinist regime itself. Abstracted from the contradictions of capitalism, the urge towards socialism becomes merely an idealistic chimera.

Attitude to the Stalinist Parties

From the assumption that Bureaucratic Collectivism is more reactionary than capitalism, Shachtman draws the conclusion that if a choice has to be made between Social Democratic Parties which support capitalism and Communist Parties – agents of Bureaucratic Collectivism – a socialist should side with the former against the latter.

Thus Shachtman wrote in September 1948:

Stalinism is a reactionary, totalitarian, anti-bourgeois and anti-proletarian current IN the labor movement but not OF the labor movement . . . where, as is the general rule nowadays, the militants are not yet strong enough to fight for leadership directly; where the fight for control of the labor movement is, in effect, between the reformists and the Stalinists, it would be absurd for the militants to proclaim their 'neutrality' and fatal for them to support the Stalinists. Without any hesitation, they should follow the general line, inside the labor movement, of supporting the reformist officialdom against the Stalinist officialdom. In other words, where it is not yet possible to win the unions for the leadership of revolutionary militants, we forthrightly prefer the leadership of reformists who aim in their own way to maintain a labor movement, to the leadership of the Stalinist totalitarians who aim to exterminate it . . . while the revolutionists are not the equal of the reformists and the reformists are not the equal of the revolutionists, the two are now necessary and proper allies against Stalinism. The scores that have to be settled with reformism – those will be settled on a working-class basis and in a working-class way, and not under the leadership or in alliance with totalitarian reaction.[13]

Again there is a lack of historical perspective, of real analysis of social forces, an oversimplification. The dual role of the Communist Parties in the West – as agents of Moscow and as a collection of fighting individual militants, strangled by the same bureaucracy – is completely overlooked. Shachtman's attitude to the Communist Parties, if adopted by any socialists in the West, would: firstly, strengthen the right-wing Social Democratic Parties; and, secondly, strengthen the hold of the Communist Party leadership on their rank and file. It is a sure way to liquidate any independent working-class tendency.

In Conclusion

The theory of Bureaucratic Collectivism is supra-historical, negative and abstract. It does not define the economic laws of motion of the system, explain its inherent contradictions and the motivation of the class struggle. It is completely arbitrary. Hence it does not give a perspective, nor can it serve as a basis for a strategy for socialists.

References

Chapter 1

[1] For a very good description of the changes in the management of the Russian economy see G.Bienstock, S.M.Schwartz and A.Yugow, *Management in Russian Industry and Agriculture*, Oxford University Press 1944

[2] A.Baykov, *The Development of the Soviet Economic System*, London 1946, p. 115

[3] *ibid.* p. 116

[4] *All-Union Communist Party (Bolsheviks) in Resolutions and Decisions of the Congresses, Conferences and Plenums of the Central Committee* (hereafter referred to as *AUCP in Resol.*), (Russian) Moscow 1941, 6th ed. Vol. II p. 811

[5] *ibid.* p. 812

[6] *Socialism Victorious*, London 1934, p. 137

[7] *Za Industrializatsiu* (Organ of the Commissariat of Heavy Industry), Moscow, 16 April 1934

[8] L.Gintsburg and E.Pashukanis, *Course of Soviet Economic Law* (Russian), Moscow 1935, Vol. I p. 8

[9] *Pravda*, 11 March 1937

[10] E.L. Granovski and B.L.Markus (eds.), *The Economics of Socialist Industry* (Russian), Moscow 1940, p. 579

[11] *ibid.* p. 563

[12] H.Johnson, Dean of Canterbury, *The Socialist Sixth of the World*, London 1944, 19th imp. p. 280

[13] *Trud* (trade union daily), Moscow, 8 July 1933. Quoted by M.Gordon, *Workers Before and After Lenin*, New York 1941, pp. 104–105

[14] G.K.Ordzhonikidze, *Selection of Articles and Speeches, 1911–1937* (Russian), Moscow 1939, p. 359

[15] *Pravda*, 29 December 1935

[16] Decision of the All-Union Central Council of Trade Unions, 2 January 1933 *Labour Legislation in USSR* (Russian), Moscow-Leningrad 1933, p. 320

[17] V.I.Lenin, *Works* (Russian), 4th ed. Vol. XX pp. 6–7. (hereafter the 4th ed. is always quoted unless otherwise stated)

[18] *Eleventh Congress of the Russian Communist Party (Bolsheviks). Stenographic Report. Held in Moscow, March–April 1922* (Russian), Moscow 1936, p. 275

[19] *Wage Labour in Russia* (Russian), Moscow 1924, p. 160; and *Trade Unions in USSR 1926–1928* (Russian), Moscow 1928, p. 358

[20] *Trud*, 23 April 1949

[21] G.N.Aleksandrov (ed.), *Soviet Labour Law* (Russian), Moscow 1949, p. 166

[22] *Professionalnye Soiuzy* (monthly organ of the trade unions), Moscow 1940, Nos. 4–5

[23] *ibid.* 1947, No. 2

[34] I.T. Goliakov (ed.), *Legislation Regarding Labour* (Russian), Moscow 1947, p. 15

[35] G.N.Aleksandrov and D.M.Genkin (eds.), *Soviet Labour Law* (Russian), Moscow 1946, p. 106. See also G.N.Aleksandrov and G.K.Moskalenko (eds.) *Soviet Labour Law* (Russian), Moscow 1947, pp. 100–101

[36] *Labour Code of RSFSR* (Russian), Moscow 1937, Article 58, p. 28

[37] Goliakov, *op. cit.* p. 15

[38] *Trud*, 13 April 1952

[39] F.Neumann, *Behemoth*, London 1942, pp. 352–353

[40] *ibid.* p. 353. My emphasis

[41] Baykov, *op. cit.* p. 222

[42] G.Sorokin, *Socialist Planning of the National Economy of USSR* (Russian), Moscow 1946, p. 95

[43] *The Large Soviet Encyclopaedia*, Vol. USSR (Russian), Moscow 1948, Column 1751

[44] *Trud*, 20 April 1949

[45] A.I.Beskin, *Organisation and Planning of Production in the Oil Extraction Industry* (Russian), Moscow-Leningrad 1947, p. 134

[46] *Bolshevik* (Organ of the Central Committee of the Party), Moscow 1952, No. 5

[47] *Za Industrializatsiu*, Moscow, March 1936 ˙

[48] A.A.Arutinian and B.L.Markus (eds.), *Development of Soviet Economy* (Russian), Moscow 1940, p. 492

[49] A.Yugow, *Russia's Economic Front for War and Peace*, London 1942, p. 193

[40] *ibid.*, p. 194

[41] *Trud*, 17 April 1941

[42] *Mashinostroenie* (Organ of the Commissariat of Machine Construction), Moscow, 11 May 1939

[43] *Izvestia*, 2 April 1936

[44] J.Maynard, *The Russian Peasant: And Other Studies*, London 1942, p. 340

[45] For the earliest reported cases of the murder and sabotage of Stakhanovites after the introduction of Stakhanovism, see *Izvestia*, 23 August 1935, 27 September 1935, 2 and 5 October 1935; *Pravda*, 2, 21 and 22 November 1935; *Trud*, 1 November 1935. Many more could be quoted

[46] Beskin, *op. cit.* p. 31

[47] V.I.Lenin, *Works* (Russian), *op. cit.* Vol. XXI, p. 135

[48] *Labour Code 1922* (Russian), Moscow 1922, Article 37.

[49] Quoted by V.Serge, *Russia Twenty Years After*, New York 1937, p. 66

[50] *A Collection of Laws and Ordinances of the Worker-Peasant Government of the USSR* (hereafter referred to as *Coll. Laws USSR*), (Russian) Moscow 1932, No. 84, Article 516

[51] *Izvestia*, 17 December 1930

[52] *Labour Code of RSFSR* (Russian), Moscow 1937, Article 37, p. 20

[53] *Za Industrializatsiu*, 12 February 1931; *A Collection of Decisions and Ordinances of the Government of USSR* (hereafter referred to as *Coll. Decisions USSR*) (Russian), Moscow 1938, No. 58, Article 329

[54] Serge, *op. cit.* p. 68

[55] *A Collection of Laws and Ordinances of the Workers' and Peasants' Government of RSFSR* (hereafter referred to as *Coll. Laws RSFSR*) (Russian) Moscow 1932, No. 85, Article 371

[86] *Decisions of the Central Committee of the All-Union Communist Party (Bolsheviks) and the Council of People's Commissars of USSR, concerning Most Important Problems of Socialist Construction* (Russian), Leningrad 1933, pp. 127–130

[87] *Coll. Decisions USSR*, 1939, No. 1, Article 1

[88] *Supreme Soviet USSR Gazette* (Russian), Moscow 1940, No. 20

[89] *Izvestia*, 30 December 1940

[40] *Bloknot Agitatora* (Organ of the Propaganda and Agitation Department of the Moscow Committee of the Party), Moscow, 1952, No. 4 pp. 41–42

[41] *Supreme Soviet USSR Gazette* (Russian), Moscow 1940, No. 42

[42] Aleksandrov and Genkin, *op. cit.* p. 278

[43] *ibid.* pp. 273–274

[44] *ibid.* p. 275

[45] See G.N.Aleksandrov, *Soviet Labour Law*, 1949

[46] *Coll. Laws RSFSR*, 1927, No. 49, Article 330; and *Criminal Code of RSFSR* (Russian), Moscow 1937, Article 58, Item 14. My emphasis

[47] V.Gsovski, *Soviet Civil Law*, Ann Arbor 1948, Vol. I p. 805

[48] *Labour Code 1922* (Russian), Moscow 1922, Article 129, p. 18

[49] 'Women Workers and their Protection in Russian Industry', *International Labour Review*, October 1929

[70] G.N.Serebrennikov, *Zhenskii Trud v. SSSR*, Moscow 1934, p. 204. Quoted by J.Grunfeld in 'Women's Work in Russia's Planned Economy', *Social Research*, February 1942. Serebrennikov was careful, of course, not to include such information in his book, *The Position of Women in the USSR*, London 1937, written specially for non-Russian readers

[71] *Russian News Bulletin*, 30 July 1941

[72] S.Wolfsson, 'Socialism and the Family', in *Pod Znamenem Marksizma* (Theoretical Organ of the Party), Moscow 1936, quoted by R.Schlesinger, *The Family in the USSR*, London 1949, p. 287

[73] International Labour Conference, Eighteenth Session, *Employment of Women on Underground Work in Mines of All Kinds*, Geneva 1934, Report VI

[74] C.Haldane, *Russian Newsreel*, London 1942, p. 151

[75] M.Hindus, *Russia Fights On*, London 1942, p. 135

[76] *Pravda*, 1 January 1939

[77] D.J.Dallin and B.I.Nicolaevsky, *Forced Labour in Soviet Russia*, London 1948, p. 153

[78] *ibid.* p. 52

[79] *ibid.* pp. 54–62

[80] A.Ciliga, *The Russian Enigma*, London 1940, p. 249

[81] Y.Gluckstein, *Stalin's Satellites in Europe*, London 1952, pp. 309–310

[82] W.Kolarz, *Russia and her Colonies*, London 1952, p. 185

[83] *Supplements to the Order of the Council of People's Commissars of USSR and the Central Committee of the All-Union Communist Party* (Russian), No. 127, 17 January 1941. No date or place of publication given. Photographic copy by the Universal Press for the American Council of Learned Societies, New York 1950

[84] *ibid.* p. 10

[85] Dallin and Nicolaevsky, *op. cit.*, p. 165

[86] *Pravda*, 28 March 1953

[87] *Izvestia*, 20 December 1937

** A.Ya.Vyshinsky (ed.), *The Law of the Soviet State* (Russian), Moscow 1938, pp. 514–515

** *Five-Year Plan of National Economic Construction of USSR*, 3rd ed. (hereafter referred to as *I Plan*) (Russian), Moscow 1930, Vol. I, p. 132; *The Second Five-Year Plan for the Development of the National Economy of USSR* (hereafter referred to as *II Plan*) (Russian), Moscow 1934, Vol. I, p. 429

** *I Plan*, Vol. II Part I p. 250; *II Plan*, Vol. I pp. 172, 522, Vol. II pp. 291–292, 296; *Pravda*, 19 February 1941; *Socialist Construction of the USSR, Statistical Year Book 1936* (hereafter referred to as *Socialist Construction 1936*) (Russian), Moscow 1936, pp. 192, 195, 201, 204, 206; *Socialist Construction of the USSR (1933–1938)* (hereafter referred to as *Socialist Construction 1933–1938*) (Russian) Moscow 1938, p. 73; *Pravda*, 10 March 1950; *Izvestia*, 17 April 1951

** *Socialist Construction (1933–38)*, pp. xxiv–xxv

** A.Baykov, *Soviet Foreign Trade*, Princeton 1946, Appendix Tables IV and VI.

** *I Plan*, Vol. I pp. 145, 147; Vol. II, Part I pp. 248–251; *II Plan*, Vol. I pp. 172, 522; Vol. II pp. 276, 278–280, 291–292, 296; *Law on the Five-Year Plan for the Reconstruction and Development of the National Economy of USSR for 1946–50* (hereafter referred to as *IV Plan*) (Russian), Moscow 1946, pp. 11–13; *Pravda*, 6 October 1952.

** Calculated from: *I Plan*, Vol. I pp. 145, 147; Vol. II, Part I pp. 248–251; *Summary of the Fulfilment of the First Five-Year Plan of Development of the National Economy of USSR* (hereafter referred to as *Ful. I Plan*) (Russian) Moscow 1933, pp. 83, 95, 105, 121; *II Plan* Vol. I, pp. 172, 522, Vol. II pp. 276, 278–280, 291–293, 296; *IV Plan*, pp. 11–13; *Izvestia*, 17 April 1951. (There is no reference to the fulfilment of the Third Five-Year Plan (1938–42) because the war interrupted it and no fulfilment figures were published).

** *Socialist Construction 1936*, p. 3

** S.N.Prokopovicz, *Russlands Volkswirtschaft unter den Sowjets*, Zurich 1944, p. 302

** *I Plan* Vol. I p. 20; V.P.Diachenko (ed.), *Finance and Credit in USSR* (Russian), Moscow 1938, p. 184; *IV Plan*, p. 9; *National Economy of USSR* (Russian), Moscow 1948, Vol. II, p. 185

** *National Economy of USSR* (Russian), Moscow 1948, Vol. II, p. 129

** Prokopovicz, *op. cit.*, p. 306

100 N.Jasny, *The Socialised Agriculture of USSR*, Stanford 1949, pp. 777–778

101 K.Kautsky, *Die Agrarfrage*, Stuttgart 1899, pp. 24, 31

102 N.A.Voznessensky, *The War Economy of the USSR in the Period of the Patriotic War* (Russian), Moscow 1948, p. 126

103 N.Jasny, *The Soviet Economy During the Plan Era*, Stanford 1951, p. 74

104 *ibid.* p. 76

105 Calculated from figures of the output of consumers' goods on p. 35

106 V.V.Kuibyshev, *Articles and Speeches, 1930–1935* (Russian), Moscow 1935, p. 131

107 *I Plan* Vol. II Part 2 pp. 292–293; *Ful. I Plan*, p. 186; *II Plan*, Vol. I p. 533

108 *Workers' and Employees' Budget, Vol. I. The Budget of a Worker's Family in 1922–1927* (Russian), Moscow 1929, p. 55; *II Plan* Vol. I p. 533;

B.B.Veselovsky, *Course of Economics and Planning of Communal Economy* (Russian), Moscow 1945, p. 174

[109] United Nations, *The European Housing Problem*, Geneva 1949, p. 41

[110] United Nations, *Economic Survey of Europe in 1949*, Geneva 1950, p. 31

[111] *International Labour Review*, May 1932, p. 627

[112] *Soviet News*, 23 January 1952

[113] V.L.Kobalevsky, *Organisation and Economics of Housing in USSR* (Russian) Moscow-Leningrad 1940, p. 109

[114] Veselovsky, *op. cit.* p. 176

[115] *IV Plan*, p. 55

[116] Veselovsky, *op. cit.* pp. 132, 473

[117] *Soviet News*, 23 January 1952; *Pravda*, 18 October 1937

[118] *International Labour Review*, May 1932, p. 627

[119] A.G.Zverev, *State Budgets of the USSR, 1938/1945* (Russian) Moscow 1946, pp. 15, 22, 47, 104; K.N.Plotnikov, *Budget of a Socialist State* (Russian), Moscow 1948, pp. 142, 146, 216, 218; *The National Economy of the USSR* (Russian), Moscow 1951, Vol. IV pp. 127, 340; *Planovoe Khoziaistvo* (monthly organ of the State Planning Commission), Moscow 1952, No. 2, p. 24

[120] These figures are taken from *State Plan of Development of National Economy of the USSR for 1941*, No. 127, 17 January 1941, *op. cit.* p. 11

[121] L.P.Shulkin, *Consumption of Iron and Steel in the USSR* (Russian), Moscow-Leningrad 1940, pp. 20 ff; M.Gardner Clark, *Some Economic Problems of the Soviet Iron and Steel Industry* (unpublished dissertation), Cornell University 1950, p. 42

[122] Voznessensky, *op. cit.* p. 126

[123] Arutinian and Markus, *op. cit.* p. 484

[124] Prokopovicz, *op. cit.* p. 306

[125] *USSR and the Capitalist Countries; Statistical Handbook* (Russian), Moscow 1939, pp. 75–80

[126] *Soviet Weekly*, Supplement, 18 December 1947

[127] Ministry of Labour, *Labour Survey of British Workers*, April 1947

[128] N.Jasny, *The Socialised Agriculture of USSR, op. cit.* pp. 374–375

[129] *ibid.* p. 375

[130] A.Arina, 'Kolkhozes in 1938', *Sotsialisticheskoe Selskokhoziaistvo* (monthly organ of the Commissariat of Agriculture), Moscow 1939, No. 12

[131] Arina, *op. cit.* and Jasny, *The Socialised Agriculture of USSR, op. cit.* p. 684

[132] T.L.Basyuk, *The Organisation of Kolkhoz Production* (Russian), Moscow 1946, pp. 272–273

[133] Prokopovicz, *op. cit.* p. 164

[134] F.Semenov, A.Pankratova and others, *The Proletariat in the Revolution of 1905–1907* (Russian), Moscow-Leningrad 1930, p. 232

[135] M.P.Osadko (ed.), *Problems of Organisation of Kolkhoz Production* (Russian), Moscow 1945, p. 94

[136] *ibid.*

[137] *ibid.* p. 95

[138] *ibid.* p. 191

[139] *ibid.* p. 201

[140] *ibid.* p. 212

[141] *ibid.* p. 217

[142] V.I.Lenin, *Selected Works*, Vol. I p. 179

[143] K.Marx, *Capital*, New York, Modern Library n.d. Vol. I p. 193

[144] K.Marx and F.Engels, *Selected Correspondence*, London 1941, pp. 509–510

[145] M.Dobb, *Soviet Economic Development since 1917*, London 1948, p. 364

[146] A.K.Suchkov (ed.) *Revenues of the State Budget of USSR* (Russian), Moscow 1945, p. 14; Plotnikov, *op. cit.* pp. 17, 26, 102, 181, 259; N.N.Rovinsky, *The State Budget of USSR* (Russian), Moscow 1949, p. 72; *The National Economy of USSR 1950* (Russian), Moscow 1950, p. 393; *The National Economy of USSR 1951* (Russian), Moscow, 1951, p. 337; *Planovoe Khoziaistvo* 1952, No. 2 p. 20

[147] Suchkov, *op. cit.* p. 16

[148] N.Jasny, *The Soviet Price System*, Stanford 1951, pp. 164–165.

[149] M.Dobb, *Soviet Planning and Labour in Peace and War*, London 1942, pp. 61–62

[150] M.Dobb, *Soviet Economic Development since 1917*, *op. cit.* pp. 371–372

[151] Prokopovicz, *op. cit.* p. 316; *Bolshevik* No. 12, 1950

[152] *AUCP in Resol.* Moscow 1932, 4th ed. Vol. I, p. 22

[153] *ibid.* p. 506

[154] *Socialist Construction, 1935*, p. 644: Jasny, *The Soviet Price System*, *op. cit.* p. 78

[155] *Socialist Construction, 1936*, pp. 646–647; Jasny, *ibid.*

[156] Zverev, *op. cit.* p. 43

[157] *Coll. Laws USSR* 1932, No. 62, Article 360

[158] J.V.Stalin, *Works* (Russian), Vol. VIII, p. 209

[159] This extract and the following two are quoted from Gluckstein, *op. cit.* pp. 93–95

[160] *Pravda*, 5 June 1947

[161] *ibid.*

[162] *Pravda*, 9 July 1947

[163] *Criminal Code of RSFSR* (Russian), Moscow 1937, pp. 70–71

[164] *ibid.* p. 74

[165] *Code of Laws on Marriage, Family and Guardianship of RSFSR* (Russian), Moscow 1948, p. 19, Article 69

[166] *ibid,* p. 19, Article 70

[167] *Coll. Laws USSR*, 1935, No. 19, Article 155

[168] Quoted by M.Yvon, *L'URSS, telle qu'elle est*, Paris 1938, p. 243

[169] *Vecherniaia Moskva*, 19 April 1935, in N.S.Timasheff, *The Great Retreat*, New York 1946, p. 325

[170] See *Sovetskaia Ustitsiia*, 1935, No. 10. Quoted by Timasheff, *op. cit.* p. 321

[171] *Supreme Soviet USSR Gazette*, 1941, No. 25

[172] I.T.Goliakov (ed.) *Criminal Law* (Russian) 3rd ed. 1943, p. 137. Quoted by Gsovski, *op. cit.* Vol. I p. 122

[173] Dallin and Nicolaevsky, *op. cit.* p. 84

[174] K.Marx and F.Engels, *Works* (Russian) Vol. IV p. 312

[175] V.I.Lenin, *Works* (Russian) Vol. XXIV, p. 5

[176] K.Marx, *Critique of the Gotha Programme*. Quoted by Lenin, *State and Revolution*, London 1942, p. 70

[177] Lenin, *op. cit.* p. 76

[178] *ibid.* p. 77

[179] *ibid.* p. 78

[180] *ibid.* p. 40

[181] V.I.Lenin, *Works* (Russian), Vol. XXVII, p. 132

[182] *ibid.* Vol. XXIX, p. 159

[183] *ibid.* Vol. XXXIII, p. 64

[184] *AUCP in Resol.* 4th ed. Vol. I p. 337

[185] *ibid.* p. 444

[186] *Minutes of the Tenth Congress of the Russian Communist Party (Bolsheviks) held in Moscow, March 1921* (Russian), Moscow 1933, p. 317

[187] S.G.Strumilin, *Wages and Labour Productivity in Russian Industry in 1913–22* (Russian), Moscow 1923, p. 35

[188] M.N.Pokrovsky (ed) *1905* (Russian), Moscow-Leningrad 1925, Vol. I p. 439

[189] *Labour in USSR, Statistical-Economic Survey, October 1922 – March 1924* (Russian) Moscow 1924, p. 158

[190] S.Zagorsky, *Wages and Regulation of Conditions of Labour in the USSR,* Geneva, 1930, pp. 176, 178

[191] L.Lawton, *Economic History of Soviet Russia,* London 1932, Vol. II, pp. 359–361

[192] From Z.M.Chernilovsky (ed.) *History of State and Law* (Russian) Moscow 1949, p. 29

[193] Quoted by D.I.Chernomordik, *The Economic Policy of USSR* (Russian), Moscow-Leningrad 1936, p. 240

[194] *Labour Code 1922* (Russian), Moscow 1922, Article 57, pp. 9–10

[195] *ibid.* Abrogated 17 March 1934 (*Coll. Laws USSR 1934,* No. 15, Article 109)

[196] *Coll. Laws USSR 1937,* No. 71, Article 340

[197] L.A.Bronstein and B.N.Budrin, *Planning and Accounting in Automotive Transport* (Russian), Moscow 1948, p. 150

[198] *Coll. Laws USSR 1936,* No. 20, Article 169

[199] G.Poliak, 'On the Director's Funds in Industrial Enterprises', *Planovoe Khoziaistvo,* 1938, No. 4

[200] *Socialist Construction 1933–38, op. cit.* p. 138

[201] L.Vilenski, 'Financial Questions of Industry', *Planovoe Khoziaistvo,* 1938, No. 10

[202] Quoted by Yvon, *op. cit.* p. 111

[203] *Pravda,* 27 June 1937

[204] *Socialist Construction 1936, op. cit.* p. 513

[205] *First Session of the Supreme Soviet of the USSR, Stenographic Report* (Russian). Moscow 1948, pp. 124, 205

[206] *Izvestia,* 18 January 1938

[207] *New York Times,* 23 August 1943

[208] *Pravda,* 21 December 1939

[209] *Izvestia,* 6 April 1940

[210] A.Werth, *The Year of Stalingrad,* London 1946, p. 126

[211] *ibid.* p. 104

[212] *ibid.*

[213] See above pp. 57

[214] Jasny, *The Soviet Price System, op. cit.* pp. 44–45

²¹⁵ *Coll. Laws RSFSR*, 1918, No. 34, Article 456
²¹⁶ *Coll. Laws USSR*, 1929, No. 8, Article 78
²¹⁷ R. Bishop, *Soviet Millionaires*, London 1945, p. 3
²¹⁸ I.I.Evtikhiev and V.A.Vlassov, *Administrative Law of USSR* (Russian), Moscow 1946, pp. 164, 418
²¹⁹ *ibid.* p. 408
²²⁰ *Pravda*, 4 April 1951
²²¹ *Pravda*, 17 March 1949
²²² *Large Soviet Encyclopaedia*, Vol. *USSR* (Russian), Columns 1225, 1228 and 1233
²²³ *Cultural Construction USSR* (Russian), Moscow 1940, pp. 111–112
²²⁴ *ibid.* p. 114
²²⁵ *Coll. Decisions USSR*, 1940, No. 27, Article 637
²²⁶ *The People's Education in RSFSR in 1943* (Russian), 1944, p. 42
²²⁷ *Directives of the All-Union Communist Party (Bolsheviks) and the Decisions of the Soviet Government on Education. Collection of Documents 1917–1947* (Russian), Moscow-Leningrad 1947, Vol. II pp. 109–111
²²⁸ Decree of 28 December 1940, *Supreme Soviet USSR Gazette* (Russian), 1941, No. 1
²²⁹ *ibid.* 1947, No. 21
²³⁰ *I Plan*, Vol. I, Part 1, p. 329
²³¹ *ibid.* pp. 324–325
²³² *Socialist Construction 1933–38, op. cit.* pp. xxiv–xxv
²³³ *I Plan*, Vol. I, p. 94
²³⁴ *Ful. I Plan*, p. 170
²³⁵ *Pravda*, 27 October 1940
²³⁶ I.P.Bardin and N.P.Banny, *Iron and Steel Industry in the New Five-Year Period* (Russian), Moscow-Leningrad 1947, p. 166
²³⁷ *ibid.* p. 165
²³⁸ *Izvestia*, 24 May 1952
²³⁹ *Meeting of the Supreme Soviet of USSR (Third Session), 20–25 February 1947* (Russian), Moscow 1947, p. 20
²⁴⁰ N.Jasny, *Soviet Prices of Producers' Goods*, Stanford 1952, pp. 83–84
²⁴¹ Jasny, *The Soviet Price System, op. cit.* pp. 9–10
²⁴² *ibid.* p. 10
²⁴³ J.V.Stalin, *Economic Problems of Socialism in the USSR*, Moscow 1952, pp. 24–25
²⁴⁴ *Planovoe Khoziaistvo*, 1946, No. 3, pp. 38–39
²⁴⁵ H.G.Berman, *Justice in Russia: An Interpretation of Soviet Law*, Cambridge, Mass. 1950, p. 66
²⁴⁶ *ibid.* pp. 76–77
²⁴⁷ Stalin in *Pravda*, 7 November 1929, *Problems of Leninism*, p. 301. In Stalin's *Works* (Russian), Vol. XII, p. 129, the same article is reproduced with the substitution of 40–50,000 hectares for 50–100,000 hectares.
²⁴⁸ *Izvestia*, 20 January 1930
²⁴⁹ G.K.Ordzhonikidze, *Industrial Development in 1931 and the Tasks for 1932*, Moscow 1932, pp. 40–41
²⁵⁰ *Planovoe Khoziaistvo*, 1931, Nos. 5–6, p. 29; *II Plan*, Vol. II pp. 276, 278–280
²⁵¹ *Izvestia*, 8 March 1931

[338] *Komsomolskaia Pravda*, 6 December 1935. Quoted by Gordon, *op. cit.* 389–390

[339] K.Marx and F.Engels, *The Communist Manifesto* in *Selected Works*, London 1942, Vol. I, pp. 208–210

Chapter 2

[1] K.Marx, *Selected Works*, Vol. I, pp. 226–227

[2] F.Engels in *Neue Zeit*, Vol. XX, No. 1, p. 8. Quoted in K.Marx and F.Engels, *Selected Correspondence*, London 1943, p. 486

[3] Engels' Introduction to K.Marx, *The Civil War in France*, London 1941 p. 19

[4] *ibid.* pp. 40–41

[5] *ibid.* p. 18

[6] F.Engels, *The Origin of the Family, Private Property and the State*, London 1943, p. 195

[7] V.I.Lenin, *The State and Revolution*, London 1942, p. 10

[8] L.Trotsky, *The Revolution Betrayed*. London 1937, p. 211

[9] *AUCP in Resol.*, 4th ed. Vol. I, p. 22

[10] *Coll. Laws RSFSR*, 1917, No. 9, Article 138

[11] *ibid.* Article 139.

[12] Ya L.Berman (ed.) *The All-Union Communist Party (Bolsheviks) and Military Affairs*, in *Resolutions of Congresses and Conferences of the AUCP* (Russian), Moscow 1928, 2nd ed. pp. 71–73

[13] L.Trotsky, *How the Revolution Armed Itself* (Russian), Moscow 1924, Vol. II, Book 1, p. 118

[14] *ibid.* Vol. II, Book 2, p. 16. The same idea is again put forward in a thesis published by Trotsky on 16 December 1919, *ibid.* pp. 33–36

[15] Berman, *op. cit.* pp. 84–85

[16] I.Smilga, *Fundamental Problems of the Construction of the Red Army* (Russian), Moscow 1921, pp. 16–17. The same ideas are elaborated in M.N.Tukhachevsky's article 'The Red Army and the Militia' in his *War of the Classes. Articles 1919–1920*, (Russian) Moscow 1923, pp. 60–77. The only difference between Smilga's arguments and those of Tukhachevsky lies in the emphasis the latter puts upon the incompatability of the militia system with 'Soviet Russia's military mission of disseminating socialist revolution throughout the world'.

[17] Quoted in *Soviet Military Encyclopaedia* (Russian), Moscow 1932, Vol. I, Column 619

[18] D.F.White, *The Growth of the Red Army*, Princeton 1944, pp. 63–64

[19] Trotsky, *How the Revolution Armed Itself*, *op. cit.* Vol. II, Book 1, pp. 84–86. Quoted by White, *op. cit.* p. 121

[20] White, *op. cit.* p. 252

[21] *ibid.* p. 223

[22] E.Wollenberg, *The Red Army*, London 1940, pp. 182–183

[23] *ibid.* p. 188

[24] White, *op. cit.* p. 303

[25] *ibid.* p. 304

[26] *ibid.* p. 305

[27] K.Voroshilov, in *The Land of Socialism Today and Tomorrow*, Moscow 1939, p. 288

[28] A.Bergson, *National Income and Product of the USSR*, Appendix: 'Sources and Methods', New York 1950, hectographed, p. 8

[29] *New York Times*, 23 August 1943

[30] Evtikhiev and Vlassov, *op. cit.* pp. 166–167

[31] *Coll. Laws USSR*, 1935, No. 57, Articles 468–469

[32] *ibid.* 1937, No. 51, Article 219

[33] *Supreme Soviet USSR Gazette* (Russian), 1940, No. 15

[34] *ibid.* 1945, No. 36. For an enumeration of the decrees introducing ranks into the army, air force and navy, see Evtikhiev and Vlassov, *op. cit.* pp. 156–157

[35] *Krasnaia Zvezda* (Soviet Army daily), Moscow, 4 September 1940

[36] *Small Soviet Encyclopaedia* (Russian), Vol. VI, p. 624

[37] *Krasnaia Zvezda*, 7 January 1943

[38] *ibid.* 23 May 1940

[39] *Daily Worker*, 9 July 1943

[40] *Krasnaia Zvezda*, 22 October 1940

[41] *ibid.* 15 October 1940

[42] *ibid.* 22 October 1940

[43] *Pravda*, 6 October 1940

[44] J.Towster, *Political Power in the USSR*, New York 1948, p. 210

[45] Speech of Sverdlov, 5 July 1918. Quoted by J.Bunyan, *Intervention, Civil War and Communism in Russia, April-December 1918. Documents and Materials*, Baltimore 1936, p. 205

[46] *Izvestia*, 1 September 1939

[47] *Pravda*, 7 March 1952

[48] *Pravda*, 12 April 1954

[49] Johnson, *op. cit.* p. 353

[50] J.V.Stalin, *Speeches at Pre-Election Meetings of Electors of the Stalin Election District in Moscow Province. 11 December 1937 and 9 February 1946* (Russian), Moscow 1946, p. 5

[51] A.R.Williams, *The Soviets*, New York 1937, p. 49

[52] *Pravda*, 22 December 1947

[53] B. Newman, *The New Europe*, London 1942, p. 159

[54] *New York Times*, 25 November 1937

[55] *AUCP in Resol.*, 4th ed. Vol. I, p. 126

[56] *AUCP in Resol.*, 6th ed. Vol. I, pp. 154–160

[57] L.Trotsky, *History of the Russian Revolution*, London 1932, Vol. I, p. 59

[58] *ibid.* and V.I.Lenin, *Works* (Russian), Vol. XXI, p. 432

[59] A.Shliapnikov, *The Year Seventeen* (Russian), Moscow 1924, Vol. I, p. 197

[60] A.S.Bubnov and others, *The All-Union Communist Party (Bolsheviks)* (Russian), Moscow-Leningrad 1931, p. 113

[61] *Pravda*, 15 March 1917. Quoted by Trotsky, *History of the Russian Revolution*, *op. cit.* Vol. I, p. 305

[62] *Pravda*, 8 April 1917

[63] Bubnov, *op. cit.* p. 114

[64] *AUCP in Resol.*, 4th ed. *op. cit.* Vol. I, p. 258

[65] V.I.Lenin, *Works* (Russian), 3rd ed. Vol. XX, p. 652

[66] *ibid*, Vol. XXI, p. 526

[67] J.Reed, *Ten Days that Shook the World*, London 1932, pp. 223–224
[68] *ibid.*
[69] L.Trotsky, *Stalin*, London 1947, pp. 341–342
[70] Bubnov, *op. cit.* p. 511
[71] *ibid.* p. 512
[72] V.I.Lenin, *Works* (Russian), 2nd ed. Vol. XXVI, p. 232
[73] *AUCP in Resol.*, 4th ed. Vol. I, pp. 372, 543; Vol. II, p. 212
[74] *ibid.* 6th ed. Vol. II, p. 592
[75] V.I.Lenin, *Works* (Russian), *op. cit.* Vol. XXX, p. 414
[76] *Social and National Composition of the All-Union Communist Party [Bolsheviks]* (Russian), Moscow-Leningrad 1928, p. 41
[77] Towster, *op. cit.* p. 328
[78] S.N.Harper and R.Thompson, *The Government of the Soviet Union*, 2nd ed. New York 1949, p. 80
[79] *Partiinaia Zhizn* (Organ of the Central Committee of the Party), Moscow, No. 20, October 1947, p. 83
[80] *Pravda*, 22 April 1942
[81] Bubnov, *op. cit.* p. 626
[82] *USSR, The Land of Socialism* (Russian), Moscow 1936, p. 94
[83] Bubnov, *op. cit.* p. 624
[84] K.Voroshilov, *Articles and Speeches 1925–1936* (Russian), Moscow 1939, p. 94
[85] *The Land of Socialism Today and Tomorrow*, *op. cit.* p. 148
[86] *Pravda*, 23 July 1940
[87] Malenkov's Report, *Pravda*, 14 March 1939
[88] Bubnov, *op. cit.* p. 612
[89] *ibid.* p. 620
[90] *AUCP in Resol.*, 4th ed. Vol. I, p. 315
[91] L.Trotsky, *Stalin*, *op. cit.* p. 484
[92] White, *op. cit.* p. 387
[93] *Bolshevik*, No. 5, March 1937
[94] *The Land of Socialism Today and Tomorrow*, *op. cit.*, pp. 195–196
[95] V.I.Lenin, *Works* (Russian), *op. cit.* Vol. XXV, p. 442
[96] J.V.Stalin, *Works* (Russian), *op. cit.* Vol. X, p. 95
[97] *Constitution, Basic Law, of the Russian Socialist Federated Soviet Republic*, Moscow 1919, Article 9, pp. 4–5
[98] P.F.Yudin, 'The Most Important Source of the Development of Soviet Society', *On Soviet Socialist Society* (Russian), Moscow 1948, p. 22
[99] *ibid.*
[00] Ts.A.Stepanian, 'The Conditions and the Paths of Transition from Socialism to Communism', *On Soviet Socialist Society*, *ibid.*, p. 526

Chapter 3

[1] K.Marx, *The Poverty of Philosophy*, London n.d. p. 146
[2] F.Engels, *Herr Eugen Dühring's Revolution in Science (Anti-Dühring)*, London, n.d. p. 320
[3] K.Marx, *Capital*, Vol. I, pp. 396–397

4 K.Marx and F.Engels, *Selected Correspondence*, London 1942, p. 493

5 K.Marx, *Selected Works*, *op. cit.* Vol. 1, p. 221

6 K.Marx, *Capital*, *op. cit.* Vol. I, p. 652

7 K.Marx, *Selected Works*. *op. cit.* Vol. I, pp. 563–566

8 V.I.Lenin, *Works* (Russian), 4th ed. Vol. XXXI, pp. 7–8

9 C.Clark, *The Conditions of Economic Progress*, 2nd ed. London 1951, p. 268

10 F.Engels, *The Peasant Question in France and Germany* (Russian), St. Petersburg 1920, pp. 37, 39

11 E.A.Preobrazhensky, 'The Law of Primitive Socialist Accumulation', an article published in 1924 and then included as a chapter in his *New Economics* (Russian), Moscow 1926, Vol. I, Part 1, p. 100

12 See Trotsky's Speech to the Twelfth Party Congress, *Twelfth Congress of the Russian Communist Party [Bolsheviks] Stenographic Report* (Russian), Moscow 1923, p. 321

13 Preobrazhensky, *op. cit.* pp. 57–58

Chapter 4

1 V.I.Lenin, *Works* (Russian), Vol. XXVII, p. 387

2 K.Marx, *Die Moralisierende Kritik und die Kritische Moral. Beitrag zur deutschen Kulturgeschichte. Gegen Karl Heinzen. Aus dem literarischen Nachlass von Marx Engels und Lassalle*, Stuttgart 1902, Bd. 2, p. 456

3 C.Clark, *The Conditions of Economic Progress*, London 1940, pp. 79, 83, 91, 98

4 K.Marx, *Die Moralisierende Kritik und die Kritische Moral*, *op. cit.* My emphasis

5 F.Engels, *The Peasant War in Germany*, London 1927, pp. 135–136

6 F.Engels, 'Socialism Utopian and Scientific' in Marx-Engels, *Selected Works*, Vol. I, p. 183

Chapter 5

1 L.Trotsky, *The Revolution Betrayed*, London 1937, pp. 232–233

2 J.Burnham, *The Managerial Revolution*, London 1945, pp. 103–104

3 V.I.Lenin, *Works* (Russian), Vol. XXV, p. 51

4 K.Marx, *Capital*, Vol. III, Chicago 1909, p. 712

5 *ibid.* p. 517

6 V.I.Lenin, *Imperialism, the Highest Stage of Capitalism*, London 1942, p. 20

7 V.I.Lenin, *Collected Works*, London, Vol. XXI, Book 1, pp. 210–211

8 N.Bukharin, *Oeknomie des Transformationsperiode*, Hamburg 1922, pp. 131–133

9 F.Engels, *Anti-Dühring*, *op. cit.* pp. 306–307

Chapter 6

1   V.I.Lenin, *Works* (Russian), Vol. XXIX, p. 388
2   N.Bukharin, *Historical Materialism*, London 1926, p. 276
3   F.Engels, *The Origin of the Family, Private Property and the State*, op. cit. p. 201
4   K.Marx, *Capital*, Vol. I, pp. 648–652
5   G.V.Plekhanov, *The Materialist Conception of History*, London 1940 p. 32
6   F.Engels, *Anti-Dühring*, op. cit. p. 309
7   R.Luxemburg, *Sozialreform oder Revolution?* 2nd ed. Leipzig 1908, p. 41
8   V.I.Lenin, *State and Revolution*. op. cit. pp. 30–31
9   *Fourth International and the Soviet Union*. Thesis adopted by the First International Conference of the Fourth International, Geneva, July 1936
10 V.I.Lenin, *Imperialism, the Highest Stage of Capitalism*, op. cit. p. 109. My emphasis
11 J.Kuczynski, *Weltproduktion und Welthandel in den letzten 100 Jahren*, Libau 1935, pp. 20–21

Chapter 7

1   F.Engels, *Anti-Dühring*, op. cit. p. 341
2   I.Lapidus and K.Ostrovitianov, *Political Economy in Connection with the Theory of Soviet Economy*, Moscow-Leningrad 1928, pp. 8–9
3   *ibid.* p. 10
4   *ibid.* pp. 131–132
5   E.A.Preobrazhensky, *New Economics*, op. cit., pp. 28–29, 36–37
6   A.Leontiev, *Political Economy. A Beginner's Course*, London 1943, p. 76. For the same ideas see A.Leontiev and E.L.Khmelnitskaia, *Outlines of Transition Economics* (Russian), Leningrad 1927, especially p. 132
7   F.Engels, *Anti-Dühring*, op. cit. p. 340
8   *ibid.* p. 341
9   *Marx and Engels Archives* (Russian), Moscow 1933, Vol. II (VII) pp. 6–7
10 *ibid.* Vol. V, p. 59
11 *Pod Znamenem Marksizma*, No. 7–8, 1943, translated in full in *American Economic Review*, September 1944. Quotations are taken from that translation
12 Stalin, *Economic Problems of Socialism in the USSR*, op. cit. p. 23
13 *ibid.* p. 42
14 *ibid.* p. 22
15 *ibid.* p. 21
16 K.Marx, *Capital*, Vol. I, p. 188
17 *ibid.* p. 49
18 *ibid.* p. 84
19 *ibid.*
20 *ibid.* p. 114
21 *ibid.* pp. 390–391
22 Marx and Engels, *Selected Correspondence*, op. cit. p. 246

[22] R.Hilferding, *Das Finanzkapital*, Vienna 1910, p. 286

[24] K.Marx, *Capital*, Vol. I, p. 105

[25] V.I.Lenin, *Works* (Russian), Vol. XXV, p. 51

[26] K.Marx, *Capital*, Vol. I, p. 49

[27] *ibid.* p. 84

[28] *ibid.* p. 126

[29] *ibid.*

[30] *ibid.* p. 633

[31] *ibid.* pp. 186–187

[32] *Foreign Trade of the USSR for 20 Years, 1918–1937, Statistical Handbook* (Russian), Moscow 1939, p. 10

[33] See Y.Gluckstein, *op. cit.* pp. 62–67

[34] N.Bukharin, *World Economy and Imperialism* (Russian), 3rd ed. Moscow 1920? p. 157n.

[35] K.Marx, *Capital*, Vol. III, p. 286

[36] *ibid.* pp. 312–313

[37] *ibid.* p. 568

[38] See, for example, Marx, *Capital*, Vol. III, p. 199

[39] *ibid.* p. 283

[40] *ibid.* p. 303

[41] *ibid.* Vol. II, p. 476

[42] *ibid.* Vol. I, pp. 694–695

[43] *ibid.* Vol. II, p. 211

[44] K.Marx, *Theorien über den Mehrwert*, Vol. II, Book 2, p. 293

[45] K.Marx, *Das Kapital*, Marx-Engels-Lenin ed. Vol. II, p. 562. Quoted by P.M.Sweezy, *The Theory of Capitalist Development*, London 1946, p. 186

[46] K.Marx, *Capital*, Vol. III, pp. 140–141

[47] *ibid.* pp. 569–576

[48] N.Bukharin, *Der Imperialismus und die Akkumulation des Kapitals*, Vienna-Berlin 1926, p. 80

[49] *ibid.* pp. 80–81

[50] K.Marx, *Capital*, Vol. III, p. 304

[51] M.Tugan-Baranovsky, *Studien zur Theorie und Geschichte der Handelskrisen in England*, Jena 1901, p. 25

[52] *ibid.* p. 231

[53] *ibid.* p. 27

[54] M.Tugan-Baranovsky, *Theoretische Grundlagen des Marxismus*, p. 230. Quoted by Sweezy, *op. cit.* p. 168

[55] *ibid.* pp. 230–231. Quoted by Sweezy, *ibid.* p. 169

[56] K.Marx, *Capital*, Vol. I, p. 649

[57] K.Marx, *A Contribution to the Critique of Political Economy*, Chicago 1918, pp. 278–279

[58] K.Marx, *Capital*, Vol. I, p. 701

Chapter 8

[1] *New International* (marxist monthly), New York, February 1942

[2] V.I.Lenin, *Imperialism, the Highest Stage of Capitalism, op. cit.* p. 81

[8] G.C.Allen, M.S.Gordon, E.F.Penrose, E.B.Schumpeter, *The Industrialisation of Japan and Manchukuo, 1930–1940*, New York 1940, pp. 10–11

[6] *ibid*, pp. 26–27

[8] F.Sternberg, *The Coming Crisis*, London 1947, p. 73

[8] E.Varga and L.Mendelsohn (eds.), *New Data for V.I.Lenin's Imperialism, the Highest Stage of Capitalism*, London 1939, p. 141

[7] Schumpeter, *op. cit.* p. 399; A.J.Grajdanzev, 'Manchuria: an Industrial Survey', *Pacific Affairs*, December 1945

[8] K.L.Mitchell, *Industrialisation of the Western Pacific*, New York 1942, pp. 75–78; Allan Rodgers 'The Manchurian Iron and Steel Industry and its Resource Base', *Geographical Review*, New York, January 1948; A.J.Grajdanzev, *op. cit.*

[9] Sternberg, *op. cit.* pp. 74, 73

[10] R.A.Brady, *Business as a System of Power*, New York 1943, p. 3

[11] Gluckstein, *op. cit.* pp. 66–67

[12] *Far Eastern Economic Review*, 27 November 1952

[13] *Prenodavaniye istorii v Shkolye*, 1950, No. 6

[14] *Voprosy Istorii*, 1950, No. 10

[15] *Literaturnaia Gazeta* (weekly organ of the Union of Soviet Writers of the USSR) Moscow, 10 July 1952

[16] *ibid.*

[17] *Pravda*, 26 December 1950

[18] *Literaturnaia Gazeta*, 16 May 1953

[19] *Proletarian*, Kharkov 1934, Nos. 15–21. Quoted by W.E.D.Allen, *The Ukraine*, Cambridge 1940, p. 326

[20] For further particulars see Gluckstein, *op. cit.* pp. 281–310

Chapter 9

[1] Ciliga, *op, cit.* p. 97

[2] Serge, *op. cit.* p. 166

[3] G.Fischer, *Soviet Opposition to Stalin. A Case Study in World War II*, Cambridge, Mass. 1952, p. 106

[4] *ibid.* p. 138

[5] *Answers to Questions of Interest to Soviet Citizens Located Abroad as Displaced Persons* (Russian), Moscow 1949, p. 3. Quoted by G.Fischer, *ibid.* pp. 111–112

[6] Fischer, *ibid.* p. 206

[7] See the UPA newspaper in Volhynia, No. 1, 1943, 'Defence of the Ukraine' Quoted by Vs.F. in 'The Russian Ukrainian Underground', *New International*, April 1949

[8] See the book, *The Position of the Ukrainian Liberation Movement*, published by the UPA illegally in the Ukraine in 1947 and re-issued by the emigration in Germany in 1948. *ibid.*

[9] *ibid.*

[10] *ibid.*

Postscript 1988: From Stalin to Gorbachev

1. Tony Cliff, *The Nature of Stalinist Russia* (duplicated, London 1948).
2. In a Fabian Society pamphlet.
3. E Germain (Ernest Mandel), in *Quatrieme International* 14 (1956) numbers 1-3.
4. In *Quatrieme International* (December 1956).
5. Tony Cliff, 'The Class Nature of the People's Democracies' (1950), reprinted in *Neither Washington nor Moscow* (London 1982) and Ygael Gluckstein (Tony Cliff), *Stalin's Satellites in Europe* (London 1952).
6. Ygael Gluckstein (Tony Cliff), *Mao's China* (London 1957).
7. Cliff, *The Nature of Stalinist Russia*, pages 134-5.
8. Some of which were reprinted in *A Socialist Review* (London, no date (1965)) and *Neither Washington nor Moscow*.
9. Tony Cliff, *From Stalin to Khrushchev* (London 1956).
10. Cliff, *Russia: A Marxist Analysis* (London 1964) page 198.
11. Cliff, *Russia: A Marxist Analysis*, page 209.
12. Cliff, *Russia: A Marxist Analysis*, page 234.
13. Cliff, *Russia: A Marxist Analysis*, page 240.
14. Cliff, *Russia: A Marxist Analysis*, page 254.
15. Cliff, *Russia: A Marxist Analysis*, page 256.
16. Cliff, *Russia: A Marxist Analysis*, page 256.
17. Cliff, *Russia: A Marxist Analysis*, page 254.
18. Cliff, *Russia: A Marxist Analysis*, page 255.
19. Cliff, *Russia: A Marxist Analysis*, pages 248-9.
20. Cliff, *Russia: A Marxist Analysis*, pages 250-4.
21. Cliff, *Russia: A Marxist Analysis*, page 274.
22. Cliff, *Russia: A Marxist Analysis*, pages 262-3.
23. See a summary of accounts by J Pajetska, Goldman and Korba, Basked, Bence and Kis, Branko Horvat and others, in Chris Harman, *Class Struggles in Eastern Europe* (London 1983) pages 288-96.
24. See for example Branko Horvat, *Trade Cycles in Yugoslavia*, special issue of *East European Economist*, volume X, numbers 3-4, and Goldman and Korba, *Economic Growth in Czechoslovakia* (Prague 1969); see also summary of these accounts in Harman, *Class Struggles in Eastern Europe*.
25. Cliff, *Russia: A Marxist Analysis*, page 263.
26. Cliff, *Russia: A Marxist Analysis*, page 274.
27. Cliff, *Russia: A Marxist Analysis*, page 283.
28. Cliff, *Russia: A Marxist Analysis*, pages 284-5.
29. Figures given in Cliff, *Russia: A Marxist Analysis*, page 291.
30. Cliff, *Russia: A Marxist Analysis*, pages 289 and 295.
31. Cliff, *Russia: A Marxist Analysis*, pages 309-10.
32. Cliff, *Russia: A Marxist Analysis*, page 318.
33. Quoted in Cliff, *Russia: A Marxist Analysis*, page 315.
34. Cliff, *Russia: A Marxist Analysis*, page 319.
35. Cliff, *Russia: A Marxist Analysis*, pages 223-4.
36. Cliff, *Russia: A Marxist Analysis*, page 327.
37. Cliff, *Russia: A Marxist Analysis*, pages 329-31.
38. Cliff, *Russia: A Marxist Analysis*, page 333.
39. 'The Class Nature of the East European States' (1949), reprinted in *Neither Washington nor Moscow*; *Stalin's Satellites in Europe* (1952); *Mao's China* (1957); and 'Deflected Permanent Revolution' (1963), reprinted as a pamphlet with the same title (London 1986).

40. Cliff, *Russia: A Marxist Analysis*, page 336.

41. Cliff, *Russia: A Marxist Analysis*, page 337.

42. I rely here on my memory of a talk he gave at the London School of Economics in 1965.

43. Figures given in M I Goldman, *Gorbachev's Challenge* (Ontario 1987) pages 32-3.

44. Figures from *Narodnoe khoziastvo* (various years), quoted in Mike Haynes, 'Understanding the Soviet Crisis', in *International Socialism* 2:34, pge 18.

45. Figures from US Congress Joint Economic Committee, *USSR: Measures of Economic Growth* (Washington 1982), quoted in Goldman, page 15.

46. Figures from *Narodnoe khoziastvo*, quoted in Goldman, page 66.

47. Nikolai Ryzhkov, Report on Draft Guidelines for Economic and Social Development, given to 27th Congress of the CPSU, March 1986.

48. Ryzhkov, Report to 27th Congress.

49. There are a number of accounts of this story; see for example C Schmidt-Hauer, *Gorbachev, the path to power* (London 1986) pages 72-3.

50. Speech by Gorbachev, quoted in *Financial Times*, 12 June 1986.

51. Figures from E Rusanov show that in Stalin's last years a 0.3 per cent rise in wages produced a 1 per cent incrase in productivity; by the late 1980s it took a 0.9 increase in wages to do so (quoted in Goldman, page 29).

52. *Pravda*, 12 December 1984 and 22 August 1985, quoted in Goldman, page 23.

53. Quoted in Goldman, page 30.

54. For accounts, see Andy Zebrowski in *Socialist Worker Review* (December 1987), and Anthony Barnett, *Soviet Freedom* (London 1988) pages 216-7.

55. *Izvestia*, 4 December 1986, quoted in Goldman, page 78.

56. The Russian news agency TASS, 27 January 1987, quoted in Zebrowski.

57. Law on State Enterprise Associations, in *Izvestia*, 1 July 1987.

58. Quoted in Zebrowski.

59. *Partiinaya zhizn*, number 5 (1969), page 5, quoted in Mervyn Matthews, *Class and Society in Soviet Russia* (London 1972) page 224.

60. *Partiinaya zhizn*, quoted in Matthews, page 224.

61. Details in *Pravda*, 15 February 1987.

62. This account is based on *The Guardian*, 12 November 1987, and Barnett, pages 174-7.

63. For a full discussion of these events see Harman, *Class Struggles in Eastern Europe*.

64. Harvey Liebenstein, 'Allocative inefficiency versus "X-inefficiency" ', in *American Economic Review*, June 1960.

Appendix

[1] *Problems of the Development of the USSR. A Draft of the Thesis of the International Left Opposition on the Russian Question*, New York 1931, p. 36

[2] *New International*, April 1943

[3] *ibid*.

[4] L.Trotsky, *The Revolution Betrayed*, London 1937, p. 235

[5] *ibid.* pp. 238–240

[6] K.Marx, *The Poverty of Philosophy*, London n.d., pp. 129–130

[7] *ibid*, p. 166

[8] Sources used on feudalism in the Arab East: A.N.Poliak, *Feudalism in Egypt, Syria, Palestine and Lebanon*, London 1939; A.N.Poliak, 'Les Révoltes Populaires en Egypte a l'Epoque des Mamelukes et leurs causes Economiques' in *Revue des Etudes Islamiques*, Paris 1934; A.N.Poliak,

various articles that appeared in Hebrew in the periodical *Hameshek Hashitufi*, Tel Aviv; A.Kremer, *Kulturgeschichte des Orients unter der Chalifen*, Wien 1875–1877; A.Kremer, *Geschichte der Herrschenden Ideen des Islams*, Leipzig 1868; C.H.Becker, *Beitrage zur Geschichte Aegyptens unter dem Islams*, Strasbourg 1902–1903

⁹ Trotsky, *The Revolution Betrayed*, op. cit. p. 110
¹⁰ *ibid.*
¹¹ Marx, *A Contribution to the Critique of Political Economy*, op. cit. pp. 285–286
¹² Trotsky, *In Defence of Marxism*, New York 1942, pp. 63–70
¹³ L.Trotsky, *Stalin*, op. cit. p. 408
¹⁴ L.Trotsky, *The Living Thoughts of Karl Marx*, London 1940, p. 9
¹⁵ Trotsky, *The Revolution Betrayed*, op. cit. p. 238
¹⁶ L.Trotsky, *War and the Fourth International*, New York 1934, p. 22
¹⁷ Engels, *Anti-Dühring*, op. cit. p. 312
¹⁸ Quoted by L.Laurat, *Marxism and Democracy*, London 1940, p. 69

Appendix 2

1. 'China in the World War', *New International*, June 1942.
2. *La Bureaucratisation du monde*, page 31.
3. *Ibid*, page 95.
4. *Ibid*, page 56.
5. *Ibid*, pages 72-4.
6. *Ibid*, page 283.
7. *Ibid*, page 284.
8. Max Shachtman, *The Bureaucratic Revolution* (New York 1962) page 32.
9. Engels, 'Socialism Utopian and Scientific', in Marx/Engels, *Selected Works*, Volume 1, page 183. My emphasis – TC.
10. Kautsky describes this regime: 'The Spartans made up the minority, perhaps a tenth of the population. Their state was based on real War Communism, the barrack communism of the ruling class. Plato drew his ideal of the State from it. The ideal differed from real Sparta only in that it was not the military chiefs but the "philosophers", that is, the intellectuals, who directed the war communism.' *Die Materialistische Geschichtauffassung*, Zweiten Band, Berlin 1927, pages 132-3.
11. Karl Kautsky, *Thomas More and his Utopia*, page 38.
12. *New International*, December 1947.
13. Max Shachtman, *op. cit.*, pages 306, 308-9. A by-product of this hysterical anti-Stalinism is softness, even idealisation, of Social Democracy: 'In most of the countries of Europe west of the barbed-wire frontiers, the socialist parties not only represent the sole serious alternative to the futile and futureless parties of the *status quo* but are the political instrument of the democratic working class.'

Index

Eiche, Commissar, 260
Elections, 121-2
Engels, F, 104, 136, 174, 189, 192, 194, 320, 328; and 'primitive accumulation', 64-5; and the workers' state, 106-8; and division of labour, 138, 140; and 'premature' workers' revolution, 161; on social class, 162-3, 179; on state capitalism, 177; and law of value, 201, 203-4

Female labour, 39-41; in prison camps, 45
Five-Year Plans: and workers' control, 24; and growth of piecework, 31; and labour mobility, 34-5, 37-8; and egalitarianism, 81-93; and female labour, 39-41; and forced labour, 42-6; and accumulation, 47-56; fixing of targets, 49; and consumption, 50-56; and production, 56-9; and labour productivity, 60-62; and agriculture, 62-7; financing of through turnover taxes, 67-71; legal protection of state property, 71-7; and inequalities in distribution, 81-93; and pricing policy, 98-100; and transformation of bureaucracy into a ruling class, 164-6, 194; after Stalin, 196-7
Forced labour, 72-7 in passing; of teenagers, 91-2; in prison camps, 42-6
Frunze, M V, 113

Gamarnik, J, 132
Gertsenzon, A A, 44-5
Gibbons, J, 116-7
Glebov-Avilov, N P, 132
Goloded, 260
Gomulka, 264
Gorbachev, M, 13, 15, 179, 298-303; limits of his reforms, 299-302, 304

Haldane, C, 41
Herzen, A, 189
Hilferding, R, 210, 213
Hindus, M, 41
Housing, 54-6
Hungary, uprising in, 14, 278

Ignatiev, A, 117
Imperialism: Lenin's theory of, 245-6; Japanese, 247-51; after First World War, 249-50; nature of Stalinist, 251-4; and Russia's satellites, 254-7
Industrial production, 47-51; before the revo-

lution, 159-60; *see also* Military production, Five Year Plans
Industry: control of, 23-30, 80; directors' remuneration, 83-4; mismanagement of, 93-103; crisis of 1950s, 283-9
Inheritance of property, 87

Jasny, N, 53, 71, 98-9
Johnson, H, Dean of Canterbury, 26, 120

Kaganovich, L M, 25
Kaganovich, M M, 25
Kamenev, L B, 123, 125, 127, 131
Kardelj, 264
Kerensky, A F, 124
Khrushchev, N S, 127, 279-95; 'secret speech', 13, 277; orders invasion of Hungary, 14; fall from power, 295
Kossior, S V, 122
Kostov, 266
Kostubinsky, 260
Kosygin, 296
Kovnar, 260
Krylenko, N V, 132
Kuibyshev, V V, 57

Labour discipline, 34-9; in general, 140-41
Labour power: a commodity in Russia? 218-20
Lapidus, 201-3
Law, 184-7; and labour, 25, 29-30, 34-9, 81-2; in agriculture, 65; and property, 71-7; and crimes against persons, 74-6; and juveniles, 75-7
Law of combined and uneven development, 154-8, 161-2, 331
Law of value, 171, 206-10; Stalin on, 99, 205; partially negated by state regulation of economic activity, 171-3, 201-12; operation in Russia denied, 201-3; and affirmed after 1943, 204-5; monopoly and, 201-12; state monopoly capitalism and, 212-14; operation in Russia viewed in isolation, 214-21; operation in Russia viewed in context of world economy, 221-4
Lenin, V I, 27, 127, 131-2, 177, 193; on Taylorism, 33; on officials, 77-8, 84; on agrarian question, 65; on the state, 27-8, 108; and party democracy, 123-6; his testament, 131-2; and socialism in one country, 156-7; on historical mission of bourgeoisie,

and state capitalism, 174-7; fusion of economics and politics in, 191-2; and transition to a capitalist state, 193-5; Trotsky's two definitions of, 310-12; Russia not a, 313-14, 326-31; the 'new democracies' and, 327-9